RESTORATION OF THE END TIME CHURCH

Dr Johanna E Carstens

© 2025 Print on Demand

Dr Johanna Carstens

End Time Revelation

All rights reserved. No part of this publication may be reproduced, stored in a retrieval system or transmitted in any form or by any means, electronic, mechanical, photocopying, recording or otherwise without the prior permision of the publisher or in accordance with the provisions of the Copyright, Designs and Patents Act 1988 or under the terms of any licence permitting limited copying issued by the Copyright Licensing Angency.

Published by: Unlocking Digital

Text Design by: Karien Smith

Cover Design by: Dr Johanna Carstens

A CIP record for this book is available from the Library of South Africa Cataloging-in-Publication Data

ISBN-13: 978-0-7961-3351-9

Distributed by:

J Carstens

Boschenmeer, Paarl, 7680

Printed and bound in Location by Print on Demand

DEDICATION

I dedicate this book to my dear Heavenly Father to whom salvation belongs, to my Lord and Saviour Jesus Christ and to the Holy Spirit, the mind of Christ who called and mantled me through His grace and mercy to write all the revelations received through His Spirit concerning the end times.

I also dedicate it to my precious family, my children Pieter, Andre, Johanna and Alwyn and to my grandchildren Emily, Johannes, Kai and Andre

APPRECIATION

I want to express my sincere appreciation to my spiritual father and mother in the faith, Apostle Surprise Sithole and Prophet Triphina Sithole who have and are still guarding over my ministry in Christ Jesus.

Thank you Apostle Surprise for being the watchdog over doctrine concerning this book. I want to also thank Apostle Dr Francois Engelbrecht for raising me in the faith, believing in me and always encouraging me, especially concerning my Doctorate studies.

A deep thank you to my sister Rynette Spray who sacrificed her time to edit and tirelessly type all documentation Finally I want to thank our intercessors, Special Forces and Ahava International Revival who earnestly prayed for this work.

Foreword

Dear readers,

It is with great joy and anticipation that I present to you this profound and timely book, "Restoration of the End Time Church, "written by the insightful and anointed Pastor Johanna E Carstens. In these uncertain and challenging times, it is essential for us to understand the important role that the Church plays in God's divine plan. This book will undoubtedly serve as a guiding light on this crucial topic.

Pastor Carstens has dedicated her life to studying, teaching, and experiencing the manifestation of God's restorative power within the Church. In "Restoration of the End Time Church," she brings forth a message of hope, clarity, and restoration for those who may feel disillusioned, discouraged, or uncertain about the future of the Church.

Through her deep understanding of the biblical prophecies concerning the end times, Pastor Carstens unveils the divine blueprint for the restoration of the Church. She skillfully guides us through the pages of Scripture, revealing the signs, patterns, and principles that will usher in a renewed and powerful Church, fully equipped to face the challenges of the end times.

What sets this book apart is Pastor Carstens' unwavering conviction that the Church, despite its current state of decline, will experience a remarkable restoration. Drawing from her immense knowledge of the Scriptures and her personal encounters with the Spirit of God, she expertly navigates through the misconceptions and misunderstandings that have hindered the Church's potential.

Within the pages of this book, you will find enlightening discussions on topics such as the role of prayer and intercession in the restoration process, the importance of unity and love within the Body of Christ, and the crucial need for spiritual discernment in these deceptive times. Pastor Carstens' passionate and persuasive writing style, combined with her practical insights and real-life examples, make these profound truths accessible and applicable to all readers.

"Restoration of the End Time Church" is not just a book of theoretical knowledge; it is a divinely inspired guidebook for individuals, church leaders, and believers alike who desire to see the Church restored and revived. Each chapter is designed to challenge, inspire, and empower readers to play an active role in this restoration process, becoming vessels of revival and agents of change within their spheres of influence.

I believe that as you embark on this transformative journey through the pages of this book, you will be stirred to action and propelled into a deeper relationship with God. You will gain a renewed sense of hope, faith, and expectation for what He is about to do in and through His Church.

May this powerful and enlightening book be a catalyst for change within your heart and a beacon of hope for the Church as we eagerly anticipate the restoration of the end-time Church.

THE AUTHOR OF VOICE IN THE NIGHT
love and blessings to you from
Surprise Sithole
www.surprisesithole.com

Preface

It is an honour and a privilege to introduce this powerful book, *The Restoration of the End-Time Church*, written by Dr. Johanna Carstens. Having known her for many years as a colleague, postgraduate student, and dear friend, I have been deeply inspired by her unwavering dedication to God and her profound obedience to His voice. Her relentless pursuit of His Kingdom has taken her to the most remote corners of the earth, where she has shared the Gospel of Jesus Christ with open-hearted people hungry for His truth.

What sets Dr. Johanna apart is that she does not merely teach about the Glory of God, Holiness, Mount Zion, or the Sevenfold Spirit of God as academic subjects - she lives and breathes them as a tangible reality. She walks in the supernatural realm daily, embodying the ascension lifestyle that this book so powerfully unveils.

In a time where the world is shifting rapidly, and prophetic events are unfolding before our eyes, this book is not just informative—it is essential. Every believer must gain a biblical understanding of what is happening now and what is to come, so we may stand firm, victorious, and prepared for the days ahead.

As you embark on this journey through the pages of *The Restoration of the End-Time Church*, I encourage you to allow the Holy Spirit to lead you into deeper revelations of His glory. May these insights transform your walk with God, lifting you to your rightful place -seated with Christ in heavenly places. As you are moulded into His image, may you step into your divine calling to rule and reign as priests and kings, bringing heaven's reality to earth.

This is more than a book; it is an invitation to be part of God's divine restoration in these crucial times. May you arise as a mighty instrument in His hands and play a pivotal role in the fulfilment of His end-time purposes.

With great expectation,
Dr Francois Engelbrecht.

Table of Contents

DEDICATION	3
APPRECIATION	3
Foreword	4
Preface	6
CHAPTER 1	**10**
HIS GLORY REVEALED	*10*
WHY IS RESTORATION NEEDED?	12
CHAPTER 2	**28**
THE HIGHWAY OF HOLINESS	*28*
THE HIGHWAY OF HOLINESS	28
What are the seven spirits of God, or the seven-fold Holy Spirit?	43
SPIRIT OF THE LORD	45
THE SPIRIT OF WISDOM	46
THE SPIRIT OF UNDERSTANDING	47
THE SPIRIT OF COUNSEL	47
THE SPIRIT OF KNOWLEDGE	48
THE SPIRIT OF MIGHT	49
THE SPIRIT OF THE FEAR OF THE LORD	50
EFFECTS OF THE REVERENTIAL FEAR OF THE LORD THROUGH THE SPIRIT OF THE FEAR OF THE LORD	50
HEADSHIP AND GATHERING TOGETHER OF ALL THINGS IN CHRIST	*53*
HEADSHIP AND GATHERING OF ALL THINGS TOGETHER IN CHRIST	53
PREPARATION	55
SEPARATION	56
HEADSHIP OF CHRIST	57
HEAVENLY REALM	58
EARTHLY REALM	62
MARKS OF THE TRUE REMNANT CHURCH	62
PURPOSE OF GATHERING ALL THINGS	66
Chapter 4	**76**
RESTORATION OF THE TABERNACLE OF DAVID	*76*
RESTORATION OF THE TABERNACLE OF DAVID	76
WHY IS REBUILDING NECESSARY?	79
WHAT DOES THE TABERNACLE OF DAVID REFER TO?	79
FOUR COMPONENTS OF THE TABERNACLE OF DAVID:	80
DAVID ESTABLISHING A NEW WORSHIP ORDER IN JERUSALEM:	82
HOW WILL WE BUILD AND WHAT IS NEEDED?	87
CHAPTER 5	**90**
MOUNT ZION: THE MOUNTAIN OF THE LORD	*90*
MOUNT ZION: THE MOUNTAIN OF THE LORD	90
THE LORD'S REIGN IN ZION:	92
AN ABIDING PRESENCE IN ZION:	94
THE FOUNDATION OF ZION:	95
TIMES AND SEASONS:	96
HOLINESS IN ZION:	97
GOD'S LOVE IN ZION	99
POWER OF MALCHIZEDEK - PRIESTHOOD AND MARKET PLACE IN ZION	99
WARFARE FROM ZION	101

FALSE PROPHETS AND FALSE TEACHERS	102

CHAPTER 6 — 106
AUTHORITY, TRUE IDENTITY SONSHIP — *106*

FACE OF THE SONS	107
Why is this significant?	108
SONSHIP THROUGH THE SPIRIT	110
TRUE IDENTITY	111
ACCOUNTABILITY CALLS UP TO:	115
EFFECTS OF TRUE IDENTITY	115
PROCESS OF ESTABLISHING TRUE IDENTITY	116
HOW CAN THIS HEAVENLY PERSONA BE ESTABLISHED?	118
TRUE IDENTITY WILL BE TESTED	121
PRAYING FROM YOUR IDENTITY	123
HOW IS THE GODLY TRI-UNE KNOWN IN HEAVEN?	125
GOD, THE FATHER	125
JESUS, THE SON OF GOD	127
Jesus was baptized, being filled with the Holy Spirit, returned from the Jordan and was led by the Spirit into the wilderness, where He was tempted by satan and in final preparation of His call.	127
HOLY SPIRIT	128
ANGELS	130

CHAPTER 7 — 132
HABITATION OF THE SOUL AND THE SEVEN-FOLD HOLY SPIRIT — *132*

HABITATION OF THE SOUL AND THE SEVEN-FOLD HOLY SPIRIT	132
HABITATION OF THE SOUL	134
DWELLING PLACE OF THE SPIRIT	135
FUNCTION OF THE CHURCH	135
HOW ARE STRONGHOLDS BUILT?	136
KEY TO CHANGE	137
THE SEVEN SPIRITS OF GOD	139
MANIFESTATIONS OF THE SEVEN SPIRITS OF GOD	140
FUNCTIONS OF THE SPIRIT OF THE LORD	140
OPERATION OF THE SPIRIT OF THE LORD	141
MIRACLES BY THE SPIRIT OF GOD	143
THE SPIRIT OF WISDOM	144
WHERE IS WISDOM FOUND?	145
HOW CAN WISDOM BE FOUND?	146
What does all of this mean from the book of Job?	146
SPIRIT OF UNDERSTANDING	147
HOW IS THE SPIRIT IMPARTED?	149
FUNCTIONS OF THE SPIRIT OF COUNSEL	150
EXAMPLES OF THE SPIRIT OF COUNSEL AT WORK	150
SPIRIT OF KNOWLEDGE	152
FUNCTION OF THE SPIRIT OF KNOWLEDGE	153
WHY DO WE NEED THIS REVELATION ON THE LOVE OF GOD?	153
THE SPIRIT OF MIGHT	154
FUNCTIONS OF THE SPIRIT OF MIGHT	155
SPIRIT OF THE FEAR OF THE LORD	155
CONCLUSION	157

CHATER 8 — 158
PROCESS OF BEING MADE READY — *158*

THE PROCESS OF BEING MADE READY	158
Who is prepared to build the house of the LORD?	160
THERE ARE THREE LEVELS OF ANOINTING	162
FUNCTION AND ROLE OF THE FIE-FOLD MINISTRY	164

PURPOSE OF THE FIVE-FOLD MINISTRY	165
FUNCTION OF THE CHURCH	171
FUNCTION OF THE FIVE-FOLD LEADERSHIP GIFTS	173
FIVE-FOLD MINISTRY OFFICES AND THEIR FUNCTIONS	176
APOSTLE DEFINED	176
THE CALL OF THE APOSTLE	177
HARDSHIPS OF THE APOSTLE	180
PROPHET DEFINED	181
THE CALL OF THE PROPHET	181
The prophet is called	182
CHARACTERISTICS/ATTRIBUTES OF A PROPHET	182
LEADERSHIP SKILLS	183
FUNCTIONS OF THE PROPHET	184
HARDSHIPS OF THE PROPHET	184
SIGNS OF A MATURE PROPHET	184
EVANGELIST DEFINED	185
CALL OF THE EVANGELIST AND HIS BURDEN	185
LEADERSHIP SKILLS OF THE EVANGELIST	186
FUNCTIONS OF THE EVANGELIST	186
HARDSHIPS OF THE EVANGELIST	187
PASTOR DEFINED	187
THE FUNCTION OF THE PASTOR	187
ATTRIBUTES AND CHARACTER OF THE PASTOR	188
LEADERSHIP SKILLS OF THE PASTOR	189
FUNCTIONS OF THE PASTOR	189
HARDSHIPS OF THE PASTOR	190
TEACHER DEFINED	190
CALL OF THE TEACHER	191
There are two types of teachers:	191
ATTRIBUTES OF A TEACHER	192
LEADERSHIP SKILLS OF THE TEACHER	192
FUNCTIONS OF THE TEACHER	192
HARDSHIPS OF THE TEACHER	192
CHAPTER 9	**195**
THE ORDER OF MELCHIZEDEK	*195*
THE ORDER OF MELCHIZEDEK	195
WHO IS MELCHIZEDEK	196
PURPOSE OF THE ORDER OF MALCHIZEDEK	201
FUNCTIONS OF A KING	209
EFFECTS OF THE ORDER OF MELCHIZEDEK BEING RESTORED	210
CHAPTER 10	**212**
THE RISING OF THE SPIRIT OF ELIJAH PREPARING THE WAY OF THE LORD	*212*
THE RISING OF THE SPIRIT OF ELIJAH PREPARING THE WAY OF THE LORD:	212
ELIJAH OVERCOMING JEZEBEL AND THE FALSE PROPHETS	216
POWER AND MIRACLES BY THE ANOINTING UPON ELIJAH	219
CHAPTER 11	**223**
THE SHAKING OF ALL THINGS AND THE JUDGEMENT OF GOD	*223*
REASONS WHY THIS END TIME SHAKING WILL TAKE PLACE	225
HOW DO WE THEN DEAL WITH PRIDE?	226
THE JUDGMENT OF GOD	227
IN CONCLUSION	*228*
Bibliography	**229**

CHAPTER 1

HIS GLORY REVEALED

Whilst singing in tongues I was in the Spirit encountering a vision of a cylinder filled with bright light. It sucked me in as I found myself inside of His glory. Caught up in the light of His glory.

From this place in Him everything seemed clear, peaceful, easy, full of joy and restored in His fullness. Healing came forth from this place in Him.

He spoke to me from the light of His glory, saying that sickness and evil cannot stand here. Total restoration, provision, revelation, wholeness, and the fullness of Him is found in the glory in His light. The enemy has no access here and loses its power. Nothing that is not of Him can stand in His manifested presence – His glory. I encountered Him in His light – the light of His glory. This place is meant for every believer to dwell in and corporately we are being built together as a dwelling place of God in the Spirit.

In whom you also are being built together for a dwelling place of God in the Spirit.
Ephesians 2:22

Jesus Christ is the brightness of the Father's glory and the express image of His Person and He upholds all things by His Word.

Who (Jesus) being the brightness of His glory and the express image of His Person, and upholding all things by the word of His power, when He had by himself, purged our sins, sat down at the right hand of the Majesty on high.
Hebrews 1:3

From this place in Him, in the light of His glory the redeemed of the Lord will say so. We will speak and declare from a realm of what we have seen and become aware of. The realm of heaven where the throne of God is seated. We will declare a thing in the earth and God will establish it.

You will also declare a thing and it will be established for you. So light will shine on your ways.
Job 22:28

The light of His manifested presence will shine and from that realm as sons, we will declare and decree His purposes and His mind with authority. God will establish our decrees in the earth, and we will walk in His light. The end time ecclesia will carry the answers, the revelation, power and authority. In this great move of God upon the earth He will once again restore His glory back to the ecclesia.

What are we referring to when we talk about His glory?

His glory is expressed in His visible, manifested, tangible presence. The original intent of Christ is that His glory – His manifested presence – will rest upon the redeemed and corporately we grow into a Holy temple in the land, a dwelling place of God in the Spirit. This will be an abiding glory and final restoration that we will see and experience as part of the end time move of God in the earth.

At the end of this age the church will be glorious. When Solomon built the temple, he was praying, after his prayer fire came down from heaven and consumed the burnt offering and the sacrifices, and the glory of the Lord filled the temple. This glory will be restored to the end time ecclesia. In this dispensation we find the church lacking His glory, as the glory has left the church for several reasons, which we will be discussing shortly. God's purpose is to complete His church as Christ is returning for a victorious and glorious end time ecclesia. Ecclesia meaning the legislative governing body of Christ – the church. A church filled with the glory of God as He resides amongst His people. As a result, the church will come forth shining and reflecting the brightness of Christ, and she will carry authority, fire and power. The whole earth will be covered with His glory.

But truly, as I live, all the earth shall be filled with the glory of the Lord.
Numbers 14:21

Also, the earth will be filled with the knowledge (revelation) of the glory of the Lord, as the waters covers the sea. What does the revelation of the glory of the Lord refer to?

It is the sons and daughters of God being revealed in their true identity and full authority, as He glorified the redeemed. His glory will be revealed in and through us for the earnest expectation of the creation eagerly waits for the revealing of the sons of God.

Moreover whom He predestined, these He also called, whom He called, these He also justified, and whom He justified, these He also glorified　　　　　　　　　　Romans 8:30

An army moving and manifesting glory and power is arising in this hour of restoration. In His light, His truth is revealed.

WHY IS RESTORATION NEEDED?

God's glory left the church for several reasons. One of these foremost reasons is because of the church deviating from the original plan and intent.

The spirit of religion with it's five tentacles of legalism, debate, criticism, opinion and judgment reigning over the church is now coming down and being removed by God and replaced by the five-fold ministry. We will see a restoration of the five-fold ministry as Christ's governing system for His church. There will be no more hiding in the church. Every member will take up their place in the end time army of God.

God's government will be set up as religion and tradition is replaced with the five-fold ministry. Jesus' model for leadership and equipping of the body of Christ will not be reinstated. These five-fold leaders will walk with God and do what God wants.

And He himself gave some to be apostles, some prophets, some evangelists and some pastors and teachers, for the equipping of the saints for the work of the ministry, for the edifying of the body of Christ, till we all come to the unity of the faith and the knowledge of the Son of God, to a perfect man, to the measure of the stature of the fullness of Christ.
　　　　　Ephesians 4:11 – 13

This is the process of the redeemed being made ready. Religion withstands this process. The five-fold ministry will equip the body unto unity of faith and the acknowledgement of Christ, united by the headship of Christ. The corporate body will display Christ in His full representation to the world. There will be a gathering of His sheep under the headship of Jesus Christ, the chief Cornerstone.

Restoration is further needed as the church is specifically desolate in three areas:

- The first area of desolation is the area of demon infiltration, thus rendering the body of Christ powerless. The body needs healing and deliverance as part of equipping through the five-fold ministry.
- Another area of desolation seems to be the lack of the presence of the Holy Spirit and power. The seven-fold Holy Spirit needs to return to the church. The fear of the Lord needs to return to the church. The Spirit of the Lord, the Spirit of wisdom and understanding, the Spirit of counsel and might, and the Spirit of knowledge are all aspects of the Spirit of God and should be welcomed in the church. All these aspects of the Holy Spirit need to become the habitation of the soul. This will result in full alignment to the Spirit of God. The Holy Spirit will lead the ecclesia.

The Spirit of the Lord shall rest upon him, the Spirit of wisdom and understanding, the Spirit of counsel and might, the Spirit of knowledge and of the fear of the Lord.
Isaiah 11:2

He has given to the church the former rain faithfully during *Acts 2*. This was the first outpouring of His Spirit during Pentecost. Now He will cause the latter rain, the outpouring of His Spirit, to come upon all flesh, especially the children, the youth, the elderly and leaders.

And it shall come to pass afterward that I will pour out My Spirit on all flesh; your sons and your daughters shall prophecy, your old men shall dream dreams, your young men shall see visions and also on My men servants and on My maid servants I will pour out My Spirit in those days.   *Joel 2;28 - 29*

"those days" has arrived. This outpouring will not only come upon believers, but it will be a universal outpouring for the sake of bringing the end time harvest of souls.

- The third area of desolation to be restored by God, is the fact that the church seems to be far away from its inheritance (sonship). The sons and daughters of God need to be made manifest. It is the season and time for the sons of God to be revealed and to walk in the fullness of their true identity and authority. This requires a lot of equipping via the five-fold ministry. Believers need to understand their authority, walk in purity and take up their position in the body of Christ. This function of the five-fold ministry requires for a process of mentoring these sons and daughters.

Full restoration will encompass the gathering of His sheep under the headship of Jesus Christ. The sons and daughters of God being executives involved in His purposes, and finally the outpouring of the Holy Spirit on all flesh.

This outpouring will result in judgment where full alignment to the Holy Spirit is required, and people will be forced to make a decision to choose either for Him or against Him.

CONDITIONS FOR HIS GLORY TO RETURN

- Repentance - The glory of God will only be restored upon the church by confession of sin and a full repentance of the old ways. By confession we bring that which is hidden to the light and the evil one loses its power. By repentance we turn away from evil and turn towards God's ways and thoughts. There needs to be a repentance from the soul ruling over the human spirit. The soul is rebelling against the Spirit of God. Submit your soul to your spirit that is joined to Christ in becoming one spirit with Him. Thereby yielding to the Spirit of God.

Confession and repentance both leads to restoration. David, in Psalms 51, acknowledged and confessed his sin. He asked for mercy and acknowledged God as judge. David explained his case to God and declared God's desire for uprightness. David was pleading with God for restoration. All of this led to David being purged and cleansed. A clean heart resulted, and steadfast spirit was renewed in him. The Holy Spirit was not taken from him, and he was not cast away from God's presence. The joy of his salvation was restored. He was upheld by God's Spirit and all of that resulted in a condition of the heart that is freed up to teach transgressors His ways and for sinners to be converted to Him. This is a prerequisite and will be needed again for the bringing in of the final harvest of souls.

In other words, the harvest can be gathered in and discipling can take place as a result of confession and repentance. Repentance is key to the end time move of God. God's manifested presence can only be on display under these conditions – a clean heart and a repentant heart. (pure heart) A heart that is turned and surrendered.

Let the wicked forsake his way and the unrighteous man his thoughts, let him return to the Lord, and He will have mercy on him; and to our God, for He will abundantly pardon. For My thoughts are not your thoughts, nor are your ways My ways, says the Lord.
Isaiah 55:7 - 8

Now therefore, says the Lord, turn to Me with all your heart, with fasting, with weeping and with mourning. So rend your heart and not your garments. Return to the Lord your God, for He is gracious and merciful …….   Joel 2:12 - 13

Confession and repentance combined with fasting will usher in the second outpouring of the Holy Spirit upon all flesh. The Spirit of God is returning in all glory to His end time remnant church, who will walk in purity and unity of heart, as they agree upon heaven's agenda.

- Love Light, love and life are intertwined. His love ushers in His glory. His glory is connected to His love. Love leads to light as He is love and He is light.

In Him was life and life was the light of men.   John 1:4

Light again leads to revelation. Light illuminates and reveals from a place in Him where His light is. Much revelation comes forth as His presence is manifested. A heart that does not love is a selfish and dark heart. Christ is love and He is the Cornerstone of His church. Foundations are being restored by love. Concerning the end time remnant church, it will be earmarked by light and abiding glory. His manifested continual presence.

The vile will be removed from the precious. The precious being a pure remnant walking on the highway of holiness. A separation will take place. God will remove from His body slander, religious activities earmarked by criticism, opinions of men, debating of the Word of God, judging one another and legalism. All of this will be replaced by the five-fold ministry. Appointed five-fold leaders who will walk with God and govern with Him and legislate from mount Zion. These leaders will equip the body of Christ.

All division will be removed. This will all happen to make room for the original plan and intent of Jesus Christ to be fulfilled in the church – His glory. Love as bond of perfection amongst believers will be the norm and will lead us into a place in His heart. Those who love God with a sacrificial love, to those He will reveal Himself. Love will cost you something. It surely has a price tag to it. We need to love Him with all our heart, with all our strength and with all our mind. You earn a place in the heart of the Father by laying down your life. This type of laid down life, a sacrificial love, is a life that the Spirit of truth is drawn to. Light illuminates this pathway and revelation flows from it.

A sacrificial love for one another satisfies the heart of the Father. In this way we draw near to the heart of the Father, touching His heart. When He turns His face towards us on account of us loving through His nature, the result is eternal light which carries life and revelation in it. A fusion takes place between His Spirit and our spirit and in His light, we become one.

Jesus prayed and petitioned His Father in *John 17*.

And the glory (His presence/His light) which You gave Me, I have given to them, that they may be one, just as We are One. I in them, and You in Me, that they may be made perfect in one and that the world may know that You have sent Me, and I have loved them as You have loved me. Father, I desire that they also whom You gave Me may be with Me where I am that they may behold My glory which You have given Me, for You loved Me before the foundation of the world.
John 17:22 – 24

It all starts with covenant relationship and love. When we behold Him through love, we are drawn into His heart and as a result we will see and walk in the light of His glory.

He reveals His glory to those who He can trust with His love and His heart. To those who seek His face, remains in Him and radiates with love for the only reason to love Him and to please Him. They are not seeking His face to receive anything from Him, but to minister His love back to Him by ministering His love to a broken world. This is the type of stewardship He is looking for, a selfless life totally surrendered to Christ and yielded to His Spirit.

Pure love is crucified and its desires. True love's desire is to please Him only. To go where He goes.

I beseech you therefore, brethren, by the mercies of God, that you present your bodies a living sacrifice, holy, acceptable to God, which is your reasonable service.
Romans 12:1

On those He will pour out His glory. It will be seen upon them, and they will carry the power of God as the end time remnant – His true bride. This is the face of His Joel 2 army that He is preparing.

- Renewed Mind
- To be a glory carrier the thick darkness over the soul (will, emotions, intellect) also refer to as the mind, needs to be removed.

For behold darkness shall cover the earth and deep darkness the people. But the Lord will arise over you and His glory will be seen upon you.   Isaiah 6:2

Deep darkness refers to the mind or soul dimension of people in this age being darkened by depression, fear and anxiety. This is not the portion of the believer. A clear distinction is being made between people out there and God's people by the phrase *"but the Lord"*. The Lord will arise over His remnant which He prepared to carry His glory, and the effect will be that Gentiles will come to the light of His remnant church and kings to the brightness of their rising. His glory attracts a new rising.

But we all with unveiled face beholding as in a mirror the glory of the Lord, are being transformed into the same image from glory to glory, as just by the Spirit of the Lord.
2 Corinthians 3:18

Being transformed into His image means to see both the realm of the Spirit and the realm of the natural as one. We need to be set free from the bondage of the mind with its limitations to "see" the realm of the Spirit. We need to be governed and directed by the realm of the Spirit of God. That is what it means to behold His glory. That which you behold you will become.

And do not be conformed to this world but, be transformed by the renewing of your mind that you may proof what is the good and acceptable will of God.

Romans 12:2

The mind needs to be redeemed and delivered from bondage and renewed to "see" what God sees. The mind, surrendered soul dimension with its limitations and reasoning opposes the life in the Spirit. It needs to be freed up and transformed, renewed and governed by what God reveals and speaks. This is done by tearing the veil that overshadows the mind by the Spirit of God and allow the seven-fold Holy Spirit to become the habitation of the soul. By allowing the seven-fold Spirit of God to feed your soul with His wisdom, power, counsel, knowledge, understanding, might and the reverential fear of the Lord it results in Him leading you in all these aspects.

The soul needs to be subjected to the spirit as we are spirit beings living in a body that has a soul.

- Unity

- Unity attracts God's glory. The five-fold ministry leadership model that Jesus demonstrated to govern the church, and from which the church has deviated in part, is responsible for equipping the saints for the work of the ministry. It is for the edifying of the body of Christ till we all come to the unity of the faith and of the knowledge of the Son of God, to a perfect man, to the measure of the stature of the fullness of Christ. An acknowledgement of Christ united by the headship of Christ is the road to unity. Christ acknowledged unity.

This calls for maturity. All believers need to be empowered and prepared through a process of mentoring, discipleship training and impartation until they reach full maturity and thereby, through faith, take up their function in the body of Christ. In unity the body grows into a temple, a dwelling place for the Spirit of God.

Spiritually functioning people gather, and the body is being built up in unity by mutual efforts of all the members supplying their contribution to the whole.

True spiritual unity flows from the presence of the Holy Spirit. However, the Holy Spirit will not dwell amongst divisions, strife and slander. God is looking for "singleness of heart". Where there is unity, singleness of heart, you will find obedience to God and godly appointed leadership.

Also the hand of God was on Judah to give them singleness of heart to obey the command of the king and the leaders, at the word of the Lord. 2 Chronicles 30:12

As fellow believers we have koinonia-fellowship. Koinonia is unity brought about by the Holy Spirit. Koinonia cements the believers to the Lord Jesus and to each other in a bond of love. The power of this unity was displayed by the early church in Acts 2 in as much as they "continued steadfastly" in the apostle's' doctrine which is the Word of God, and in prayer. They enjoyed a deep sense of spiritual community and union with the Lord and with each other. They were likeminded as they stood in spiritual unity. When brothers and sisters together in unity, the Spirit of the Lord dwells amongst them. In such an environment you will find oil - an anointing, an ability from God flowing to His people. It is likened to the dew of Hermon descending upon the mountains of Zion. In other words, it is a dimension of God's presence coming down from above providing life, resulting in revelation and spiritual growth.

Where there is unity, the Lord commands a blessing. What is a blessing?

Life forevermore. There is power in unity. God dwells amongst His people in unity of the Spirit. Spiritual life, abundance, revelation and provision comes forth where there is unity as His presence will manifest in such an environment. The Spirit of the Lord is attracted to unity amongst His people. Therefore, unity attracts His glory. The army of the Lord moving in unison will be marching by revelation from the throne of God in the days to come.

- Righteousness

    - Righteousness means to be in right standing with God and needs to be worked out. In other words, there is nothing hindering the flow of the Holy Spirit between a believer and God. For the glory of God to be released over an individual, righteousness becomes a prerequisite. Righteousness ushers in His glory.

God is seeking a generation who walks uprightly, who works out righteousness and speaks the truth with boldness. A generation who does not backbite with the tongue, nor does evil to their neighbor. God requires clean hands and a pure heart. A generation who will not be lifted up to idols, but sold out to God's purposes. Such a generation will receive righteousness from the God of their salvation. A generation who seeks His face. Where these character traits are found it results in the King of glory entering in. His manifested presence will descend, the light of His glory. Light needs to become brighter on your pathway. The time for compromise and neutrality is over. Only those with a pure heart and clean hands can descend the mountain of the Lord, His dwelling place, Mount Zion. This is confirmed in the word of God in *Psalms 24 and Psalms 15.*

- Suffering - This is a time and season when we will know Jesus in His suffering. A vessel needs to be broken for the light to manifest. Jesus, through the suffering of death, was crowned with glory and honor. He brought many sons and daughters to glory and, in the process, the Captain of our salvation was made perfect through sufferings. Though He Himself was a son, yet He learned obedience by the things He suffered, and, having been perfected, He became the Author of eternal salvation to all who obey Him. How much more do we need to be willing to go through suffering, trials and tribulation to be made perfect before Him. This is a dispensation in the church where we will not escape these things, especially as we see the end of the age draw closer. Our eyes must be fixed on Him only, the Author and finisher of our faith. Through suffering His glory will be ushered in. As sons we are heirs of God and joint heirs with Christ, if indeed we suffer with Him that we may be glorified together. As glory carriers we will rule with Him even in the realm of the earth. The end time church will be ruling and reigning with Him, legislating from mount Zion, from suffering to glory. Paul said the following:

For I consider that the sufferings of this present time are not worthy to be compared with the glory which shall be revealed in us. For the earnest expectation of the creation eagerly waits for the revealing of the sons of God.   Romans 8:18,19

- Refinement - *No glory without refinement. God refines His sons and daughters for His glory. He refines and tests His people in the furnace of affliction for His Name's sake as He will not give His glory to another.*

Behold, I have refined you, but not as silver; I've tested you in the furnace of affliction. For My own sake, for My own sake, I will do it; For how should My name be profaned? And I will not give My glory to another.   Isaiah 48:10,11

The way will be prepared before our Lord for the second coming in this season. The Lord will come His temple suddenly, for this very purpose. When He comes, He is likened to the refiner's fire and the launderer's soap. He will sit as refiner and as a purifier of silver. He will purify the sons of Levy, (sons and daughters ministering as priests), and purge them as gold and silver, that they may offer to the Lord an offering of righteousness. This is confirmed in the word of God in Malachi 3:2,3.

It is time for the remnant to rise in purity and to bring God a sacrifice of right doing. Through such a lifestyle His glory will arise and rest upon us. The church will end strong and powerful. Refinement leads to holiness; holiness leads to righteousness and righteousness leads to eternal life and ushers in His manifested presence - His glory.

EFFECTS OF HIS GLORY UPON THE CHURCH

The restoration of God's glory upon His church will be an abiding glory. The church will arise and shine for her light has come.

*Arise, shine; for your light has come! And the **glory** of the Lord is risen upon you. For behold, the darkness shall cover the earth, and deep darkness the people; but the Lord will rise over you, and His glory will be seen upon you. The gentiles shall come to your light, and kings to the brightness of your rising.*

Isaiah 60: 1 - 3

The gentiles, far off nations that do not know God shall come to the light that has come upon the church. They will come to be saved and healed.

- God's provision for harvest - Kings will come to the brightness of the rising of the church. Kings resemble the marketplace entrepreneurs. This is the time when the church will carry the revelation that the marketplace needs and the kings will carry the provision for the end time harvest. There will be a cross pollination between these two arenas, and the wealth of the gentiles (nations) shall come to the church. By this fusion the order of Melchizedek will be restored. There will be a definite transfer of wealth for the end time church to fulfill her mandate of bringing in the final harvest. God will glorify His house. The answers for all seven mountains of society - mountain of religion, family, education, government, media, arts and business - will be found within the ecclesia. As a result of the abiding glory upon the remnant church, there will be a continual harvest of souls, especially the young generation.

- *Behold, the days are coming, says the Lord, when the plowman shall overtake the reaper, and the treader of grapes, him who sows seed: the mountains shall drip with sweet wine, and all the hills shall flow with it.*

Amos 9:13

- Nations will gather. The effect of God's glory upon the church will cause nations to gather to the mountain of the Lord. They will be drawn to the light of His glory and the intense worship that will be going forth as the tabernacle of David will also be restored. His light, His presence brings forth revelation, healing manifests, provision is at hand and clarity goes forth. The remnant church will carry the answers in the end times. Rulers of nations will turn to the church for answers. The church will become an eternal excellence and a joy for many generations.

This is what the house of the Lord will look like when it is restored.

Now it shall come to pass in the latter days that the mountain of the Lord's house shall be established on the top of the mountains, and shall be exalted above the hills; and all nations shall flow to it. Many people shall come and say "come, and let us go up to the mountain of the Lord, to the house of the God of Jacob; He will teach us His ways, and we shall walk in His paths".   Isaiah 2:2,3

- Power restored to the church. Where the church was rendered powerless and defeated it will now rise in the light of His glory to a point where those who despised the church will come bowing down. The church will be called the city of the Lord. Our God will be our glory, and everlasting light which produces an abiding glory. His people will be righteous walking on the highway of holiness and the Lord will be glorified. Christ will return for a victorious bride.

- Worship restored. High praises and worship invite His glory. The young generation will hear the sound of the worship, be attracted to it, will assemble and be delivered and redeemed in the manifested presence of the Lord. The lame and the outcast will come. They will come to the brightness of His light and to the joyous sound of continual worship and praise as the tabernacle of David is being restored. In the presence of this atmosphere sinners will be convicted and convinced, fall on their faces and say this is the true living God. The Spirit of the Lord will come down on them as latter rains. They will be set free in His presence. An influx of young people and a harvest of young souls will manifest as a direct result of His glory upon the ecclesia.

During the time of Acts 2 the Holy Spirit was poured out on believing Jews only. The evidence was the speaking of tongues that came forth. Each speaking in a foreign language as the fire of the Spirit fell upon them. However, in Joel 2 the Spirit is poured out upon all flesh and comes down as the latter rains.

- Latter rain and revelation released. We are now in the days of Joel 2 when the latter rains of the Spirit will be released upon all flesh. Those who belong to Him by covenant as well as on unbelievers. The evidence of these latter rains will be seen through prophecy being released through the mouths of children, the youth, the elderly, as well as on the leaders of the ecclesia. The prophetic will become very eminent. The church shall start to "see in the Spirit" and flow together in unity. Many churches will gather in one river and stand in unity as the end time move of God will be an apostolic and prophetic team effort. No more wandering of ministries on their own. These streams will culminate and become an ocean of revival.

Water will start to flow from the altar as the altar of God is being restored, cleansed and purified. This move of God will start as a river flowing ankle deep and will proceed deeper to the knees and to the waist. It is the river of His glory and manifested presence. The river will become very deep and will cause a separation between the vile and the precious. The river will become too deep to cross, but people will swim in it. The waters of this river, His Spirit, will bring healing to the nations and it will manifest as a culmination of streams coming together. Ministries will join forces, and healing will flow in the body of Christ. When all ministries are joined to the Head, Jesus Christ, the water will flow strongly as we stand in unity, and it will result in a great healing and revival. And it shall be that every living thing, wherever the river goes, will live. Life in the Spirit will come forth from this river. Wherever the river goes, life comes forth. Everything will live wherever the river goes. There will be a great multitude of fish resembling the harvest of souls. This is the river of life spoken of in Revelations 22.

And He showed me a pure river of water of life, clear and crystal, proceeding from the throne of God and of the Lamb in the middle of its street, and on either side of the river, was a tree of life, which bore twelve fruits, each tree yielding its fruit every month. The leaves of the tree were for the healing of the nations.

Revelations 22:1,2

It shall be that fishermen will stand by it from En Gedi to En Eglaim, they will be places for spreading their nets. Their fish will be of the same kinds as the fish of the Great Sea, exceedingly many. But its swamps and marshes will not be healed: they will be given over to salt. Along the bank of the river, on this side and that, will grow all kinds of trees used for food: their leaves will not wither, and their fruit will not fail. They will bear fruit every month, because their water flows from the sanctuary. Their fruit will be for food and their leaves for medicine.

Ezekiel 47:10 - 12

The nets of different ministries joining forces in unity will be cast to bring in the harvest from desolate places and from the ends of the world. The harvest will be brought in through a team effort. These nations from afar off will join the sons and daughters of God and they will all join together as His sons and daughters. All differences will be eliminated. It will be an exceedingly great harvest. Outside of this river there will be no healing, neither provision, as it will be swamps and salt lakes. Outside of this river of God desolation and destruction will be seen as God's judgment comes down upon those who reject Him.

Because this river, the river of His glory flows from the altar, there will be a continual supply of healing and provision unto the nations. The continual fruit of these ministries, joined together in the flow of this river, will supply food and medicine in and out of season without ceasing. There will be continual supply from the altar. The streams of this river shall make glad the city of God, the tabernacle of the most high. God is in her midst, and she will not be moved. God will be exalted among the nations and be exalted in the earth through the true remnant church. The confirmation for this word is found in Psalms 46.

It is imperative that you are joined to an apostolic prophetic altar or ministry in this end time dispensation. The word of God is clear on it. The water flows from the altar. Therefore, it is of utmost importance that the altars of churches and ministries are purified as the church needs to be holy, sanctified, walking in purity to ensure a continual flow of the river of His glory. The time is over to sit in the church and be defiled or to defile the altars of God. Such ministries, leaders and congregation members will find themselves in the marshes and swamps given over to salt. There will only be safety in the ecclesia, the pure, holy legislative, governing body of Christ, registered in heaven.

This is a totally new era. The old has passed. This end time move of God will be earmarked by the church being purified, standing in unity as ministries culminates in one stream of flow. Directed and gathered together under the headship of Christ. There will be no cursing of one another's nets, nets resembling one another's ministries. No slandering and backbiting. God's people will walk in holiness before Him covered with His glory, an abiding glory. A continual flow in the Spirit and God will be in the midst of the true remnant.

- Shaking. The time preceding the outpouring of the latter rains of His glory will be marked by different shakings all over the world. Only that which is of God will stand. That which is founded on the foundation of the apostles and the prophets, with Jesus Christ as the chief Cornerstone. His house will be filled with His glory. We are commanded to work hard and not to fear when we see the shaking take place. For the coming glory of God's house, He first need to shake that which is man made and not pleasing unto Him.

For thus says the Lord of Hosts: once more (it is a little while) I will shake heaven and earth, the sea and dry land; and I will shake all nations, and they shall come to the Desire of All Nations and I will fill this temple with glory, says the Lord of hosts. The silver is Mine, and the gold is Mine, says the Lord of hosts. The glory of this latter temple shall be greater than the former, says the Lord of hosts, and in this place I will give peace, says the Lord of hosts.
Haggai 2:6 - 9

From the scripture in Haggai 2 we see five areas of shaking: one, the heavens will be shaken, two, the earth will be shaken, three, the sea, four, the dry land, and fifthly, the nations. Everything will be shaken worldwide, starting with the nations which we have already seen a little bit of. This will all happen before the great outpouring of the latter rains, His glory that will manifest on all flesh and cause the prophetic to come upon all flesh, especially the infants and children.

God makes Himself known as the Lord of hosts. This means He is manifesting Himself as the Head of the armies of the living God. Jesus will head His army in these final days prior to the rapture. We as leaders need to prepare the body of Christ to stand and take up their places in this great army to take their mantles and spiritual weapons and fight. Time for complacency in the church is over. You will no longer be able to hide. Every believer needs to take up their place in the body for the final quest. The church needs to be prepared for this function. True sons and daughters will be revealed in this hour as we approaching the final move of God in the earth. The victory belongs to the church by His Spirit. His temple will be filled with His glory. Throughout scripture we see the dwelling places of His glory within the tabernacle of Moses, the tabernacle of David and the arc of the covenant with its mercy seat being covered by cherubim angels. It was covered by a cloud during the day and the pillar of fire by night resembling His manifest presence amongst His people. The twentieth century church has lost this dimension, but it will be restored in this dispensation.

There was also the temple of Solomon in Jerusalem where His presence dwelt and now again His presence will dwell amongst His people within the ecclesia. In this dispensation of the church, His presence resides inside of us, our bodies serve as a tabernacle in the earth. However, His presence also covers us and rests upon a holy human vessel. When we all gather together, we grow into a holy temple in the Lord, built together for a dwelling place of God in the Spirit. This is confirmed by the apostle Paul in Ephesians 2:21 and 22.

When God's word declares that His temple will be filled with glory, it means that He will descend by His Spirit and dwell amongst His children within the ecclesia. The Word declares that the silver and gold belongs to God. Why is He making such a statement? There will come a time not long from now when we will not be able to trade, buy or sell without the implanting of the microchip, the mark of the beast referred to in Revelations 13.

He causes all, both small and great, rich and poor, free and slave, to receive a mark on their right hand and on their foreheads, and that no one may buy or sell, except one who has the mark or the name of the beast, or the number of his name. Here is wisdom. Let him who has understanding calculate the number of the beast, for it is the number of a man. His number is 666.

Revelations 13: 16 - 18

However, God says that the silver and the gold, resembling al trading belongs to Him. He says this so that we can know that within the remnant church, God will make provision for His children to live through these times. The remnant will not be controlled by the anti-Christ. You can only be controlled if you partner with the evil one. As children of God, we need to walk in full authority and legislate from mount Zion. It is the days where we as sons and daughters of God will declare a thing and it will be established for us, so that light will shine on our ways.

You will also declare a thing, and it will be established for you: so light will shine on your ways.   *Job 2:28*

If we do not have bread to eat, we will declare a bread and God will allow a bread to manifest. This is part of the powers to come concerning the end time church. That is how powerful the end time church will be. However, there are some prerequisites for this power to manifest, which we will discuss. He will provide for us. Should you take the mark of the beast on your right hand or forehead, you will not enter God's Kingdom. The mark of the beast is part of the anti-Christ agenda.

Finally, God says that, in this place, referring to the ecclesia, the true remnant church, He will give peace. Peace is not the absence of trouble and strife. It is the Presence of the Prince of peace, Jesus Christ. Where His presence is, there is light, the light of His glory that manifests all that we need. He will take His children through to their final destination in this hour, as He is a faithful Son over the house and our heavenly Father is the builder of the house. But be warned through this, take heed of the book of Revelations and bow only to our Lord, Jesus Christ. This is war against the church, and it is real. The Lord of Hosts, the Commander of the armies of God, is with us and will lead us to victory. Obedience is key.

CHAPTER 2
THE HIGHWAY OF HOLINESS

THE HIGHWAY OF HOLINESS

Concerning the future glory of the church, God is calling her to reign and declare from mount Zion. The Lord reigns from mount Zion and the glorious end time church will reign with Him from this place. Mount Zion is the legislative governmental seat of heaven and courts of heaven. This is where verdicts are passed by the Judge, our heavenly Father, and executed by the angels on the earth. This is the seat where the church needs to be seated with Him in heavenly places to rule and reign.

"Raised us up together, and made us sit together in the heavenly places in Christ Jesus"
Ephesians 2:6

Now it shall come to pass in the latter days that the mountain of the Lord's house shall be established on the top of the mountains and shall be exalted above the hills; and peoples shall flow to it. Many nations shall come and say, "come let us go up to the mountain of the Lord, to the house of the God of Jacob; He will teach us His ways and we shall walk in His paths". For out of Zion the Lord shall go forth and the Word of the Lord from Jerusalem.
Mica 4:1,2

Through intimacy and holiness, the end time remnant will carry authority in the courts of heaven. God wants to establish cities like this in the earth where He dwells amongst His people and releases His glory. His tangible presence that brings change about. The end time remnant church will not be defeated but walk in authority and glory, and rule in Zion.

There will be a road called the highway of holiness between mount Zion in heaven and these established places of dominion in the earth.

"A highway shall be there, and a road, and it shall be called the Highway of Holiness. The unclean shall not pass over it, but it shall be for others. Whoever walks the road, though a fool, shall not go astray. No lion shall be there, nor shall any ravenous beast go up on it. It shall not be found there. But the redeemed shall walk there"
Isaiah 35:8,9

What does all of this mean? The prophet Isaiah was prophesying about a future dispensation where the saints will have access to the governing system in heaven from where declarations are made, and from where God's law and judgments goes forth. This pathway will require holiness.

However, the church right now is far from it and needs to be restored to overcome in the last days when great darkness will cover the earth and the hour of trial which shall come upon the whole world, to test those who dwell on it is at hand.

"For behold, darkness shall cover the earth, and deep darkness the people; but the Lord will arise over you and His glory will be seen upon you" Isaiah 60:2

"Because you have kept My command to persevere, I will also keep you from the hour of trial which shall come upon the whole world, to test those who dwell upon the earth".
Revelations 3:10

Hereby we can know that the hour of trial will come, and that darkness will come upon the whole world.

God, through the blood of His Son, Jesus Christ, gave us access to the governmental mountain and place in the Spirit, Mount Zion. The church needs to learn to access this mountain. To have access there the condition to be met is holiness. Therefore, it is called a Highway of Holiness. It is a pathway through which we have access to the throne of God. The Word is clear about it, that the unclean will not pass over it. It shall be for those who keep their garments and live a holy life. You need to be pure and clean to have that privilege as righteousness was imputed to us through the blood of the Lamb. However, there is a deeper level as righteousness needs to be worked out by the saints.

No lion shall be there, referring to satan himself. Nor any ravenous beast, referring to high ranking demons. It is a pathway for the redeemed and the ransomed by the blood of the Lamb. Joy and gladness is found is there. From this place sighing and sorrow will flee. It is a sacred place where God wants all His sons and daughters through a holy, sacrificial and self-denied life, to regularly come and receive. From mount Zion we will make a decree, and it will be established in the earth and light will be on our pathway. Without this lifestyle we will not be able to navigate the end times.

It is clear that God is calling His church up higher. Therefore, we need to fully comprehend holiness and how to walk in it on this highway, this pathway between God's throne and the realm of the earth.

What then is holiness? Let us start by what it is not. Holiness is not a set of rules. God does everything for His glory. His end result is His glory and a glorious, victorious church. God wants His church to be permeated by His presence. He seeks a dwelling place amongst His people in the earth. Where holiness and God's presence is on display you will also find the fire of God. That is what Christ died for. Holiness is radical obedience to God, total surrender to Christ and yielded to the Holy Spirit. Holiness is part of the preparation of the bride as where we are going, our bridegroom is holy. Holiness ushers in His glory. Without holiness there will be no glory - tangible presence of God that invokes change. The glory of God is summed up in holiness and worship is the response to God's holiness.

Holiness means to be sensitive to the voice of God and follow a lifestyle of hearing and obeying. Without holiness no one will see the kingdom of God. Holiness revealed will lead to repentance.

"Pursue peace with all people, and holiness, without which no one will see the Lord"
Hebrews 12:14

Holiness is seated in the heart of the redeemed. It calls for a circumcised heart, pure and upright heart, undefiled. Clean from mental defilement.

REQUIREMENTS FOR WALKING IN HOLINESS

- Righteousness. A prerequisite to holiness. We have already stated that righteousness is imputed to us through faith in the blood of Jesus unto salvation. We also stated that righteousness needs to be worked out. Once you are saved, you cannot remain in the outer courts. You must work out your salvation with fear and trembling.

- *"Therefore, My beloved, as you have always obeyed, not as in my presence only, but now much more in my absence, work out your salvation with fear and trembling"*
Philippians 2:12

As you work out your salvation, it means that you need to watch and keep your garment of righteousness. Our righteous robe needs to be kept clean from sin and dead works. Righteousness means to be in right standing with God with a clean conscience. This way you will become a conduit for the Spirit of God to flow through you and hear His voice in order to obey what He requires.

God is calling His remnant church out from the world to be holy and consecrated unto Him in this hour.

Therefore "come out from among them and be separate, says the Lord. Do not touch what is unclean, and I will receive you. I will be a Father to you and you shall be My sons and daughters, says the Lord almighty"   2 Corinthians 6:17,18

This is covenant language. God sets His standard for righteousness and holiness. God wants us free from all sorts of mental defilement. We need to be careful as to what we are looking at and what we are exposing the Holy Spirit inside of us to through our natural senses. The church needs to make herself ready.

"Let us be glad and rejoice and give Him glory, for the marriage of the Lamb has come, and His wife has made herself ready." And to her it was granted to be arrayed in fine linen, clean and bright, for the fine linen is the righteous acts of the saints"
Revelations 19:7,8

From the above it is clear that our garments are made up of the righteous acts of the saints. A person can be righteous without being holy but cannot be holy without being righteous. There are specifically three areas of righteous acts that God requires from the church:

- *"Pure and undefiled religion before God and the Father is this: to visit orphans and widows in their trouble, and to keep oneself unspotted from the world"*
  James 1:27

God Himself becomes the Father of the fatherless and a husband to the widow. This counts as a righteous act before God and we will be rewarded by God at the white throne judgment seat, when we involve ourselves on behalf of the orphans and the widows. These righteous acts make up the fine linen robe of righteousness, the garment.

> *"Go therefore and make disciples of all the nations, baptizing them in the name of the Father and of the Son and of the Holy Spirit, teaching them to observe all things that I have commanded you; and lo, I am with you always, even to the end of the age"* Matthew 28:19,20

This is God's requirement, that we will bring in the harvest and baptize them in the name of the Father and the Son and the Holy Spirit by immersing them in water. Then they are marked by the Holy Spirit as a seal that they belong to God and to the body of Christ. This is the reason why a born-again believer cannot take the mark of the beast, microchip, that resembles the mark of the beast, and the number is of man 666. Being marked either by the Holy Spirit or by the beast resembles ownership.

We also need to teach them the unprecedented word of God, through a process of teaching, training and mentoring we need to develop them until they have reached the fullness of Christ. They need to be trained by the five-fold ministry to bring them to full maturity as sons and daughters of God. This is lacking in the church and needs to be corrected. How can we pursue holiness if we are disobedient to the word of God? It is obedience that leads to righteousness and righteousness leads to holiness and holiness leads to eternal life according to Romans. All of this which God requires of the church makes up the fine linen of the robe.

"And this gospel of the Kingdom will be preached in all the world as a witness to all the nations, and then the end will come" Matthew 24:14

The gospel of Jesus Christ refers to the acknowledgement that Jesus Christ is the Son of God, died on the cross of Calvary and was resurrected on the third day. Is seated at the right hand of God on the throne where He rules and reigns. Should you believe this in your heart and confess it with your mouth, it leads to salvation by the blood of Jesus Christ through the Holy Spirit.

The gospel of the Kingdom of God is the manifestation of Jesus Christ. This manifestation of the powers of the Kingdom might be the only message that unbelievers may understand. It will certainly cause them to come to salvation. We owe the world an encounter with God.

Without pleasing God by walking in radical obedience, there will be no holiness. Righteousness may still be imputed by the blood of Christ, but disobedience disqualifies you from a deep relationship and carrying His Presence. It creates a barrier between you and God.

"Do you not know that to whom you present yourselves slaves to obey, you are that one's slave whom you obey, whether of sin leading to death, or of obedience leading to righteousness? "   Romans 6:16

"But now having been set free from sin, and having become slaves of God, you have your fruit to holiness, and the end, everlasting life"   Romans 6:22

This is God's word on it. No eternal life without holiness. The remnant church will be made up of believers only carrying the uncorrupted seed of God. No mixed seed. In order to produce holiness as a fruit after God. We are being prepared for eternity. God is holy, so let us be holy, so that we will see Him in this age and the age to come.

- Right relationships. *"Pursue peace with everyone with all people, and holiness, without which no one will see the Lord"*   Hebrews 12:14

We can also not have holiness without right relationships. There are times when peace is not possible, but we need to pursue peace with all people. Relationships that are troubled will hinder holiness before God and will impact on you hearing His voice.

*"bearing with one another, and **forgiving** one another, if anyone has a complaint against another; even as Christ forgave you, so you also must do"* Colossians 3:13

Forgiveness is key before God in a pursuit of a clear and clean heart. Guard your heart above all. God sees and looks at the heart. Let your conscience be clean before God and the heart's condition pure. He will draw near to you as you seek His face in purity. The presence of God and holiness needs to be stewarded well as the price at the cross of Calvary was high and God will only entrust His mind and His heart to those who meet His conditions. There is a call for the remnant church to be pure. There must be no uncorrupted seed found in us. We cannot carry any of the seed that the enemy is carrying as we will have no authority to legislate in this hour. This is a serious call to the bride in preparing herself for the coming of the King of glory and to be victorious. Christ is coming for a warrior bride that will not be defeated but be victorious. The bride of Christ will reign through her decrees. The natural will be overridden by the decrees of the pure and holy bride. We can only decree His will, His mind over matters as we hear His voice and "see" what our Father is doing. The warrior bride will please Him only. It is the time for preparation, come before the throne of God and repent.

- Condition of the heart. Those who are pure in heart will see the Lord.
- *"Blessed are the **pure** in heart, for they shall see God"*   Matthew 5:8

God requires purity. A generation is rising that will walk in purity and it will allow them to "see" Him even in this age. They will "see" Him in the Spirit. They will know His heart on matters and declare His will and mind in the earth. This is not only reserved for eternity, but it is intended for this life. God wants to redeem nations and has plans for individual lives as well as for nations, which are connected to their true identity and destiny. For this to be fulfilled in the earth, He seeks a generation to agree with Him from mount Zion. Holiness gives you access to mount Zion, the hill and city of God via the highway of holiness. We will be covering mount Zion later in this book for you to fully comprehend. Right now, we are dealing with God's requirements for holiness.

"Therefore, as the elect of God, holy and beloved, put on tender mercies, kindness, humility, meekness, long-suffering; bearing with one another, and forgiving one another, if anyone has a complaint against another, even as Christ forgave you, so you also must do. But above all these things, put on love, which is the bond of perfection"
Colossians 3:12 - 14

Mercy, kindness, long-suffering, humility and meekness are attributes of the persona of the Holy Spirit. This was the condition of the heart of the Son of Man. The Spirit of Christ acknowledges its own and is drawn to a heart like this. It is all He knows. When the Holy Spirit finds these conditions present in a heart, He will make His abode there. Life in the Spirit will come forth as the Spirit is life. Where there is much love and a pure heart, you will find much of the presence of the Holy Spirit. This opens the realm of the unseen in the heavenlies where you engage with your spiritual senses to be able to hear His voice clearly. The bride will rely on the Holy Spirit to speak and to lead. In the final move of God, it is make or break. Time for practice will then be over. We need to conquer with Him. Let there be no hindrances in your heart.

- His Word. Without His Word we are not fit for His Presence. God is seeking stewardship over His Word as He is ready to perform His Word. He will not entrust the heavenly treasures to those who do not make time or have respect for His Word. His Word washes us.

- "Husbands, love your wives, just as Christ also loved the church and gave Himself for her, that He might sanctify and cleanse her with the washing of water by the Word, that He might present her to himself a glorious church, not having spot or wrinkle or any such thing, but that she would be holy and without blemish"
Ephesians 5:25 - 27

It is the Word that sanctifies us unto holiness. A proper knowledge and understanding of the Word are required. Therefore, He gave the command to teach all newborn believers. Many are not prepared for the sacrifice. In this season there will be a price to pay both ways. What the church could get away with under the old will not be possible under the new move of God, as we are living in perilous times and the onslaught of the enemy, and the rising of the anti-Christ is a reality. Jesus Christ is making sure that His bride will be ready and victorious as He is a faithful Son over His house.

"It is the Spirit who gives life, the flesh profits for nothing. The words that I speak to you are Spirit and they are life"   John 6:63

The church is entering a period of time where the Word of God will be declared over situations to bring about change. As the Word of God is Spirit, when it is released, it seeks a resting place. When the Word which is Spirit, goes out and finds such a resting place, it will bring life into that situation and resurrect. The Word is powerful and is a two-edged sword.

The Word of God needs to dwell in us richly in all wisdom to teach and admonish. The Word of God is the end time sword. God will swing His sword against His offenders in the end time which is at hand and bring about judgment. We as the ecclesia will proclaim His Word over all evil in an effort to push the enemy back, especially the anti-christ. We are in a war. The battle is real, and the threat is real.

"For the Word of God is living and powerful and sharper than any two-edged sword, piercing even to the division of soul and spirit and of joints and marrow, and is a discerner of the thoughts and intents of the heart. And there is no creature hidden from His sight, but all

things are naked and open to the eyes of Him to whom we must give account"
Hebrews 4:12 - 13

A great tribulation will come over the whole earth and its inhabitants will be tested. We cannot escape this and already see the evidence of this in the earth. Now what should we do then?

We need to be watchful, position ourselves before the throne of God, strengthen that which remains in Him after the shaking of all things. This way we will find mercy and grace in a time of need. The end time ecclesia will carry authority in the Spirit. That is the reason why holiness and all God's requirements need to be met. Nothing is hidden from the eyes of God. All is naked before His eyes, and we have an accountability towards Him. God will expose the plans of the enemy in the end time to His prophets, sons and daughters and servants who live a holy life and seek His face. Once the plans of the enemy are being exposed we have accountability to push the enemy back by decreeing the Word of God over the situations **until** the situation turns. This is a real war. The enemy also has his plans and incantations. If the church is weak the enemy and evil will have its way.

The Word of God pierces through the unseen realm as well as through that which is seen. We need to know the Word and the Word needs to be in our hearts and in our mouths so that by the time when we are persecuted and the Word might no longer be available in different nations, we have hidden it in our hearts. Ready to pull the sword in prayer and decree from mount Zion. The end time bride will work in unison with heaven in agreeing on God's purposes in the earth. We will stand united as the body of Christ in a team effort in the last days. Division in the church will no longer be tolerated by God.

"So shall My Word be that goes forth from My Mouth: it shall not return to Me void, but it shall accomplish what I please, and it shall prosper in the thing for which I sent it"
Isaiah 55:11

Who will send the Word? We as the ecclesia will decree and declare His Word and He will establish it and accomplish that which He sent it forth to do. The Word will prosper as it is sent from God through the mouth of a holy vessel. We have a responsibility before God to come to know His Word like never before. It is part of our inheritance and part of our preparation.

- Intercession.

"Justice is turned back, and righteousness stands afar off; for truth is fallen in the street, and equity cannot enter. So truth fails, and he who departs from evil makes himself a pray"
Isaiah 59:14

Are we not seeing this in the nations currently? There is no justice for the pure, no right standing of evil doers before the only true living God. Truth has failed as it has fallen in the streets, evil is rising up. Should you depart from evil, it is accounted to you to become prey. Falling prey to the evil one. Unrighteousness prevails. God will never be satisfied with this condition in the nations, in the lives of the people He created. He is a just God and is calling the ecclesia up to intercession. He is a Redeemer of His people. How will God then deal with this and what does He expect of the ecclesia when we see such injustice on the rise?

"Then the Lord saw it, and it displeased Him that there was no justice. He saw that there was no man, and wondered that there was no intercessor; therefore His own arm brought salvation for Him; and His own righteousness, it sustained Him.
Isaiah 59:15,16

We serve a just God. The scepter of His throne is righteousness. God is looking down from His throne to the dimension of the earth and seeks for a people that will agree with Him on justice to be served and righteousness to be exercised. It is His nature, His persona. He is a sovereign God and cannot turn against His Word. He upholds all by His Word.

These conditions in the nations displeases God and calls for judgment. However, because He is loving God, He is first looking for an intercessor, a man that will stand in the gap and build a wall before His throne so that He will not destroy but restore. The Kingdom of God is a judicial system. Agreement with heaven from the realm of the earth is necessary as the ecclesia partners with God on His will, His truth and Mind over matters. He has established His throne in heaven and His Kingdom rules overall. It displeased God that there was no justice in the land. God's first choice of weapon is that we rule and reign and decree with Him from heavenly places. His manifold wisdom needs to be on display through the church to the powers and principalities in the heavenlies. He calls His true sons and daughters forth to action when we see these detestable things in the earth. We are to know His plans and purposes for individuals, families and nations and agree with Him for His purposes to be fulfilled. As intercessors we stand in the gap for individuals, our families and nations before the throne of grace to petition God on their behalf. Therefore, we repent on their behalf from any sin, iniquities or anything that is displeasing to God. The ecclesia stands on behalf of people and nations.

"So I sought for a man among them who would make a wall, and stand in the gap before Me on behalf of the land, that I should not destroy it, but I found no one"

Ezekiel 22:30

God's eyes go to and through the whole earth to look for a righteous man to stand in the gap between a righteous God and a sinful situation. He will pardon on behalf of the righteous man the sins of the unrighteous. He is a merciful God and want the ecclesia to rise and build a wall of righteousness before His throne for salvation to come. He is clothed with mercy and loving kindness towards His creation. How will we escape if we do not adhere to His call and salvation and truth will be afar off? Should God's Name be blasphemed by the disobedience of His sons and daughters? God is love and calls for a righteous remnant to arise through intercession to stand in the gap so that the gates of hell will not prevail against the church.

As there will be an outpouring of the latter rains according to *Joel 2*, in other words an outpouring of His Spirit upon all flesh, the direct result that follows is a prophetic release from heaven and much revelation. Prophecy, visions and dreams will come forth and earmark this era which has already started. Thereby the manifold wisdom of God will be on display to the powers and principalities in the heavenlies as God reveals His strategies and mysteries to His intercessors. Therefore, intercession will take on a new form. It will take on the form of prophetic intercession with decrees and declarations of His Word over nations and situations.

"And I also say to you that you are Peter, and on this rock I will build My church, and the gates of Hades shall not prevail against it"   Matthew 16:18

Jesus Himself speaking.

Peter means rock and comes from the root word "petra", which means rock bed. Christ is the Rock Bed and Peter was chosen to be instrumental in building the early church. In this passage in Matthew 16, Peter's persona, his call was made known to him by the Spirit of Knowledge, which is one of the aspects of the Holy Spirit, which we will be dealing with in a short while. The gates of Hades is a pit underneath the earth where souls will be kept that rejected the blood of Jesus and the sacrifice of His life through the cross of Calvary.

This is a profound statement that Jesus made to Peter, as it revealed Peter's persona and identity but also serves as proof that revelation knowledge by the Spirit of God is a powerful weapon against the enemy. The evil one will not prevail against the end time remnant or ecclesia as a direct result of the revelation knowledge by the Spirit of God made known to us in order for us to use it as a decree. What we decree from mount Zion, God will establish in the earth. This is the authority that a holy remnant will carry in these last days. And the elect of the Lord will say so!

We as the ecclesia have no option in these last days than to be holy and pure before our God to enable us to stand and fulfill His purposes in the earth.

- Fasting, prayer and repentance. Humble yourself with fasting. No holiness without fasting. Fasting is the abstaining from food and drink for a period of time for spiritual purposes. Fasting requires humbling of yourself, confession of your sins and seeking His will.

"Your kingdom come, Your will be done, on earth as it is in heaven" Matthew 6:10

The true remnant will seek His will and declare it in the earth. His will is made known through prayer and fasting.

"And when you pray …. and when you fast…." Matthew 6:5

This is Jesus speaking when He says, "when you fast and when you pray", it does not leave an option for choice. It comes forth as a command, followed by instruction. This indicates a lifestyle that is required which will enable us to be properly humbled and purified before God.

God uses fasting as a measure of restoration in many instances. Right now, we ought to be concerned over the overall condition of the church. A condition of desolation is present whereby the church is far from its inheritance as sons and daughters. Many sons and daughters not knowing their identity or understanding their calling. The church is demon infiltrated as many of God's sons and daughters need healing and deliverance. As a result, the church renders herself powerless through the spirit of religion and tradition hindering the manifestation of God's true sons and daughters. The spirit of witchcraft that operates through control also is responsible for withholding the true sons and daughters from their destinies in Christ. These spirits will be abolished in the end time church and replaced with the five-fold ministry tasked with the equipping of the saints.

Restoration will come forth through fasting and prayer, and only through fasting and prayer. This will result in the gathering of His sons and daughters under the headship of Jesus Christ. There is an urgency for this to happen now as the church has deviated from the original plan and intent. Hence the glory, His manifested tangible Presence left as a result. This will be restored in the end time church. His sons and daughters will be executives being involved in His end time purposes and there will be second outpouring of the Holy Spirit on all flesh with the evidence of prophecy. His voice will be everywhere in a company and community of the prophetic. We will be raising prophetic communities.

His judgment will start at His church first before it is executed to the nations. This will result in a full alignment to the Holy Spirit. People will be forced to choose in the end times. You will have to position and choose either for Him or against Him as revival will break out as a direct result of His Spirit being released upon all flesh. Revival will break loose from South Africa and will go all the way to Cairo and to the rest of the world. Revival is messy and it forces you to make a decision. The battle is real. It is full-on war now between God's armies and the agenda of the anti-Christ. Strong principalities are rising to oppose God's purposes for the end time ecclesia. The church needs to position, take up their position in the body of Christ and know how to use their spiritual weapons. Everyone needs to be healed and delivered for the enemy not to have a foothold over the soul.

All of this will come forth by prayer and fasting.

"And it shall come to pass afterward that I will pour out My Spirit on all flesh, your sons and your daughters shall prophecy, your old men shall dream dreams, your young men shall see visions, and also on My men servants and on My maid servants I will pour our My Spirit in those days."   *Joel 2:28*

Sons and daughters refer to children and infants, young men refers to the youth and also includes young daughters, old men is the elderly and also includes older women, men servants and maid servants refer to the leaders in church. This is God's final Word on it and we have reached that time and dispensation in the history of the church now. The question is whether we are ready for, this outpouring will proceed a period of fasting and prayer.

Are we prepared to sacrifice and pay the price for God's purposes to prevail and prepare ourselves for the Bridegroom as we see the time drawing near?

A call to repentance. This outcry is directed to the church and all peoples upon the earth.

"Now, therefore," says the Lord, "turn to Me with all your heart, with fasting, with weeping and with mourning. So rend your heart and not your garments. Return to the Lord your God for He is gracious and merciful, slow to anger and of great kindness; and He relents from doing harm. Who know if He will turn and relent and leave a blessing behind Him - a grain offering and a drink offering for the Lord your God?" Blow the trumpet in Zion, consecrate a fast, call a sacred assembly, gather the people, sanctify the congregation, assemble the elders, gather the children and nursing babes. Let the bridegroom go out from his chamber and the bride from her dressing room. Let the priests who minister to the Lord, weep between the porch and the altar. Let them say, spare Your people, o Lord, and do not give Your heritage to reproach, that the nations should rule over them. Why should they say amongst the peoples, "where is their God?"
                Joel 2:12 - 17

It is clear that nations are on God's heart and that the final outpouring will be superceded by intense fasting and prayer, a seeking of His face. I thoroughly believe that the darkness that will cover the earth in the days and the deep darkness that will cover the people according to the prophet Isaiah in Isaiah 60:2, will play an instrumental role in wakening the sleeping giant - the church. Such darkness as depression, anxiety and fear will grip the people and the only place for them to turn to will be to God through repentance, prayer and fasting.

Then only the promise of restoration in Joel 2 of the latter rains will come to fulfillment. The final outpouring of His Spirit upon all flesh, and prophecy will be everywhere as well as revival will break loose. This outpouring and the gathering of the harvest will be the final move of God in the earth concerning the restoration and preparation of His end time bride. There is no other way. The end result will be the ultimate goal of holiness, the original intent of the church being restored as a glorious church carrying tangible Presence to impact and change the world. A Presence that can be seen and perceived by the spiritual senses. His glory will be seen upon the church to a point where it cannot be denied. Everyone whom God has drawn near to Him and whom He has called will run to the ecclesia for safety, healing and deliverance. They will run to the mountain of the Lord, to His house of the Lord to be taught His ways.

HOLINESS RESTORED - THE MIND OF CHRIST

The Holy Spirit recognises its own. Where holiness abides the condition of the heart will carry the persona of the spirit of God. Humbleness, meekness, kindness, lovingkindness, forgiveness, tender mercies and long-suffering. The Holy Spirit feels at ease in a heart that carries His persona and will make His abode in such a heart as He recognes Himself. As the presence of the Holy spirit is evident, the fruits of the Spirit will be eminent, love, joy, peace, long-suffering, kindness, goodness and faithfulness. These fruits are cultivated in the presence of the Lord and calls for a holy conduct before our Father.

The gifts of the Spirit will flow through a pure and clean conduit. There will be a manifestation of the Spirit to profit all. A word of wisdom through the Spirit, a word of knowledge through the same Spirit, faith by the same Spirit, gifts of healing by the same Spirit, working of miracles and prophecy. Discerning of spirits, different kinds of tongues and the interpretation of tongues by the Spirit of God. One and the same Spirit works all these things, distributing to each as He wills. The proof of this word is found in 1 Corinthians 12.

As true sons and daughters God has sent forth the Spirit of His Son into our hearts, crying out "Abba Father". We have the mind of Christ.

We were created in the likeness and image of God the Father, Jesus Christ and the Holy Spirit according to Genesis 1:16. We were created to have dominion over the earth. During this end time move of God we will see the manifestation of the sons and daughters of God rising in full authority and dominion over the evil works of the devil.

The seven-fold Holy Spirit becomes the habitation of the soul. Habitation refers to a dwelling place. The Holy Spirit in all its facets should rule over the soul of the sanctified believer walking in holiness before God. It is the responsibility of every believer to build a habitation for the Holy Spirit. This is the aim of Christ in these last days for His church. That He will be formed in all of His sons and daughters by having our souls as a habitation for His Spirit. A renewed mind, a mind that is not conformed to this world, but is continually being fed by all the facets of the Holy Spirit, the Spirit of Christ. This way the church will become a dwelling place for Him in the Spirit. The church will be a hundred percent effective and rule and have dominion as the soul dimension is fed by the Spirit of the Lord, by His wisdom, understanding, knowledge, counsel, might and the fear of the Lord. This way the church will become Kingdom orientated as the manifold wisdom of God will be available and on display to the powers and principalities in the heavenlies. The end time ecclesia will stand united in the Spirit.

For the sake of the above it is imperative that the soul dimension of every believer is healed and delivered from demon oppression. The soul feeds off a spiritual dimension which is either demon oppression or the mind of Christ - the seven-fold Holy Spirit. As a blood washed believer, you cannot be possessed by a demon as possession indicates ownership and you are already owned by Jesus Christ as His own. However, the soul dimension can be oppressed and influenced by demon oppression as the enemy has access to the mind through the five natural senses. Therefore, the soul needs to be delivered from fear and oppression and the Holy Spirit needs to feed into the soul an eternal Spirit dimension, as the soul needs to be subjected to your spirit-man and receive instruction from the Holy Spirit to be directed according to God's plans and purposes.

What are the seven spirits of God, or the seven-fold Holy Spirit?

"And from the throne proceeded lightnings, thundering and voices. Seven lamps of fire were burning before the throne, which are the seven Spirits of God"

Revelations 4:5

From this verse we notice that the seven Spirits of God is represented in heaven at the throne of God.

"And I looked, and behold, in the midst of the throne and of the four living creatures, and in the midst of the elders, stood a Lamb as though it had been slain, having seven horns and seven eyes, which are the seven Spirits of God, **sent out into all the earth***"*
Revelation 5:6

From this verse we learn that the seven Spirits of God is also sent out to the realm of the earth and represented on earth.

"There shall come forth a Rod (Jesus predicted by the prophet Isaiah) from the stem of Jesse (His lineage) and a Branch shall grow out of his (Jesse's) roots"

Isaiah 11:1

Jesus was from the lineage of David, who was Jesse's son.

"The Spirit of the Lord shall rest upon Him, the Spirit of wisdom and understanding, the Spirit of counsel and might, the Spirit of knowledge and of the fear of the Lord"
Isaiah 11:2

Notice that the word "Spirit" is written with a capital letter, which indicates that this is Jesus' Spirit. The Holy Spirit has seven aspects or manifestations depicting His character. This resembles the fullness of Christ and is our inheritance as true sons and daughters. What the church is lacking at the moment is for true sons and daughters corporately to be led only by the seven aspects of the Spirit of God as the situation calls for it.

"For as many as are lead by the Spirit of God, these are sons of God"

Romans 8:14

Sons and daughters walking in the fullness of His Spirit, the Spirit without measure. Therefore, we have a great task ahead of us raising the sons and daughters to full maturity as part of the preparation of the bride of Christ for the coming of the King. It is a late hour for the church already. It is the fullness of His Spirit, the Mind of Christ, that will allow us to be effective in this age. The fullness of Spirit leads to quick understanding, insight and the fear of the Lord. Without the restoration of the reverential fear of the Lord, His latter rains, His glory will not be released.

It is clear that the seven Spirits of God are seven manifestations of the Holy Spirit that rested on Jesus and now ought to rest upon us in order to legislate, govern and have dominion on the earth and in heavenly realms. This calls for purity, holiness and maturity. Remember Christ is returning for a victorious bride.

"His delight is in the fear of the Lord, and He shall not judge by the sight of His eyes, nor decide by the hearing of His ears; but with righteousness He shall judge the poor, and decide with equity for the weak of the earth. He shall strike the earth with the rod of His mouth, and with a breath of His lips He shall slay the wicked. Righteousness shall be the belt of His loins, and faithfulness the belt of His waist."

Isaiah 11:3 - 5

From the above it is clear that Jesus legislated and governed by the seven-fold Spirit of God upon Him. These verses speaks about the outcome of the Spirit "upon" Him, His fullness. This is another dimension. As born-again sons and daughters we all have the Holy Spirit inside of us. However, there is a further and more excellent dimension in the Spirit - the Spirit "upon" a believer. This dimension requires holiness and purity as well as righteousness not only imputed but worked out. We are created in His image. If this is what He looks like (His image) in the Spirit, we ought to look the same. We all need to carry the Spirit upon us to be effective. The church was and still is permeated with the spirit of religion and tradition most of the times. Many believers are hiding in the pews and got away with it under religious leaders. God is dethroning that dominion in this dispensation and bringing forth His true shepherds and leaders who will raise the flock to take up their place in the body of Christ and thereby be enrolled in God's end time army through the five-fold ministry.

We admitted it before, the battle is real, and it will intensify as the age draws to a close. The bride needs to position. Five-fold ministry is restored in the church and will now arise to raise God's soldiers. We will operate in the fullness of His Spirit. This now requires a thorough understanding of the seven Spirit of God in the diversity of His operations and manifestations and operate in both realms in heaven and on earth.

There are seven aspects of God's Spirit which is also referred to as the Spirit of Christ and referred to as the Mind of Christ. These seven aspects are the following:

The Spirit of the Lord, the Spirit of Wisdom, the Spirit of Understanding, the Spirit of Counsel, the Spirit of Might, the Spirit of Knowledge and the Spirit of the Fear of the Lord.

SPIRIT OF THE LORD

"And the Spirit of the Lord will rest upon Him".   Isaiah 11:2

The Spirit of the Lord can be described as the Spirit of Lordship, dominion and power. This aspect of the Holy Spirit rests upon a Spirit-filled son or daughter for the purposes of dominion to rule over a God-given domain as part of an assignment from God. The Spirit of the Lord puts you in charge of situations to declare and decree God's will over it. The Spirit of the Lord establishes.

"You will also declare a thing and it will be established for you, so light will shine on your ways"   *Job 22:28*

A matter is established by God in the realm of the earth and light (His glory) will shine on your pathways. A matter is established by the power of God through the Spirit of the Lord.

It is by the Spirit of the Lord that you are empowered to speak God's truth into a given situation.

"Therefore prepare yourself and arise, and speak to them all that I command you. Do not be dismayed before their faces lest I dismay you before them, for behold, I have made you this day a fortified city and an iron pillar, and a bronze wall against the whole city"
Jeremiah 1:17 - 18

It is by the Spirit of the Lord that the army of God is led. The Spirit of the Lord allows us to become fierce even in the face of adversity. Boldness and authority comes forth. The Spirit of the Lord is connected to His power.

THE SPIRIT OF WISDOM

The function of the church is to display the manifold wisdom of God to the powers and principalities in the heavenly realms. This is accomplished by the Spirit of Wisdom.

*"To the intent that now the **manifold** wisdom of God might be made known by the church to the principalities and powers in the heavenly places"*   Ephesians 3:10

The ecclesia will strike the earth with the rod of our mouths and nullify the plans of the enemy. This is a direct result of the Spirit of Wisdom upon the believer. The same Spirit that rested upon Jesus needs to rest upon us to engage in the final battle.

Wisdom is applied knowledge. What does knowledge refer to in this context?

It refers to revelation knowledge from the throne of God. By the Spirit of Wisdom, we will rightly judge as we will become aware of that which is not visible to the eyes, nor can be heard by the ears, but are revealed by the Spirit.

Wisdom is insight and will propel you towards executing God's purposes in the earth. Wisdom mobilizes into action. It gives direction in a given situation. It is knowing what to do and when and how to do it. The Spirit of Wisdom will direct your mind, and the mind becomes anointed with the ability from God to legislate from the throne of God into the realm of the earth. An ability from God is released through wisdom to direct your thoughts and decisions. Your mind becomes one with His mind, the mind of Christ in the executing of His purposes in the earth.

"And all Israel heard about the judgment which the king has rendered, and they feared the king, for they saw that the Wisdom of God was in him to administer justice"
                                      1 Kings 3:28

Wisdom allows you to do God's will and especially to stand for justice in the courts of heaven during intercession and also on the earth. Wisdom comes from the secret place and is found at the altar of prayer. The Spirit of Wisdom is connected to revelation and direction.

THE SPIRIT OF UNDERSTANDING

By the Spirit of Understanding we comprehend or understand the mysteries of God and His word, as well as the deep things of God are discerned through the Spirit of Understanding, the hidden mysteries.

"and He opened their understanding, that they might comprehend the scriptures"
Luke 24:45

This is a special anointing released by the Spirit of Christ (the Spirit of Understanding) to receive a deep understanding of the Word that penetrates the heart. The Spirit of Wisdom directs, and the Spirit of Understanding brings comprehension.

Our understanding needs to be activated and opened.

"that the God of our Lord Jesus Christ, the Father of glory, may give you the Spirit of Wisdom in the knowledge of Him. **The eyes of your understanding being enlightened (opened)** *that you may know what is the hope of your calling ……..”*
Ephesians 1:17 - 18

This was Paul's prayer for the Ephesian church. The Spirit of Understanding is connected to comprehension.

THE SPIRIT OF COUNSEL

The Spirit of Counsel guides you from within, directing your path.

"Your ears shall hear a voice behind you, saying, this is the way, walk in it"
Isaiah 30:21

You will hear with your heart and be directed from within.

The Spirit of Counsel is a strategist. By the Spirit of Counsel God will release strategy in any given situation. The "how" to go about. You will hear from within and know which direction to take and how to go about it. The Spirit of Counsel is connected to His strategies.

THE SPIRIT OF KNOWLEDGE

"My people are destroyed for a lack of knowledge. Because you have rejected knowledge, I will also reject you from being a priest for Me; because you have forgotten the law of your God, I will also forget your children"   Hosea 4:6

The knowledge referred to here is revelation knowledge. The Greek word for revelation knowledge is Gnosko. It is knowledge revealed by the Spirit of God from heavenly realms. We are destroyed by a lack of revelation from the throne of God through His Spirit. As priests ministering before God, we need to receive fresh revelation daily. This comes with a warning from God that we should not reject His knowledge, as it forms part of God's law, the law of the Spirit. In other words, it is our duty to receive revelation and hear from heaven. If we don't there will be consequences even concerning the next generation.

This revelation knowledge forms part of the governing system of heaven, we cannot reject it as it has an effect on the next generation, our children. God is restoring the priesthood as part of His end time restoration of the Church.

There are also different kinds of knowledge. The definition for knowledge, according to the dictionary, is "being aware of something, or knowing something with familiarity gained through experience or association or theory." This type of knowledge is head knowledge and the Greek word for this type of knowledge is Gnosis.

However, revelation knowledge (Gnosko) is exact knowledge, specific knowledge, knowledge that is separated from the mind and it is a knowledge that supersedes the mind. It is supernatural and is being released from a heavenly realm which is a higher dimension. Therefore, it is a higher knowledge. We therefore come to the conclusion that there is Gnosis, head knowledge, available in the earthly realm and Gnosko, available from the heavenly realms which is revelation knowledge.

What then is the difference? The source where it comes from is the difference.

One set of knowledge comes from the mind which is the soul, and the second set of knowledge is revealed from the throne of God by the Spirit of knowledge. Because its source is from heaven, it supersedes earthly knowledge and has a far reaching effect on generations. It reveals God's secrets and strategies. This is the type of knowledge that, when revealed you know that you know, that you know, and it will always be confirmed by two or more witnesses.

"By the mouths of two or three witnesses every word shall be established"

2 Corinthians 13:1

It becomes established knowledge. It becomes irrefutable and is part of the way God governs through us from heaven. This kind of revelation knowledge turns on the lights. It is imperative that the end time church operates in the fullness of the Spirit in this age just before the coming of our Lord Jesus Christ.

THE SPIRIT OF MIGHT

The Spirit of Might is connected to God's supernatural, overcoming strength and miraculous power. By the spirit of Might, overcoming strength to endure is made possible from above to do extraordinary exploits in boldness. The Spirit of Might is filled by righteousness and holiness.

It is an overpowering force that overcomes human strength. It takes over human senses and is a supernatural dunamis power on display.

"For this reason I bow my knees to the Father of our Lord Jesus Christ, from whom the whole family in heaven and earth is named, that He would grant you, according to the riches of His glory, to be strengthened with might through His Spirit in the inner man"
Ephesians 3:14 - 16

From this scripture it is clear that this is a working from "within" and is spontaneous and exceeds the natural mind. It covers you as a cloak. Samson who was a judge and David who was a king, both operated in the Spirit of Might to do great exploits for God.

THE SPIRIT OF THE FEAR OF THE LORD

The Spirit of the Fear of the Lord is connected to the reverential fear of the Lord. It is Godly understanding and awe-struck fear of the holiness of God as a loving Father and as a Judge.

EFFECTS OF THE REVERENTIAL FEAR OF THE LORD THROUGH THE SPIRIT OF THE FEAR OF THE LORD

- Prayer and fasting. The Spirit of the Fear of the Lord is connected to priesthood. Look at the life of Samuel who was called as a priest and prophet.

    "And has made us kings and priests before His God and Father ………..

    Revelations 1:6

Only those who fear God will take up this appointment before the throne of God.

"If My people who are called by My Name, will humble themselves and pray and seek My face, and turn from their wicked ways, then I will hear from heaven, and forgive their sin and heal their land"   2 Chronicles 7:14

It is humbleness that will lead to prayer. Humbleness is a direct result of the Spirit of the Fear of the Lord. Without the fear of the Lord upon your life your prayer life will be greatly affected.

- Godly order. Reverence for God will cause you to submit to Godly ordained leadership as these leaders need to guard over your souls and are accountable to God.

"Obey those who rule over you, and be submissive, for they watch out for your souls, as those who must give an account. Let them do so with joy and not with grief, for that would be unprofitable for you"   Hebrews 13:17

Where the Fear of the Lord is lacking disobedience reigns and God's Word is disrespected as God requires Godly submission at an altar of God.

- Godly discipline. Where the fear of the Lord is present, God's instructions and commandments according to His Word, will be obeyed. Only those who honor God will obey His commandments.

- Unity. Unity in the Spirit is a direct result of the Spirit of the Fear or the Lord being present. There God commands a blessing. The mountains of Zion will be restored and blessed. These mountains represent the ecclesia and includes the other six mountains of society that needs to be governed by the church.

  "As many as I love, I rebuke and chasten. Therefore be zealous and repent"

  Revelations 3:19

The church has to repent and return to God's ways and thoughts. The altars of God need to be restored as the Fear of the Lord return to the church. This is needed for the harvest and end time revival to break loose.

Godly order and governance need to be restored back to the altar for God's fire to fall on the altar and for the latter rains of His Spirit to be released on all flesh as promised in Joel 2. However, the church needs to meet God's conditions set out in His Word. It is our love for our Father and the Spirit of the fear of the Lord that will propel the end time church to align to heaven's purposes. This is the hour that we are living in. Therefore, God has no other alternative but to shake all things. His focus is on the harvest as He holds an eternal perspective.

By the Spirit of the fear of the Lord coming down upon the church, this Spirit will cause holiness to return to the body of Christ. We are in a window period of grace and have to prepare ourselves as part of the end time army of the Lord to be ready.

"Behold, I am coming as a thief. Blessed is he who watches, and keeps his garments, lest he walks naked and they see his shame" *Revelations 16:15*

Let us watch by prayer and fasting. Let us keep our garments by righteous acts so that we will not be caught off guard and empty handed.

Without the fear of the Lord returning to the church and holiness, we will not see the glory of God rising upon His church. However, He Who called us is faithful, and will bring a remnant forth that will be willing to sacrifice and pay the price for holiness. Those who will not deny His Name, keep his word and His commandments. It is time to prepare.

"He who has an ear, let him hear what the Spirit says to the churches"

Revelations 3:13

CHAPTER 3

HEADSHIP AND GATHERING TOGETHER OF ALL THINGS IN CHRIST

HEADSHIP AND GATHERING OF ALL THINGS TOGETHER IN CHRIST

It is the time of fulfillment of prophecy, biblical prophecy. Spiritual understanding is necessary in order for God's people to align themselves with Heaven's mandate and purposes in the earth.

"For it pleased the Father that in Him (Jesus) all the fullness should dwell and by Him to reconcile all things to Himself. By Him, whether things on earth or things in heaven, having made peace through the blood of His cross" Colossians 1:19,20

All fullness of time and divinity dwells in Christ. Therefore, we should come to full maturity and understanding of the Son of God through wisdom, knowledge as well as the length, width, depth and height of His love, to carry His fullness. Being rooted and grounded in His love. The fullness of God speaks of more than one experience of His truth and power. It points to all of His blessings, spiritual resources and wisdom. Above all, the love of Christ for the world, which surpasses all knowledge allows us to be filled with his fullness. He reconciled all things to Himself. All that is in heaven and on the earth. It was done through the blood sacrifice on the cross. Jesus brought heaven down to earth for the culmination of all things in Him. Alignment is necessary through the Holy Spirit. By this culmination and fullness, His fullness of all in all, the final end time battle will be fought on the earth. He that Indwells us has overcome the world.

He has made known to us the mystery of His will, according to His good pleasure which He purposed in Himself. It is a mystery how the end time ecclesia will rise and how heaven will back us up to fulfill end time prophecy.

The ecclesia is progressing the fulfillment of *Ephesians 1:10:*

"that in the dispensation of the fullness of time He might gather together in one all things in Christ, both which are in heaven and which are on the earth - in Him"
Ephesians 1:10

A dispensation refers to a period of time in which God relates to His people in a certain way. There was the dispensation of the patriarchs in the Old Testament during the time of Abraham. There was a dispensation of Moses and the law. We are now living in the dispensation of time just before the second coming of Jesus Christ. This is also referred to as the dispensation of the fullness of time. The word of God is clear on this, it is He who changes the times and seasons.

"And He changes the times and the seasons; He removes kings and raises up kings........
Daniel 2:21

All these seasons and times need to be fulfilled in church history according to the prophecies of the Old and New Testament.

"For there are three that bear witness in heaven: the Father, the Word (Jesus) and the Holy Spirit, and these three are one. And there are three that bear witness on the earth: the Spirit, the Water (His Word) and the Blood, and these three agree as one"
1 John 5:7 - 8

Why is this significant? Because heaven and earth will be joined to fight together in the end time battle which is approaching. The bride in all her glory, joining forces with heaven's agenda opposing the anti-Christ, Jezebel and the Babylonian world system.

We notice that in heaven all agree and there is unity. In the realm of the earth the Holy Spirit and the Word of God as well as the Blood sacrificed on the cross testifies and agrees as one. Unity is key on the earth amongst the body of Christ. Many shall be purified, made whole and refined, but the wicked shall do wickedly, and none of the wicked shall understand, but the wise shall understand. This scripture is confirmed in *Daniel 12:10*.

The kingdom of God is a judiciary system. It operates on witnessing and agreement. The agreeing and working together of the two realms, heaven and earth, culminating all things under the headship of Christ during the fullness of time that we are entering into now, will make up the final move of God in the earth. In this culmination there will be a separating of the vile from the precious. The church needs to be unified and perfected under the Head, Jesus Christ, as all in heaven is already unified. The heavenly realm will surround us in the last days. The seven-fold Holy Spirit of God will be the habitation of the remnant's souls as they will be directed by wisdom from above. Angels will be dispatched to the earth to assist the remnant in their call to complete the work of Christ, and all the saints that have already surpassed us into the heavenlies. God is bringing His ministry and purposes to full completion in the earth and then the end will come.

PREPARATION

Preparation time is now, it is at hand. The Lord is saying:

"Whom shall I send and who will go for us?"   *Isaiah 6:8*

When the prophet Isaiah saw the Lord sitting on the throne and when he saw the seraphim angel, the angel that carries fire, he was undone as he realized the holiness of God and at the same time, he realized his own condition of unclean lips as well as the unclean lips of the people amongst whom he lived. His eyes saw the Lord of hosts. The Lord of hosts is the Lord of the armies of heaven and earth. The angel touched his mouth with a coal of fire from the altar and instantly he was cleansed from iniquity and unclean lips. Then God sent him. His Presence will cause people to bow down and repent. We need to grow in the knowledge of Christ which will allow His light to rise in us. The more you grow in Him, the more you become ready to carry the weight of His glory, which is needed during this dispensation.

"And from the throne proceeded lightnings, thundering and voices. Seven lamps of fire were burning before the throne, which are the seven spirits of God"

Revelations 4:5

The seven-fold Holy Spirit will feed the souls of the ecclesia with wisdom, revelation, knowledge and counsel. This Spirit of Might and the Spirit of the Lord and the Spirit of the Fear of the Lord will be on display. However, the Holy Spirit requires holiness, a yielded spirit and surrendered life to Christ for all of this to happen.

"Behold, He is coming with the clouds, and every eye will see Him, and they who pierced Him and all the tribes of the earth will mourn because of Him. Even so amen. I am the Alpha and

the Omega, the Beginning and the End, says the Lord, Who is and was and Who is to come, the Almighty"   *Revelations 1:7*

The end time army of God is now being prepared by Heaven. The five-fold ministry in the church will raise up the saints for the final quest, prior to the second coming of Jesus Christ. All things are gathered, in the heavens and on the earth under His Headship for the purpose of showing forth His glory and power in the end time move of God that will come upon the church.

SEPARATION

Before the gathering of all things in heaven and on earth a separation will first take place on the earth. A separation between the vile and the precious. A separation between the true remnant church and the religious infiltrated church carrying mixed seed. A church where there is no differentiation between Babylon and the bride. The true remnant bride is positioning and is separated from the rest.

"And Jesus said, for judgment I have come into this world, that those who do not see may see and those who see, may be made blind"   *John 9:39*

Jesus came as the separator between those who "see" and acknowledge Him and those who think that they see, who are self-righteous in their own eyes and are blinded as a result. Only those who are righteous and has a true relationship with Him will stand in this hour. As everything will be shaken and hours of great trial and testing will come upon the whole world.

There will be those who carry on in religion after their own lusts and desires and then there will be the sanctified remnant, yielding to the Spirit of God and surrendering to Christ, lives that are purified and laid down for God's purposes in all holiness. A great apostasy, a falling away will take place before the gathering of all things. Those who loved unrighteousness and did not believe the truth, a strong delusion will come upon them in the last days. A delusion saying, what is right is wrong and what is considered wrong, is right in their eyes. They will believe this lie. The day of the return of Christ will not come unless the falling away comes first, and the man of sin is revealed, the son of perdition who opposes and exalts himself above all that is called God, all that is worship, so that he sits as God in the temple of God, showing himself that he is God.

"Let no one deceive you by any means; for that day will not come unless the falling away comes first, and the man of sin is revealed, the son of perdition"

2 Thessalonians 2:3

The great apostasy is referred to in 2 Thessalonians 2:1 - 12. It is necessary for every believer to study this portion of Scripture and be fully aware and prepared for what is coming

The remnant are those who are called unto salvation and sanctification by the Spirit and belief in the truth, which He also called for the obtaining of His glory.

HEADSHIP OF CHRIST

God's purpose is that we will all come to the unity of the faith and of the knowledge of the Son of God. To a perfect man, to the measure of the stature of the fullness of Christ. That we should no longer be children, tossed to and fro and carried about with every wind of doctrine, by the trickery of men, in the cunning craftiness of deceitful plotting, but speaking the truth in love, may grow up in all things into Him who is the head – Christ. These words are confirmed in *Ephesians 4:13 - 15.*

Jesus Christ is head of His church, His fullness of all in all. He is also the chief cornerstone.

"Having being built (referring to the church), on the foundation of the apostles and the prophets, Jesus Christ Himself being the chief cornerstone"

Ephesians 2:20

Being the cornerstone and the capstone, Christ is head of His church. As the head He directs the church and initiates the actions of His church. The governing of the church will now be restored in this dispensation. At the closing of the age the headship of Christ will also be restored. The church will govern from mount Zion.

"But I want you to know that the head of every man is Christ, the head of women is man, and the head of Christ is God" *1 Corinthians 11:3*

This is God's order for the church. God is the head of Christ, and Christ is the head of the body of Christ, the church. The church has, however, deviated from the original plan and intent. Jesus is now taking back His church and governs over her and aligns her with heaven's purposes. The true remnant will grow in the knowledge of the Son of God and become matured to a place of fullness in the Spirit of Christ, not being tossed and turned by wrong doctrine and the schemes of the enemy. This is a dispensation where the spirit of error (the anti-Christ) and heresy will be exposed and removed from the body of Christ. The church will only be directed by Christ and rule and reign with Him from a governmental seat, mount Zion, the mountain of the Lord.

As there will be a gathering of all things in heaven and on earth, under the headship of Christ, it will be necessary to understand the domain of the heavenlies and the earth. We need to acquaint ourselves as heavenly beings.

HEAVENLY REALM

"For there are three that bear witness in heaven; the Father, the Word, and the Holy Spirit; and these three are one"   1 John 5:7

All of heaven witness and are in unity. The Word refers to Jesus Christ as the Word that became flesh.

"And the Word became flesh and dwelt among us, and we beheld His glory, the glory as of the only begotten of the Father, full of grace and truth"   John 1:14

All that is present in heaven already are gathered in Jesus Christ. Therefore, heaven is ready to come to earth and assist the saints in the final battle.

The four living creatures around the throne of God in heaven are the cherubim angels. Four is the symbol of completeness. These heavenly beings move everywhere where the Spirit of God goes. They move between heaven and earth and will be dispatched to assist in the last day battle. The Spirit of the Lord was upon the prophet Ezekiel when he saw a whirlwind and four living creatures in heaven.

"Also from within it came the likeness of four living creatures. And this was their appearance: they had the likeness of a man. Each one had four faces, and each one had four wings, their wings touched one another. The creatures did not turn when they went, but each one went straight forward. As for the likeness of their faces, each had the face of a man; each of the four had the face of a lion on the right side, each of the four had the face of an ox on the left side, and each of the four had the face of an eagle. Thus were their faces. Their wings stretched upwards, two wings of each one touched one another and two covered their bodies. And each one went straight forward; they went wherever the Spirit wanted to go, and they did not turn when they went. As for the likeness of the living creatures, their appearance was like burning coals of fire, like the appearance of torches going back and forth among the living creatures. The fire was bright, and out of the fire went lightning"

Ezekiel 1:5 - 13

These cherubim angels carry the fire of the Lord and play a role in the sanctification of the end time church. They will be sent to the earth with fire to purge the leaders within the body of Christ. They are the angels protecting the glory of God.

The faces of the living creatures resemble the following. The face of man refers to sonship and the authority of the sons of God being released on the earth. The face of the Lion refers to the apostolic foundations and governing of the church being restored. The face of the ox refers to the bride who will serve the Head, Jesus Christ and His church on the earth in these last days. She will carry a breaker's anointing. The horns refer to the authority the church will carry to break through impossible barriers in the end times. The face of the eagle refers to the prophetic being restored and poured out on all flesh in the last days. It also refers to the prophets restoring the foundation of the church.

How can we know for certain that the four living creatures are cherubim angels from heaven, sent to the earth to fulfill God's purposes?

"This is the living creature I saw under the guard of Israel by the River Chebar, and I knew they were cherubim. Each one had four faces and each one four wings, and the likeness of the hands of a man was under their wings. And the likeness of their faces was the same as the face which I had seen by the River Chebar, their appearance and their persons. They each went straight forward"

Ezekiel 10:20 - 22

Angelic help will be available in the final battle on the earth assisting the saints and they will form part of the army of God. In this final battle the true bride of Christ will prepare the way for the second coming of our Lord Jesus Christ and directly oppose Jezebel who is preparing the way for the anti-Christ to be ushered in as part of the end time tribulation. That is the reason why the remnant needs to be holy, pure and unblemished, stand in unity as to be able to work in unison with heaven. Heaven is holy ground. There can be no division in the body of Christ, neither between the two realms, the realm of heaven and the realm of earth. He is gathering all things in heaven and earth under His authority.

The seraphim angels around the throne of God are fiery angelic beings. They are burning flames of fire. The Hebrew root is the verb "seraph" and means "to burn or set on fire." These angels are flame-like in motion. It appears in the Word of God in Isaiah 6 as seraphim.

Their function in the earth is to either purify or destroy. The prophet Isaiah saw the Lord sitting on a throne, high and lifted up, and the train of His robe filled the temple.

"Above it stood seraphim; each one had six wings: with two he covered his face, with two he covered his feet, and with two he flew. And one cried to another and said: "Holy, Holy, Holy is the Lord of Hosts; the whole earth is full of His glory"

Isaiah 6:2 - 3

"Then one of the seraphim flew to me, having in his hand a live coal which he had taken with the tongs from the altar. And he touched my mouth with it, and said: "behold, this has touched your lips; your inequity is taken away, and your sins purged".
Isaiah 6:6 - 7

Here we can clearly see that the seraphim angels carry the fire from the altar and have a function to sanctify and purify. In the same way these seraphim angels will be engaged in the final judgment of God that will come upon the people and the nation who deliberately denies His name and turn from truth and righteousness. These angels will be dispersed to the church to purify in the last days. All of heaven will be engaged in the final hour, the hour of great trial that will come upon the whole earth.

"The throne of God in heaven - *after these things I looked and behold, a door standing open in heaven. And the first voice which I heard was like a trumpet speaking with me, saying, "come up here, and I will show you things which must take place after this." Immediately I was in the Spirit, and behold, a throne set in heaven, and One sat on the throne. And He Who sat there was like jasper and sardis stone in appearance; and there was a rainbow around the throne, in appearance like an emerald. Around the throne were twenty-four thrones, and on the thrones I saw twenty four elders sitting, clothed in white robes, and they had crowns of gold on their heads. And from the throne proceeded lightning, thundering and voices; seven lamps of fire were burning before the throne, which are the seven Spirits of God"* Revelations 4:1 - 5

God who sits on the throne is described in terms of brilliance and glory. It is from His throne where He is seated, that He rules and reigns over the earth and have dominion. He has established His throne in heaven, and His kingdom rules overall. The stone jasper suggests purity and holiness. The stone sardis is deep red in color and depicts God's avenging wrath. Emerald appearing as a rainbow symbolizes His mercy. The twenty-four elders are the celestial representatives of all the redeemed, glorified and enthroned, who worship continuously. Their white robes symbolize purity and righteousness. The crown suggests victory and joy.

Lightnings and thundering describe the awe and wondrous power of God. The seven lamps of fire represent the seven-fold Holy Spirit of God, the Holy Spirit in all its' facets. From His throne the counsel of His will go forth, when earth is aligned with heaven's end time purposes. Heaven joins and is engaged with the ecclesia as an end time army. The gold is the ultimate triumph of Jesus Christ, who culminates history with His final coming and reigns with and through His church forever.

There is a cloud of witnesses. They testify in the courts of heaven. They are heroes of faith who were forerunners and went before us, and have faithfully overcome, they are surrounding us.

"Therefore we also, since we are surrounded by so a great cloud of witnesses, let us lay aside every weight, and the sin which so easily ensnares us, and let us run with endurance the race that is set before us" Hebrews 12:1

Jesus Christ left an unfinished work behind concerning the church when He ascended on high to be seated at the right hand of His Father on the throne. He left the completion of His work to His followers. He trusted the Holy Spirit for this work on the earth. As we are now surrounded by those who went before us, let us pick up their mantles, take the baton and complete the race, each one completing the assignment that was given to us by Jesus Christ.

EARTHLY REALM

"And there are three that bear witness on earth; the Spirit, the Water, and the Blood; and these three agree as one"   1 John 5:8

The Blood of Jesus, the Spirit of Christ and His Word bear witness on earth and they agree as one. This forms the foundation of every believer. Righteousness is imputed to the believer by the Blood of Jesus Christ. The believer being filled with the Holy Spirit, washed and sanctified by the Word, whom is Jesus Christ Himself. This represents the foundation of the believer.

In these last days God will assemble for Himself a true remnant. A bride who will be made ready for the coming of the bridegroom, Jesus Christ. This invitation is open to all. However, in the last days, as the times become trying, not all would want to pay the price to live a holy surrendered life to Christ, yielding to His Spirit and obedient to His Word. There is a price to be paid in this dispensation of time as we will come to know Him in His suffering. As the anti-Christ will be on the rise, there will also be a great apostasy taking place. People who are not willing to sacrifice, denying His Name in the face of adversity. Also, people who will deny the truth for their own self-righteousness.

MARKS OF THE TRUE REMNANT CHURCH

The remnant church will keep His Word and not deny His name, especially when the mark of the beast is introduced. The microchip will be implanted on the foreheads of the people and also on the thumb on their right hand. This microchip has embedded into it the mark of the beast - 666.

"He causes all, both small and great, rich and poor, free and slave, to receive a mark on their right hand or on their foreheads, and that no one may buy or sell, except one who has the mark of the name of the beast, or the number of his name"
                                      Revelations 13:16 - 17

The number of his name is 666, the number of man. The microchip will carry the number 666 which is the mark of the beast that is already in the world. Whoever takes the mark of the beast will not enter the kingdom of God. Without it you will not be able to buy or sell. In the last days the church will be challenged by the world system introducing the microchip. The anti-Christ will mislead many. However, there will be a remnant who will not love their lives more. The remnant will overcome satan by the blood of the Lamb and by the word of their testimony and by the fact that they do not love their lives more. They will be willing to be martyred to a point of death for the sake of His Name and His Word.

"And they overcame him by the blood of the Lamb and by the word of their testimony, and they did not love their lives to death"   Revelations 12:11

We are entering the season where we will see martyrdom and great persecution.

The remnant will persevere and keep His commandments to the end.

"Because you have kept My commandment to persevere, I also will keep you from the hour of trial which shall come upon the whole world, to test those who dwell on the earth"
Revelations 3:10

We have already entered this hour of trial.

The remnant will abide with Him on mount Zion, His dwelling place.

"Then I looked and behold, a Lamb standing on mount Zion, and with him one hundred and forty-four thousand having His Father's name written on their foreheads"
Revelations 14:1

"But you have come to mount Zion and the city of the living God, the heavenly Jerusalem, to an innumerable company of angels, to the general assembly and church of the first-born, who are registered in heaven, God the Judge of all to the spirits of just men made perfect, to Jesus the Mediator of the new covenant, and to the blood of sprinkling that speaks of better things than that of Abel"
Hebrews 12:22 - 24

Mount Zion is the governmental and legislative seat in heaven. The true ecclesia will constantly be in the presence of the Lord, legislating and decreeing from mount Zion in the final move of the earth. The church will walk in authority and victory. We will further discuss the city of the Lord, Mount Zion, in another chapter of this book. But for now, it is important to note who is represented on this mountain. An innumerable amount of angels, the church (ecclesia) who's names are registered in heaven, written in the book of the Lamb, God in His capacity as Judge, the spirits of just men made perfect - all those who went before us, Jesus Christ, the mediator, the Blood of Jesus that is sprinkled on the mercy seat speaking of better things. All of these witnesses will stand with the ecclesia, the remnant church in the final battle. The ecclesia will constantly be in the atmosphere and presence of God legislating from mount Zion, although we are on the earth, as His glory will be everywhere.

The remnant will be the Acts 2 church of old. They will stand in spiritual unity. Koinonia, a spiritual communion with the Lord and with each other will signify the end time church. The priorities of the followers of Christ will focus on spiritual unity with the Lord and with our fellow brothers and sisters in Christ, within the church, the spiritual body of Christ. Every true believer is a member of the body of Christ and is related to Christ and to other believers through covenant relationship. This is the essence of true spiritual unity - unity in the Spirit. There will be no division as ministries will co-operate and support one another. Denominations will fall away. There will be one body united, filled with glory.

There will be no agenda and no competition amongst one another. A total surrender to the Head, Jesus Christ. The remnant will follow instructions only from the Spirit of Christ and be taught in His ways and be accustomed to wait upon Him to encounter Him.

The remnant church will serve the body in Christ through a sacrificial abounding love.

"Yet it shall not be so among you; but whoever desires to become great among you, let him be your servant"   *Matthew 20:26*

Greatness is not defined by a high position. True greatness in God's kingdom comes through sacrificial service, as Jesus chose to be a Servant, reconciling us to God by sacrificing His Life. This will be one of the marks of the true remnant.

A benchmark for success concerning the end time church will not be in how well they rule, but how well they serve. The bride will serve wholly for the love of Him Who, being endowed with heaven's complete authority, chose to take the form of a servant.

"let this mind be in you which was also in Christ Jesus, who, being in the form of God, did not consider it robbery to be equal with God, but made Himself of no reputation, taking the form of a bond servant, and coming in the likeness of men, and being found in appearance as a man, He humbled Himself and became obedient to the point of death, even the death of the cross"   Philippians 2:5 - 8

The same humility and Christlikeness will be evident in the remnant.

The Zadok priesthood will be restored. The true remnant will be ministering unto God in worship.

"But you are a chosen generation, a royal priesthood, a holy nation, His own special people, that you may proclaim the praises of Him who called you out of darkness into His marvelous light"   1 Peter 2:

As a "royal" priesthood, the kingly nature and anointing will prophetically be fulfilled in the remnant. Dominion and destiny will unfold as the priestly duty is fulfilled. True authority is related to a walk in purity and the constancy in worship. Battle will take place from a foundation of righteous worship before the Lord. The power of the remnant before God's throne, worshipping the Lamb and exalting in the Holy Spirit of praise, is confounding to the adversary. Worship will be all unto the Leader of the end time army. Jesus Christ, the Ruler over the kings of the earth, loved us and washed us from our sins in His own blood, also made us kings and priests to His God and Father.

"And has made us kings and priests to His God and Father, to Him be glory and dominion for ever and ever"   Revelation 1:6

This is a very important aspect concerning the end time church, in as much as under the King of Kings, we are the new breed to whom God has delegated authority to extend and administrate the powers of His rule.

The end time army will have one vision and be focused on the end time harvest, whatever it takes.

PURPOSE OF GATHERING ALL THINGS

I believe God is releasing an anointing, an ability from God to gather all things under the headship of Christ. The remnant church will be gathered from all over the world in all purity, holiness, humbleness, meekness and power. Those who are likeminded, who have been tested, chastened and humbled in the wilderness. They will now come forth by the Hand of God. They will harken unto His voice *and lead the end time army to victory. They will establish, build God's Kingdom and equip the saints for the final battle. A building anointing is also released, the anointing of the ox. The foundation of the church will be secured by the true, tested apostles and prophets. Those who were tested in the heat of His oven and found worthy. The foundation of the church will be laid afresh and be secured before the rebuilding will start. God is doing a new work in the hearts of His sons and daughters to purify them. They will render their hearts before Him and be purified. He will once again come as the launderer's soap and as the refiner's fire to purge and to bring His people forth as pure gold. This will result in them bringing Him sacrifices of right doing.*

We will see God's sons and daughters be brought to full maturity in Christ Jesus, to a knowledge of the Son of God, to a perfect man, to the measure of the stature of the fullness of Christ, through the Spirit of Knowledge and Wisdom. The body of Christ will speak the Truth in love and will grow up in all things into Him Who is the Head - Christ. The evidence of the aforesaid is found in Ephesians 4:13 - 15.

As members of the household of God having been built upon the foundation of the apostles and prophets, Jesus Christ Himself, being the chief cornerstone, in whom the whole building, being fitted together, grows into a holy temple in the Lord. In whom you are also being built together for a dwelling place of God in the Spirit. The evidence for this word is found in *Ephesians 2:20 - 22.*

The Spirit of the Lord is seeking a dwelling place for Himself in the earth. When all the saints come together in unity, purity and love, we become this dwelling place where He will dwell amongst His people. A place from where His glory will manifest. A place of His dominion in the earth. A place from where the ecclesia will decree and declare, where His provision and protection will be at hand. A safe place for the world to run to and be saved. A place of worship and Presence. The resting place where our Father will abide in the earth.

God is raising up "seers" carrying the seven-fold Spirit of God. As the Spirit of God will be poured out on all flesh, we will see an explosion of the prophetic on earth. God's voice will be everywhere, being released through children, the youth, the elderly and also church leaders and prophets. "Seers" will rise who will continually release what they see in the Spirit, as the seven-fold Holy Spirit will rest on these "seers". God is gathering these "seers" to be Elijah voices unto Him in the earth. Those who were formed in the desert, in the caves, under hard circumstances, tried and tested. All the sons and daughters globally will be one family to complete the last day purposes of God. There will be a gathering of prophets and prophetic communities will be established.

"The watchmen shall lift up their voices, with their voices they shall sing together, for they shall see eye to eye, when the Lord brings back Zion"   Isaiah 52:8

God is bringing His people forth to complete the race and finish off His work on the earth.

As mentioned, before we will see a separation, a coming out from among them.

"Therefore come out from among them, and be separate, says the Lord. Do not touch which is unclean, and I will receive you"   2 Corinthians 6:17

God is separating His people and gathering those who are clean. Those who bear the vessels of the Lord must be clean. The vessels are the weaponry that we will carry as an end time army and ecclesia. These vessels refer to and include our swords, the sword of the Word of God, our prayer life and His Presence. Everything about us and concerning us as well as God's weaponry needs to be clean, pure and holy in order for the enemy not to be able to take us out. If the evil one finds anything in us that is also in him, he will take us out as it will count as agreement. We are only protected under the Blood Covenant, therefore we need to be separate and to be holy, as He is holy. We carry the Arc of the Covenant in us, His Spirit and Presence, therefore we must be holy and pure.

For indeed the Kingdom of God is in you.   Luke 17:21

To receive Him - the King - is to receive His kingly rule, not only in your life but through your life and by your service and love. *The true remnant was humbled in the desert phase of their lives. Now he is seeking a habitation, a continual presence that will lead to an abiding glory to be seen upon us. Jesus said: "If anyone loves Me, he will keep My Word, and My Father*

will love him, and We will come to him and make our home with him"
John 14:23

This requires a tender and humble heart. Are you prepared to seek Him and wait for Him to encounter Him? The end time bride walks in close relationship with the King and He has His abode in her and upon her.

RESTORATION BEFORE THE GATHERING

There are some things concerning the church that hinders the gathering of all things in heaven and on earth under the headship of Christ. It will now be taken care of by God as He is perfecting His bride and preparing the end time army. The church will be restored back to an Acts 2 church. The restoration of all things will first take place before Jesus will return to the earth to rapture His victorious bride. Repentance will be restored, and times of refreshing will come to the body of Christ. Heaven has received Jesus and will keep Him until the restoration of all things in heaven and earth. Heaven's part is completed, however, a great restoration concerning the church on the earth needs to be restored first.

"Repent therefore and be converted, that your sins may be blotted out, so that times of refreshing may come from the Presence of the Lord, and that He may send Jesus Christ, Who was preached to you before, whom heaven must receive until the times of restoration of all things, which God has spoken by the mouth of all His holy prophets since the world began"
Acts 3:19 - 21

It is now the time of restoration; however the following are hindering this process:

Self-seeking and hidden agendas of self-promotion in the church. God is the One who promotes when He has tested and completed the process in you. David never promoted himself, he allowed God's process and remained faithful. We need to be willing to suffer for the sake of the Kingdom. We will go through many trials and tribulations until Christ is formed in us.

"My brethren, count it all joy when you fall into various trials, knowing that the testing of your faith produces patience. But patience have it's perfect work, that you may be perfect and complete, lacking nothing"   *James 1:2 - 5*

A spirit of entitlement will arise should we not yield to the process of growing a leader. As we are entering the end of this age, how much more do we need to heed to the Word of God. The battle is fierce, and we will not stand if we were not prepared in the furnace. "Self" needs to die, and our only agenda should be to please Jesus Christ. These things hinder koinonia and needs to be removed from the church.

Q

We will be persecuted for the truth.

"You will be betrayed even by parents and brothers, relatives and friends, and they will put some of you to death. And you will be hated by all for My Name's sake. But not a hair of your head shall be lost. By your patience possess your souls"

Luke 21:16 - 19

Therefore, we need to die to ourselves in order for Christ to protect us. We have entered these days. All signs of the end times are already on display in this world. Do not let your hearts be troubled, as these things need to take place. Christ is seeking a holy people, pure, humble and surrendered to Him. He is seeking those that He will gather under His Headship in these times that we are facing now.

The love for money and the merchandising of the anointing in church is another hindrance for the gathering of all things. We cannot use the Gospel to make money. God will judge this conduct within the church, and He will certainly purify His church. This is the sin of Balaam. It did not please God that Balaam wanted to accept money from Balak to go out and prophecy, in this case to curse the Israelites or to speak the word of God. Balaam's way was perverse before the Lord, and we find an account of this in the book of *Numbers 22 - 25*.

We also find that many ministers of the Word will preach a gospel that is not offensive, pleasing for man, far from the truth, in an effort to keep the big donors. The sin of Korah is flourishing in the church for this reason. Rebelling against God's appointed leadership. Korah, Datan and Abiram rebelled against Moses's leadership in Numbers 16. Moses's reply to them was:

"then Moses was very angry, and said to the Lord, do not respect their offering. I have not take one donkey from them. Nor have I hurt one of them."

Numbers 16:15

This is the exact attitude that needs to return to the church. God will not respect your offering if you cannot respect whom He has put in place to guard over your soul. Many a time what you need comes in a packaging that is not pleasing unto you. But it is pleasing to the Lord, for He chooses and appoints leaders. Let God be God. Let appointed leaders not be too weak to withstand rebelling against God for the sake of offerings and money. Only preach the Word and the Truth of the Gospel as it is stipulated in His Word. The ministry cannot be turned into a money-making venture, neither from relenting to tell the truth in a pursuit to keep donors and sponsors. Jesus cleansed the temple.

"Then Jesus went into the temple of God and drove out all those who bought and sold in the temple, and overturned the tables of money changers and the seats of those who sold doves" *Matthew 20:12*

The selling of doves refers to the selling of the anointing, as a dove symbolizes the anointing of the Holy Spirit. Christ is Head over His church and takes full responsibility for the lives and provision of ministers of the Gospel. When the apostles were sent out Jesus instructed them not to take anything with them.

"Provide neither gold nor silver nor copper in your money belts. Nor bag for your journey, nor two tunics, nor sandals, nor staffs, for a worker is worthy of his food" *Matthew 10:9 - 10*

God Himself, through the congregation, will provide for His servants, but not by the way of manipulation and undermining the Truth.

We will see an end to independent ministries and denominations. The *Acts 2* church was one church. We do not see a pattern of each running out to exalt themselves and start their own ministries. Neither do we hear or saw denominations rising. The church was united under the headship of Jesus Christ, and they worked together. Apostolic team ministry will earmark the end time church as the church is reverting to the original plan and intent. The early church fasted and prayed together in searching for the will of God in every matter. They stood united in Christ's call and purpose for the church. If leaders needed to be appointed, they unanimously fasted and prayed.

"As they ministered to the Lord and fasted, the Holy Spirit said, now separate to Me Barnabas and Saul for the work to which I have called them"   Acts 13:2

Please note that their ministry was unto the Lord, not unto themselves. They executed only the will of Christ and were led by the Spirit of God. They were officiating as priests, serving with prayers and fasting. We will see the priesthood restored before the gathering of all things in heaven and on earth under the headship of Christ. Christ cannot gather unto Himself a priesthood still wanting to run after their own desires, contrasting the desire of God. Jesus seeks one body, united, yielding to His Spirit. God builds His church. We will see a gathering of ministries becoming one church all over the globe, one stream of the working of the Spirit globally. It is teamwork and the restoration of the five-fold ministry gifts under the leading of the Holy Spirit that will cause His army to rise, to stand against the anti-Christ and to bring in the end time harvest of souls. A great harvest of souls, especially the youth will be gathered before the second coming of Jesus Christ, before the rapture takes place.

The church is currently defiled with compromise, mixed seed and self-seeking glory not pointing to Jesus Christ, but pointing to themselves. The latter rains referred to in Joel 2 will only come after much fasting and prayer. God will not share His Glory with no man. The church will be purified and will render their hearts when God's judgment comes over the evil deeds of mankind. The time is now. It will cause the body of Christ to be purified and to cry between the porch and the altar. The minds, hearts and ministries of God's people will be sanctified. A call to repentance is going out right now. Vision is restored to the church. When God's judgment is released there will be no other recourse, but to pray with fasting and humility. By declaring God's promises for the end time church through prayer, the birthing of the end time church will take place. This great army that God is raising. Salvation will come for those who call upon the Name of the Lord as they witness God's Spirit at work in His people.

Now therefore, says the Lord, turn to Me with all your heart, with fasting, with weeping and with mourning. Surrender your heart, not your garments, return to the Lord your God, for He is gracious and merciful, slow to anger, and of great kindness, and He relents from doing harm.   Joel 2:12 - 13

This passage, as well as Joel 2:14 - 17, precedes the outpouring of God's Spirit upon all flesh. The church first needs to be sanctified and freed from all defilement. She needs to be made ready for the chabod, the weight of His glory that will be poured out in order for her not to take the glory for herself, but to release His glory unto Him. This will be the greatest move of God that the world will ever see and has seen.

God rejects the prideful and shows mercy to the humble. As a result of pride, satan was abandoned from heaven in Isaiah 14. This is a season in which your gifts and your title will not take you through. Neither will your degrees, but your decrees from mount Zion will become eminent. A knowledge of the Word of God and an understanding in the knowledge of Christ Jesus will take you through. The end time church will carry much delegated authority; therefore, it is imperative that God gets rid of pride in the church. Pride and rebellion go hand in glove.

"Likewise you younger people, submit yourselves to your elders (leaders). Yes, all of you be submissive to one another and be clothed with humility, for God resists the proud, but gives grace to the humble. Therefore, humble yourselves under the mighty hand of God, that He may exalt you in due time"   1 Peter 5:5 - 6

It is God who exalts. Do not exalt yourself. Submit under the leadership God has ordained for you. If God then resists the prideful, why will we walk with them? Humility will mark the end time army. Only the humble will have reverence for God and obey His commands.

"I will exalt my throne above the stars of God. I will also sit on the mount of the congregation on the farthest side of the north. I will ascend above the clouds. I will be like the most high"   Isaiah 14:13 - 14

A picture is painted of how satan exalted himself. The farthest side of the north and the mount of the congregation refers to God's holy mountain. His resting place where the blood washed saints who walked in His statutes and commandments have access to the blood. Satan fell into pride and self-centeredness. His rebellion manifests in "I will" statements. He declared that he would take the place of the most high God, but God has the last word and God will throw him into hell. He will be made a spectacle of, he will be mocked and scorned. In the same way that God dealt with satan's pride in the book of Isaiah 14, in the same way will He deal with pride in our own lives and the church. The end time army will walk in humbleness and be cleaned of all defilement.

At the closing of the age the headship of Christ will be restored within the ecclesia. His headship entails the central governing system. Kingdom reign means governing by headship, the headship of Jesus Christ.

" Which He worked in Christ, when He raised Him from the dead and seated Him at His right hand in the heavenly places, far above all principality and power and might and dominion, and every name that is named, not only in this age, but also in that which is to come.
And He put all things under His feet, and gave them to be Head over all things to the church, which is His body, the fullness of Him who fills all in all"

Ephesians 1:20 - 23

All is put underneath His feet and underneath the feet of His true sons and daughters, as authority was delegated unto us.

"I can of Myself do nothing. As I hear I judge, and My judgment is righteous, because I do not seek My own will, but the will of the Father Who sent Me"

John 5:30

Look at heaven's apostolic order and governing system. Jesus only received instruction from His Father as He heard His voice. In a like manner the end time army will only receive instruction from Jesus Christ as we hear His voice and harken unto it, not initiating out of our own. Only the humble can be under authority.

Peace to you! As the Father has sent Me, I also send you.   *John 20:21*

This is an apostolic end time call to the church. Jesus commissioned us, set us apart for a special service and sent us out with a mission to equip and dispatch with the full backing and authority of the One who sent us.

CHARACTER AND FINAL EXPECTANCY OF THE ECCLESIA

- Hearing His voice and following His instructions. The church will follow instruction and be a follower of the Lamb.

"To him the doorkeeper opens, and the sheep hear His voice, and He calls His own sheep by His name and leads them out. And when He brings out His own sheep, He goes before them and the sheep follow Him, for they know His voice"
John 10:3,4

Mark that He calls His own by His name. The sheep follow because they know His voice. The end time ecclesia will follow after Him only.

- The true ecclesia will be truthful and faithful to the expense of losing their lives.

"And they overcame Him by the blood of the lamb and by the word of their testimony, and they did not love their lives to the death"

Revelation 12:11

The true remnant will be willing to be martyred and to die for Him.

"And I saw thrones, and they sat on them, and judgment was committed to them. Then I saw the souls of those who has been beheaded for their witness to Jesus and for the word of God, who had not worshipped the beast or his image, and had not received His mark on their foreheads or on their hands. And they lived and reigned with Christ for a thousand years"

Revelation 20:4

It is clear from the word of God that we will enter a time frame when the beast and the anti-Christ will rise. Those who remain faithful to Christ will be beheaded and lose their lives on earth, but will reign and live with Christ. It is now the time that we need to raise the church in such a way as to be prepared and be willing to stand in the hour of trial that will come upon the whole earth. The church needs to be knowledgeable about the time of tribulation that we are entering into now.

- Meekness. The real character of Christ is how the kingdom will be built in the end times that we are facing now. Meekness is power under control.

"Therefore as the elect of God, holy and beloved, put on tender mercies, kindness, humility, weakness, long-suffering"   *Colossians 3:12*

This is what the attire of the ecclesia will be made up of in the Spirit. We need to put this on to qualify in this hour as only the meek will inherit the kingdom of God"

"Blessed are the meek for they shall inherit the earth"   *Matthew 5:5*

Jesus calls for open, free and loyal relationship which enables obedience, which leads to righteousness, which leads to holiness, which leads to eternal life.

- Zealousness for God.

"I know your works. See, I have set before you an open door, and no man can shut it, for you have a little strength, have kept My word and have not denied My name. Because you have kept My command to persevere, I also will keep you from the hour of trial which shall come upon the whole world, to test those who dwell on the earth. Behold, I am coming quickly! Hold fast what you have that no one may take your crown"
        Revelation 3:8,10,11

It is only a zealousness for Christ that will cause us to persevere amid all that is taking place in the earth. The end time ecclesia will be marked by their zealousness for Christ.

- Sacrificial heart.

"I beseech you therefore, brethren, by the mercies of God, that you present your bodies a living sacrifice, holy, acceptable to God, which is your reasonable service"   *Romans 12:1*

A sacrificial lifestyle, totally sold out to Christ will also mark the end time remnant. To be sold out to Christ is a requirement to be enlisted in the end time army. No agenda of self. Directed by the King of Kings.

Chapter 4
RESTORATION OF THE TABERNACLE OF DAVID

RESTORATION OF THE TABERNACLE OF DAVID

There will be a movement in the end time church whereby a generation of worshippers will be raised. Power, prayer and worship will be restored to the house of the Lord. Churches will be open twenty-four seven as a house of prayer and worship. Much prayer will go forth from the house of the Lord, continual prayer.

"On that day I will raise up the tabernacle of David, which has fallen down, and repair its damages; I will raise up its ruins, and rebuild it as in the days of old; that they may possess the remnant of Edom, and all the Gentiles who are called by My name, says the Lord who does this thing. Behold, the days are coming, says the Lord, when the plough man shall overtake the reaper, and the treader of grapes him who sows seed; the mountains shall drip with sweet wine, and all the hills shall flow with it"
Amos 9:11 - 13

The prophet Amos prophesied the restoration of the tabernacle of David. This prophecy is to be fulfilled now in the present dispensation as part of the restoration of the end time ecclesia. The remnant will be possessed by God. The result of God's continual presence amongst the end time church will result in the plough man overtaking the reaper. Abundance will be bestowed upon the church. No longer will the church walk in poverty. The mountains will drip with sweet wines and the hills will flow with it. Revelation from the mountain of the Lord will continually be at our disposal to lead and guide us. God will live amongst the praises of His people.

King David was a worshipper who acted as king of Juda and later as king of Israel in the dispensation of the prophets, before the crucifixion and resurrection of Jesus Christ. In those days the Spirit of God came upon the prophets and they prophesied. In the current dispensation all born again believers have the Holy Spirit on the inside of us and our bodies become the temple of the Holy Spirit.

However, David was hungry for the presence of God and was seeking His face in worship and prayer continually. There was a call to David to build a tabernacle for the arc of the covenant.

"Go and tell My servant, David, thus says the LORD "Would you build a house for Me to dwell in? for I have not dwelt in a house since the time that I brought the children of Israel up from Egypt, even to this day, but have moved about in a tent in a tabernacle"
2 Samuel 7:5,6

David understood the call and the desire of God to dwell amongst His people.

To fully comprehend God's presence and the dwelling place of God amongst His people, we need to look at the different dispensations. A dispensation refers to the way God dealt with His people during a certain time period.

The Hebrew word "mishkan" implies a "dwelling place", "resting place", or "place to live in". A dwelling place for the manifested presence of God. During the dispensation of Moses and the law, God's dwelling place was in the tabernacle of Moses. The tabernacle of Moses went with the Israelites wherever they travelled. The tabernacle of Moses was located in Shilo, from where David brought it out to Zion, in Jerusalem.

Later on, David's son, Solomon, built the temple of Solomon as permanent abode for God's manifested presence in Jerusalem. Today, the dispensation prior to the return of Jesus Christ, (rapture), our bodies became the temple of the Holy Spirit as a dwelling place of God's Spirit. All the saints that are part of the end time ecclesia become a whole building, fitted together, grows into a holy temple in the Lord, in whom you are also being built together for a dwelling place of God in the Spirit. We find an account of this in the book of *Ephesians 2:21,22*

David, in the same manner as the woman at the well, because of the manifested presence of God, ushered a new dimension and order into the earth. A dimension that was meant for this coming dispensation, became a reality to David and God's people.

When David came into power after king Saul, he ushered in God's presence amongst His people, the Israelites. During the time of the end time church which we believe is part of this dispensation, the outcast and the rejected will usher in God's presence. God will now use the outcast to usher in the King of Glory. David brought the arc of the covenant to mount Zion, God's presence will bring the shift in generations. A governmental structure and system were raised up when David place the tabernacle on mount Zion. The tabernacle had no veil, it had access for everyone passing by. It was open to all twenty-four seven in those days. It was a twenty-four seven worshipping of God. The kingly and priestly anointing was restored to worship in His presence.

And He made us kings and priests to His God and father, to Him be glory and dominion for ever and ever.   Revelation 1:6

We are said to be kings in the sense that under the king of kings, we are the new breed, the reborn, to whom God has delegated authority to extend and administrate the powers of His rule. That is the ultimate function of the remnant church. It involves faithful service to humanity in the love of God. It also involves confrontation with the dark powers of hell, assertive prayer warfare and expectation of the miraculous works of God. However, this authority is only fully accomplished in the spirit of Worship, as we exercise the office of priests. The power of the believer in praise and worship before God's throne, worshipping the Lamb and exalting in the Holy Spirit of praise, is confounding to the adversary. The manifold wisdom of God will be on display to the powers and principalities in the heavenlies, by the church.

To hear from heaven during worship, receive revelation and decree a thing. This is God's original intent of man being reconnected to God. The tabernacle of David was a point of access to all under the blood of Jesus. David built a "culture" around God's presence. In the tabernacle of David, they were caught up in the Spirit. It was a foreshadowing of what was to come. This is the dispensation we live in now as the end time ecclesia. However, over the years worship in the church was confounded to half an hour or an hour. No revelation came forth this way. Nothing was decreed in the earth.

In the book of Hebrews, it was prophesied about Jesus that He is not ashamed to call us brethren.

Saying: "I will declare Your name to My brethren; in the midst of the assembly I will sing praise to You".   Hebrews 2:12

This quotation from a messianic prophecy reveals how the Spirit of Christ fills the New Testament church. Jesus identifies Himself so closely with His people and enters into songs of worship with them. His presence will return to the end time church in this way where He worships with us. He Himself enters into the gathering, in the midst and then joint praise releases the Spirit of Prophecy as the holy power of praise ignites the testimony of Jesus.

For the testimony of Jesus is the Spirit of Prophecy.   *Revelation 19:10*

This is what it is all about. His presence amongst us, prophecy flowing as a result, decreeing as kings this revelation through the Spirit and interceding. It all happens as we praise and worship with Him in our midst. This is God's order for worship being restored on the earth.

You will also declare a thing, and it will be established for you; so light will shine on your ways.   *Job 22:28*

This is the authority the church should walk in.

WHY IS REBUILDING NECESSARY?

As sons and daughters, we are to be hosting the presence of God daily.

Why did hosting of His presence fall?

There is an outward worship, but the hearts are far from God, and as a result a failure to declare the glory of God. His glory is His manifested presence. Hosting requires maturity. What you carry you will release in the earth. It all starts with the hearts of His people. An outward releasing of His glory is necessary, declaring Him to all nations. The rebuilding of the tabernacle of David is the pre-cursor in ushering in the harvest. The rebuilding of full-time worship, prayer and intercession is key to revival. Many will run and find safety in the release of God's glory upon the end time ecclesia. Pure worship will cause a young generation to be attracted to the glory. They will be healed and delivered in His presence. Nations' hearts will be turned to God, inviting nations to His glory.

WHAT DOES THE TABERNACLE OF DAVID REFER TO?

The tabernacle of David was an open tent that was set up at mount Zion in Jerusalem by David. All was welcomed to enter into the tent. The purpose was for God's presence to be hosted amongst His people and amongst the Gentiles. For a period of 33 years music, praise, worship and prayer went forth from the tent. David's first priority was to get God's presence in the center of the Israelites. He trained Levites to sing and to minister before God as priests. The Levites were trained to hear God's voice and to release God's voice from heaven. Day and night worship and prayer went forth from the tent. David realized the importance of the kingly (apostolic) and priestly anointing. David had knowledge of heaven and brought that reality to Israel. He knew God intimately. He set up in the earth what he saw in heaven by a heavenly pattern revealed to him by God. David introduced the priestly reality of worship. During the reign of David he brought in the kingly reality of rule, authority and reign. David was operating in the order of Melchizedek of the priestly and kingly joined together. He ushered in what was meant for this age whereby the kings in the market place will come to the ecclesia for revelation and whereby the priests will receive provision from the kings to establish God's kingdom in the earth.

David ushering in the reality of Christ in another dispensation. Kingdom is exalted through priestly ministry before the throne of God. God rules and reigns from mount Zion, His legislative mountain through His presence in and upon His sons and daughters, manifesting His kingdom through presence. David was pointing to Jesus and prepared the way through a model of twenty four seven worship, prayer and intercession, open to all for the Joel 2 outpouring of His spirit on all flesh. David was a forerunner.

FOUR COMPONENTS OF THE TABERNACLE OF DAVID:

1. Presence of God through worship:

But you are holy, enthroned in the presence of Israel.   Psalms 22:3

The presence of God's kingly power is directly related to the practice of God's praise. Wherever God's people exalt His name, He is ready to manifest His kingdom power in the way most appropriate to the situation, as His rule is invited to invade our setting. Heaven invades earth through our worship. God awakes the prayerful and praise-filled worship of His people as an entry point for His kingdom to "come" and to enter in, that His will be done in human circumstances. God steps into our reality by His manifested presence and power and as a result revelation from His throne becomes available. A flow of heavenly revelation start to trickle down which leads us to point 2 of the four components. However, many a times, the church treats worship on a roster of time and thereby quenches the Holy Spirit. Worship became a ritual to be completed as soon as possible in the church. God is restoring this to the original heavenly blueprint. As a result, the wall between Jew and Gentile will go down. All will worship together. The young generation, the youth will be attracted to the worship going forth and be healed, delivered and saved.

2. Revelation through worship:

Our worship ushers in the realm of heaven. As heaven invades earth by God's presence, much revelation comes forth. David received revelation from God on the functioning of ministries in the temple of his son, Solomon, when Solomon had to build the temple. He also received revelation on how the musicians should operate.

And the plans for all that he had (David) by the Spirit, of the courts of the house of the Lord, of all the chambers all-around of the treasuries of the house of God, and of the treasuries for the dedicated things. All this, said David, the Lord made me understand in writing, by His hand upon me, all the works of His plans.
1 Chronicles 28:12,19

David received the blueprint from God for a worship order that needs to be restored in these last days. David commanded the kings to establish a kingdom order of worship to the kings of Israel. The Holy Spirit is re-establishing this order globally. Prophecy comes forth through revelation which leads us to the next component.

3. Decreeing and agreement:

God's government is established in the earth through decreeing and agreement. Through our decrees God is releasing His resources in the earth.

You will also declare a thing, and it will be established for you. Job 22:28

The kingdom of God operates on agreement. Jesus was educating His disciples in the following way prior to Him ascending on high.

Again I say to you if two of you agree on earth concerning anything that they ask, it will be done for them by My Father in heaven. Matthew 18:19

God is raising up a people immersed in His presence, the culture of heaven of continual worship around the throne of God. Receiving God's revelation, prophesying all that you heard or saw, and God will establish it.

Let the redeemed of the Lord say so.   Psalms 107:2

The end time ecclesia will be a people who will not be looking at what they see in the realm of the physical, but will decree from mount Zion, the legislative mountain of the Lord. God is restoring Davids in these last days. Destinies of nations will be released through the non-stop worship, prayer and intercession of these Davids.

4.   Prayer and Intercession:

Prayer and intercession will be restored back to its original intent in these last days within the ecclesia. Voices will go forth in this generation declaring heaven's purposes. Through the spirit of religion that entered the church we were taught to pray from a place of our cognitive senses. The spirit of religion smothers God's purposes. A deliberate order will be established by God concerning prayer and intercession. An intentional act of God in raising up forerunner messengers stirring up worship and prayer as they decree heaven's purposes. Whatever is revealed by God in the heavenliness will be declared as a prayer.

DAVID ESTABLISHING A NEW WORSHIP ORDER IN JERUSALEM:

David enquired from God as to if it is from the Lord their God to bring back the ark, which represents God's presence amongst His people from Kirjath Jearim. See the order being restored by David consulting God. David did nothing without inquiring from God. The arc of God was put on a cart and taken from the house of Abinadad. Uzza and Ohio drove the cart. David and all Israel played music before God with all their might with singing and all different instruments. Trumpets and symbols were blown and played in front of the arc.

Then the oxen stumbled and Uzza grabbed a hold of the arc. The anger of the Lord was aroused and God struck him dead. David was afraid of God that day. The arc was then placed in the home of a Gentile called Obed-Edom. God blessed the home of Obed-Edom as he housed the arc.

What do we learn from this? The arc of God resembled His holy presence. When His presence was entered into by an unholy way, Uzza was struck dead by God. It was the order of God that only the Levites are appointed to minister before the arc. When they acted out of God's order it had severe consequences, as this was a non-biblical way of carrying His glory. God is sovereign over His word. We also learn that where the presence of the Lord is welcomed, a home is blessed as God blessed the home of Obed-Edom, although he was a Gentile, for hosting His presence.

David now established the correct order for worship. This will once again be restored in the end times to usher in God's glory into the earth as part of this great move that we are about to see.

So David took the arc from the home of Obed-Edom and brought it to Jerusalem as he prepared a place for the arc of God. David pitched a tent for it and covered it with tent curtains. Then David said, no one may carry the arc of God, but the Levites, for the Lord has chosen them to carry the arc of God and to minister before Him forever. Notice God's order being restored. David did things the way God wanted it to be done, restoring God's order. Listen to the sound counsel that David gave to the Levites and the priests, the leaders of his time. He called them together and said unto them, *"Sanctify yourselves, so that you may bring up the arc of the Lord God of Israel to the place he had prepared for it".* Notice the order again. Sanctification is necessary for carrying God's presence. Remember the arc of God in the Old Testament is indicative of His presence in the New Testament times that we live in. Sanctification and purity are necessary to carry His presence. This is God's order and counsel.

Then David went on to say to them that because they did not do it the first time, the Lord their God broke out against them, because they did not consult Him about the proper order. We find an account of all of this in *1 Chronicles 15:11-14.*

David setup the worship. He appointed singers and introduced all kinds of instruments to raise the voice with resounding joy. There was joy coming forth. Worship was not a passive ritual. He appointed Levites, door keepers and leaders. The priests were to blow the trumpets before the arc of the Lord their God. David placed all in order for twenty-four seven worship to go forth before God. David enquired from the Lord and restored God's order in the way He wanted it to be done. In the same way, God is restoring the order of worship in these last days. The spirit of religion will no longer dictate to the church. David as a forerunner demonstrated a worship order in the earth that was based on heaven's model. God is restoring Davidic worship. David was worshipper at heart and exercised extravagant worship to God. David had only one desire:

One thing I have desired from the Lord. That will I seek: that I may dwell in the house of the Lord all the days of my life, to behold the beauty of the Lord and to enquire in His temple.
Psalms 27:4

David continually sought God's counsel. His desire was towards God's presence in his house. This pleased God. As a result of the hunger and desire in David's heart, God entrusted to him a model whereby a whole generation changed to worship God for heaven's purposes.

David wanted to establish a God-centered worship on the earth in the same way as the four living creatures around the throne of God who do not rest day and night, crying out: *"Holy, holy, holy Lord God almighty, who was and is and is to come".*

Revelation 4:8

This is heaven's model being made available to David. The full expression of worship needs to be done God's way. Bear in mind that David did not live in the dispensation after the death and resurrection of Christ, where the Spirit of Christ lives on the inside of us. During the dispensation that David lived in, the Spirit of God came upon an individual, and he spoke as the Spirit led. How much more are we to enter into this realm of worship with the Spirit of Christ on the inside of us and a dimension of the Spirit upon us, when we live a holy life. The end time ecclesia will be filled with the glory of God as a result of extravagant worship. There will be a global outpouring of the Spirit of God on all flesh and prophecy will be in the streets as a result. These are the days of Joel. An army or worshippers arising by the example and model that David displayed. The Joel 2 outpouring of prophecy will go hand in glove with the Levites being restored to worship.

A continual twenty-four seven worship will go forth from the Ecclesia. Ministries need to work together in teams to establish this. In the end time these worshippers will be a full-time occupation. Consistent worship going forth. *It will be the duty and function of these Levites being restored. The rule, reign and government of God from mount Zion is being raised up in the end times.*

The spirit that will usher in the Anti-Christ, is the spirit of Jezebel, Leviathan and Python. Therefore, it is these spirits that will come against the apostolic and the prophetic in the end time church. By the spirit of Elijah, the ecclesia will prepare the way of the Lord.

The church will deal with the spirit of Jezebel through building the tabernacle of David, through praise and prayer. This same spirit operated through Herod by acting violently to the church in Acts 12.

Peter was therefore kept in prison, but constant prayer was offered to God for him by the church. And when Herod was about to bring him out, that night Peter was sleeping, bound with two chains between two soldiers, and the guards before the door were keeping the prison. Now, behold, an angel of the Lord stood by him, and a light shone in the prison; and he struck Peter on the side and raised him up, saying "arise quickly!". And his chains fell of his hands.

Acts 12:5 - 7

It was the constant praise and prayer without ceasing that was raised by the church for Peter that freed him from the hand of Herod. Under this new order of worship that David established, and which will be rebuilt in this season, God will take from the Gentiles a people for Himself. In the book of Acts 15 James quoted Amos' prophecy in Amos 9 concerning the rebuilding of the tabernacle of David that was in ruins. Global revival will be a result of this order and Israel will return to their land. God's counsel will be available under this new order.

WHAT WERE THE FUNCTIONS WITHIN THE TABERNACLE OF DAVID?

- Restoring God's order. David built houses for himself in the city of David; and prepared a place for the arc of God and pitched a tent for it. Then David said, "no one may carry the arc of God, but the Levites, for the Lord has chosen them to carry the arc of God and to minister to Him forever." The order of worship was restored by David giving clear direction on God's order. We can find an account of this in *1 Chronicles 15.*

- Singers were appointed. Then David spoke to the leaders of the Levites to appoint their brethren to be the singers accompanied by instruments of music, stringed instruments, harps and cymbals, by raising the voice with resounding joy.

- Offerings were brought into the tabernacle.

They brought the arc of God and set it in the midst of the tabernacle that David had erected for it. Then they offered burnt offerings and peace offerings before God. And when David had finished offering the burnt offerings and the peace offerings, he blessed the people in the name of the Lord. Burnt offerings were presented in the tabernacle. There were two types of burnt offerings. Some of the burnt offerings were mandatory. Other burnt offerings were voluntary and was an act of worship before the Lord. It called for complete submission to the ways and thoughts of the Lord. They presented themselves as a burnt offering to God. Total commitment and complete submission to God. All is on the altar for God's purposes. Total obedience to the voice of the Master. Everything surrendered to Him.

I beseech you therefore, brethren, by the mercies of God, that you present your bodies a living sacrifice, holy, acceptable to God, which is your reasonable service.
Romans 12:1

God requires total submission of our lives to His purposes. This is a New Testament example of a burnt offering.

Peace offering. Fellowship took place in the tabernacle. Peace offerings refer to their fellowship together in the presence of the Lord. Then he (David) distributed to everyone of Israel, both man and woman, to everyone a loaf of bread, a piece of meat, and a cake of raisins.   *1 Chronicles 16:3*

Resources were offered as they were sharing during their fellowship. This was done at the tabernacle of David. They shared what they had in the presence of the Lord. David blessed the people of God in His presence in the tabernacle.

- Thanksgiving. Thanksgiving took place in the tabernacle and continual worship.

And he (David) appointed some of the Levites to minister before the arc of the Lord, to commemorate, to thank, and to praise the Lord God of Israel.

1 Chronicles 16:4

David built a memorial before the throne of God to be remembered forever by God's people. Continual ministry took place in the tabernacle. It was accessible to all with only tent curtains covering it. Everyone who passed by could enter in. David set up singers and the priests regularly blew the trumpets before the arc of God.

- Acknowledgement of what God did for them went forth. David wrote a song of thanksgiving and worshipped God in the assembly of the Israelites in the tent. David declared God's glory and wonders among the nations. He made God known to the nations and everyone passing by. Prophetic insight was released by David in the tabernacle.

- General offerings were brought to the tabernacle. Everyone brought their offerings and nations (Gentiles) were also brought into the tabernacle.

- Gentiles were appointed to serve in the tabernacle. Obed-Edom was a foreigner serving in the tabernacle of David. David appointed Obed-Edom as a gate keeper as he remembered that he was a gate keeper previously. David appointed him and his brothers to be gate keepers. The arc of the covenant represented Jesus Christ as the center of worship. A Gentile was allowed to worship at the arc of the covenant. This is telling us that all are welcomed to worship God. Worship is not restricted to a certain group of people. The tabernacle in our time has been raised up by sending Jesus Christ into the world, which resulted in Gentiles being received into the kingdom of God.

HOW WILL WE BUILD AND WHAT IS NEEDED?

Maturity is needed in bringing our resources together in unity. David understood this principal. It is the time for rebuilding.

Is it time for you yourselves to dwell in your paneled houses, and this temple to lie in ruins? Now therefore, thus says the Lord of hosts; consider your ways, go up to the mountains and bring wood and build the temple, that I may take pleasure in it and be glorified, says the Lord.   Haggai 1:5,8

God is calling forth a remnant of people that will once again know how to worship Him and build His house in order for Him to have a dwelling place in the spirit amongst His people. A remnant that will sacrifice time and resources to build His house. A fountain shall once again flow from the house of the Lord.

We need to be strong as He will be with this remnant of people. His spirit will be poured out on the remnant and on all flesh according to Joel 2. The prophet Haggai prophesied that the latter glory of God's house will exceed the former glory. This calls for unity, hard work, equipping and maturity in the body of Christ.

Consider now, for the Lord has chosen you to build the house for the sanctuary; be strong and do it.   1 Chronicles 28:10

The whole building, being fitted together, grows into a holy temple in the Lord. This remnant will be built together for a dwelling place of God in the Spirit. This will be accomplished through worship as God unleashes His end time plans and army.

Much revelation comes forth as a result of extreme worship. David received all the plans from God for the rebuilding of the temple of Solomon. David then gave those plans to his son, Solomon, to start building. Those were plans for the treasuries, the upper and inner chambers of the temple and the place for the mercy seat.

And the plans for all that he had by the Spirit, of the courts of the house of the Lord, of all the chambers all around, of the treasuries for the dedicated things.
                 1 Chronicles 28:12

David did not build on his own accord, but received prophetically the strategy on how to build. In the same way the ecclesia will rebuild the house of the Lord, starting with the tabernacle of David.

Giving - giving is a form of worship to God. David understood this. Because David has set his affection on the house of God, he gave to the house of God, over and above all that he prepared for the holy house. He gave his own special treasure of gold and silver. David loved God and was an extreme worshipper. Not only in songs and music and poetry, but also in giving. His love for the house of God compelled him to give.

Then the leaders of the tribes of Israel followed his example. They all offered willingly. They gave towards the work of the house of God, five thousand talents and ten thousand grams of gold, ten thousand talents of silver, eighteen thousand talents of bronze, and one hundred talents of iron. And whoever had precious stones gave them to the treasury of the house of the Lord. Then the people rejoiced, for they had offered willingly, because with a loyal heart they had offered willingly to the Lord, and king David also rejoiced greatly. This account of matters is found in the word of God in *1 Chronicles 28:7,8*

They were extravagant givers. Worshipping God by what we give always brings tremendous joy. That which flows from the head will come down upon those you lead. They gave by the example of David and was moved by the Spirit of God to give.

No longer will we be dictated by the Spirit of religion on our giving to God's house. The remnant church must join their resources and their strength in this season for the kingdom of God to reach nations. The silver and gold belong to God. We should love the house of the Lord to the extent that we will sacrifice in offerings. Burnt offerings of total submission and obedience, peace offerings in ministering and giving of our resources.

Restoration of the tabernacle of David today means doing away with legalism, judgmentalism, condemnation, which are all religious practices to turning to the hurting people of the church and the world with open and loving arms, accepting them as they are by the ministry of reconciliation which we will explain in detail later. The Lord is inviting all to turn to Him, to let Him wipe their sins away in His presence and to receive the refreshing that only comes from His presence. All who believe in Him are being brought back into the household of God and are destined to be conformed into His image and carry His authority as they flesh out their true identities and personas. As they are known in heaven, they will be known on earth.

CHAPTER 5

MOUNT ZION: THE MOUNTAIN OF THE LORD

MOUNT ZION: THE MOUNTAIN OF THE LORD

We need to make a distinction between Mount Zion and Zion. Mount Zion is the mountain of the Lord. It is a place where God dwells amongst His people. It is a governmental seat, a place of dominion where there is to be found an abiding glory. It is a place of God's legislative governing over the earth. It is the city of the Lord where He reigns, it is the heavenly Jerusalem. A dwelling place in the Spirit for Him. A seat of power and authority. A place where the remnant gathers and will be operating from in the last days.

What will we find in Mount Zion, the city of the Lord?

But you have come to Mount Zion and the city of the living God, the heavenly Jerusalem, to an innumerable company of angels, to the general assembly and church of the first born who are registered in heaven, God the Judge of all, to the spirits of just men made perfect, to Jesus the mediator of the new covenant and to the blood of sprinkling that speaks of better things than that of Abel.

Hebrews 12:22 - 24

A company of angels as well as the general assembly of the church, all those whose names are registered in heaven, God as the Judge of all, the spirits of just men testifying, Jesus the mediator, and the blood that was sprinkled on the mercy seat are all present in the courts of heaven to agree and testify as the kingdom of God is a judicial system. In these last days the true remnant will visit Mount Zion regularly and decree from Mount Zion.

The church is rising in these last days. God is separating a remnant who will gather together and build Him a temple in the Spirit. A gathering place where He will dwell amongst His people by His Holy Spirit. All the saints whose names are registered in heaven and churches who are registered in heaven, those whom God Himself gave birth to, will join together. God is the Judge; Jesus the Mediator and the Blood speaks on our behalf. The spirits of just men, those who went before us, will testify with us and there is an innumerable company of angels joining in to lead this army on the move in the last days. The ecclesia or remnant will govern and legislate from Mount Zion as heaven is backing us up. The angels will come to the earth to engage in war with us against the dragon and the beast. God is calling a remnant to Mount Zion. The foundation of the city of God is in the holy mountains (His dwelling place), and the Lord loves the gates of Zion more than all the dwelling places of Jacob. The Lord will record, when He registers His people.

This one was born there.   Psalm 78:1

Our springs will be in Him. All revelation will flow from Him in Mount Zion.

Yet once more God will shake, not only the earth, but also the heavens. In this shaking there will be a removal of those things that are being shaken, as of things that are made (man made things) so that the things that cannot be shaken may remain. We read an account of this in the book of *Hebrews 12:27*. Everything that has gained illegal authority and has not been built by God, or where the foundation has not been laid by God will fall in this season. After the shaking all legal authority, authority from Mount Zion, will rise. Therefore we will see many churches and ministries as well as leaders fall in this season, even businesses, governments, systems, education and media. The reign in the church will be established and the church will proceed under legitimate authority. After the shake, that which remains, God will rebuild. It is now the time for the restoration and rebuilding of God's house from Mount Zion.

If we need to make a distinction between Mount Zion and Zion, who is Zion then?

Zion is the inhabitants of Mount Zion, the city of the Lord. Zion is the remnant. All the saints whose names are registered in heaven; they are Zion.

"The Lord will record, when He registers the people: "This one was born there".
                                                                                                                    Psalms 87:6

Zion refers to those who are matured and trusted with God's mandate. The remnant will enter into Zion with a new commission. Zion will bring forth the end time harvest. The youth, whom God will save, deliver and heal under the extravagant praise and worship going forth from Zion, will be equipped and be appointed as leaders in Zion.

A greater power is coming forth in the church and it is released in Zion, the company of those inhabitants of Mount Zion. There will be a new release of authority. Churches and ministries will come together and work together as teams. After fasting and much prayer we will see the Joel 2 final outpouring of God's Spirit upon all flesh. The church will move in unison and love. The power of a Melchizedek generation will rise. A generation that will take the seven mountains of society for the Lord. The priesthood and the marketplace will be dependent upon one another and will meet in Zion.

Praise and blessing will come forth from Zion. The remnant, or ecclesia, will stand united in purpose and love. They will carry God's end time mandate. Love will be unconditional amongst them and victory will be eminent. Decrees will come forth from Zion and God will establish a people for Himself in the earth. The end time ecclesia will legislate from Mount Zion and will be a force to be reckoned with.

No longer will the true church be weak, powerless, demon infiltrated, slandering one another and defeated. There is a movement of God coming and the time is now. It is the time of separation. It is a time to be holy and walk righteously. Not to love your life more and be submitted in total obedience to the call and the Spirit of God. It will be a glorious church that Christ will rapture as His second coming is very soon. Now is the time for God's final movement on the earth. As a church we need to prepare and be sanctified to cooperate with heaven in this move.

Let us now further discuss all these statements that were made about Zion.

THE LORD'S REIGN IN ZION:

Now it shall come to pass in the latter days that the mountain of the Lord's house shall be established on the top of the mountains, and shall be exalted among the hills; and peoples shall flow to it. Many nations shall come and say "Come and let us go up to the Mountain of the Lord, to the house of the God of Jacob; He will teach us His ways, and we shall walk in His paths". For out of Zion, the law shall go forth, and the Word of the Lord from Jerusalem. He shall judge between many peoples, and rebuke strong nations afar off. They shall beat their swords into plowshares, and their spears into pruning hooks. The account of this word is found in *Micah 4:1 - 3.*

We are in the latter days now and therefore the house of the Lord will be established the way God intended it to be. The modern-day church has deviated from God's original intent in many ways. The spirit of religion has infiltrated the church and cursed the church to become powerless. It hindered the true sons and daughters to be equipped and to take up their mantles and places in the body of Christ. The five-fold ministry as the original leadership pattern for the church was ignored for a long time. Many of the offices were not acknowledged and deemed Old Testament. God is restoring His reign and establishing His ecclesia. The five-fold ministry is the only appointed governing system of the church which Jesus Christ as Head of His church has ordained.

God's house will be established on the top of the mountains which is in indicative that from Mount Zion all the other six mountains of society will be influenced and brought under God's rule. These mountains are education, government, media, economy, family and arts. The seventh mountain is the mountain of the Lord, representing the church legislating from Mount Zion. This mountain is on the top of the hills. In other words, it is exalted above the other six mountains and needs to influence those mountains in society. All these mountains in society should be governed by the true remnant and should be founded in the true living God. We are currently far from it. The ecclesia or remnant, legislating, governing church of God will now rise by the hand of God.

Many nations and people shall flow to the rising of this mountain. They will find safety and will come because the answers will be in Zion. As the world spirals down and times of trial comes upon the whole world, people will flock to Zion. There they will be comforted, receive their answers and be provided for. Anxiety, fear, depression and panic will cover the people worldwide. This is not the portion of the remnant. This is God's judgment upon the unrighteous. However, God is a loving Father and has made provision for everyone to be healed and delivered in the light of His glory in Zion. Within the remnant end time church where He dwells amongst His people, an abiding glory will be present. Healing will take place in Zion.

Nations will come and be delivered. As a result of God's commandments and His ways that will go forth from Zion, as well as the unprecedented truth of His word, nations will be saved. They will be saved and delivered to such an extent that they will lay down their battle plans, their swords and their spears. As God will judge the nations through His word and the Spirit of Truth, they will lose their power and rebuild His house. No longer will nations dictate to God unless God called them to be an instrument of judgment in His hand. Nations will come to Christ.

There will be unity in Mount Zion and God will vindicate His church and nations. They will walk in the Name of their Lord forever.

AN ABIDING PRESENCE IN ZION:

"Then the Lord will create above every dwelling place of Mount Zion, and above her assemblies, a cloud and smoke by day and the shining of a fire by night. For over all the glory there will be a covering. And there will be a tabernacle for shade in the day time from the heat, for a place of refuge, and for a shelter from rain and storm"
Isaiah 4:5,6

Every dwelling tells us that there will be many of these dwelling places for the Lord in the earth worldwide. There will be many assemblies of the remnant in many nations across the world. Many remnant churches that will be established in Him where there will be habitation in the Spirit for Him. Made up of the saints who are registered in heaven and serve in their gifting and callings as a remnant church. His presence will earmark those churches. The cloud of smoke by day and the flaming fire by night is indicative of His manifested Presence, His glory, that will be upon those gatherings and churches day and night. An abiding glory as we have mentioned.

The tabernacle of shade refers to the ongoing worship that will be going forth. The heat refers to all the problems and calamities that will strike in the end times. However, under the sound of worship and praise, safety and a place of hiding will be provided. A place of refuge and safety to hide from the storms, a place to hide from all the trials that will come upon the whole world to test the inhabitants, will be provided in Zion. He will comfort nations afar off and His people in Mount Zion. There will be safety in Zion as a result of His abiding Presence.

"Thus says the Lord: I will return to Zion, and dwell in the midst of Jerusalem. Jerusalem shall be called the City of Truth, the Mountain of the Lord of Hosts, the Holy Mountain"
Zachariah 8:3

There will be a return of God's glory to His house. Why has the former glory left that the prophet Zachariah is now mentioning a return of the glory?

The glory has left for a very long time as a result of the church deviating from God's original intent, plan and commission. The church became a religious gathering place with it's own programs and agendas. The Holy Spirit was not welcomed in many churches and devoid of God's Presence. This will now be corrected in the end times.

THE FOUNDATION OF ZION:

In Zion a strong foundation will be found. A building, a temple built out of living stones. These stones are the redeemed of the Lord. It will be a temple for our God. A habitation for Him in the Spirit. Revelation will flow from Zion. God will render the heavens and come down to Zion and live among His remnants. God will come down with signs and wonders and the miraculous. No demon will survive there.

"Now, therefore, you are no longer strangers and foreigners, but fellow citizens with the saints and members of the same household of God. Having been built on the foundation of the apostles and prophets, Jesus Christ Himself, the Chief Cornerstone, in Whom the whole building being fitted together, grows into a holy temple in the Lord, in whom you also are being built together for a dwelling place of God in the Spirit"
Ephesians 2:19 - 22

We are no longer strangers and foreigners as we are all in covenant relationship with Him and with one another in Zion. We are all members of the same household. In a household there are many duties to be performed. Each one needs to walk in their call and mandate from God. This calls for maturity. Zion is a place for the matured sons and daughters of God to stand as leaders and bring in the end time harvest and to equip them. To prepare a way for the return of our Lord Jesus Christ and to make ready a bride for Him.

This church will be built on the foundation of the apostles and the prophets, Jesus the Chief Cornerstone. Jesus will personally direct the remnant church, the ecclesia. The apostolic rule and prophetic direction of the church will be established and be prominent. Everyone that is part of the remnant will be directed to an altar where they are protected under apostolic/prophetic leadership. However, all will work together in unison as a team and be part of a five-fold ministry team. The five-fold ministry will replace the five tentacles of religion, being debate, criticism, judgment, legalism and opinion. This has been dictating the church for a very long era. Religion will be uprooted by the apostles and end time prophets as it prevents God's people from fleshing out their callings and it restrains their growth to maturity. It strips the church of its power and makes it a man made entity. The Davids and Elijah's will rise with boldness against these powers and principalities. The spirit of Jezebel who controlled the church through witchcraft will also be uprooted as the true remnant will be fearless, full of power and sold out to the Lord to a point where they do not love their lives more. There will be no division in the true remnant church that God is rising up.

We will all fit together and grow into a building made out of living stones as it is made up of all the saints that are registered in heaven. This building will rise to the heavens to become a temple, the heavenly Jerusalem where God through His Spirit will dwell amongst the remnant church. He will no longer be abandoned from the church. His glory now returns as the church is being placed in order and walks in holiness and righteousness. Obedience, righteousness (right standing with God) and a sanctified people will be evident in Zion. The church will stand in unity. The spiritual language of Zion will be the language and guidance of the Holy Spirit. The Holy Spirit will lead and reposition God's people, even geographically we will see many repositioning amongst the remnant. One mind and one spirit focused on God's mandate. The word of God will go forth in all purity. Nothing that is not pure will stand in the manifested presence of God within Zion. Therefore, this will be a righteous remnant. For many the price and sacrifice will be too high and as a result they will be walking away from the Truth and despise righteousness. We will see a falling away and a great apostasy in the end times.

TIMES AND SEASONS:

The sons of Issachar were enlisted in David's army. They had understanding of the times and seasons, to know what Israel in those days ought to do. This same Issachar anointing is being released to the end time ecclesia in Zion. Everyone will know their seasons to transition and understand their area of calling. They will be enlisted in the Joel 2 end time army of God. Each one will take their place. They will not break ranks. All will be equal. No one will be more important than the other. They will not contend with one another, but each one will understand his call. However there will be different levels of authority. All will work together in unison as a team with one common goal, to overcome the dragon and the beast and to gather the final harvest just before the coming of our Lord Jesus Christ. Ministries will join forces and work together helping and supporting one another.

"He will baptize you with the Holy Spirit and fire"   Matthew 3:11

A baptism of fire will come forth from Zion. All will be baptized with the Holy Spirit and with fire.

"His winnowing fan is in His hand, and He will thoroughly clean out His threshing floor, and gather His wheat into the barn; but He will burn up the chaff with unquenchable fire"
Matthew 3:12

This baptism of fire that will come to Zion will cause a separation between that which is pure and that which is defiled. There will be a separation of the wheat, which still has purpose and the chaff which is only a by-product and has no further purpose. People will no longer be able to sit in the church and hide. No longer will they be able to sit in their sins. No longer will they be able to sit a service and return to a vile lifestyle. God will separate the vile from the precious. Many people will walk away from you and even from your ministry or church because of the heat. Those who truly serve God in Spirit and in Truth will be persecuted for their positioning. God is separating. When the fire of the Holy Spirit falls it will be messy. Many will take offense and walk away as it will be offensive to their spirit of religion.

His church will be holy and pure. This is necessary for the abiding glory to return. The remnant will not be able to stand in the last days without the abiding glory of God. Jesus Christ is returning for a pure and spotless bride.

HOLINESS IN ZION:

The remnant will be set apart, sanctified and walk on the highway of holiness.

"For God did not call us to uncleanness, but to holiness. Therefore, he who rejects this does not reject man, but God, who has also given us His Holy Spirit"
1 Thessalonians 4:7,8

Holiness is non-negotiable. It is a command from God. Whoever rejects this command, rejects God Himself and His Spirit and will certainly be judged.

Holiness is required as the remnant will war together with the angels from heaven and heavenly beings in the final conflict in the earth. In heaven there is unity. Satan and his angels were expelled from heaven as a result of their rebellion against God.

'So the great dragon was cast out, the serpent of old, called the devil and satan, who deceives the whole world; he was cast on the earth and his angels were cast out with him"
Revelation 12:9

Now all heaven is obeying God. The end time army will co-operate in unison with heaven in this final move of God. The heavens are called to war with us. As a result the remnant have to be obedient and holy before God to create unison between heaven and earth. These two realms will be engaged together in the final quest. There has never been a time such as this. God secured extra help for His sons and daughters in the earth. We need to be knowledgeable of the Scriptures. There is a war for souls and a war to destroy the bride. Satan's angry response of being cast out of heaven triggers the events of the great tribulation, as he attempts to gain even greater control over the earth and the spiritual realm. We are engaged in war. We need to prepare ourselves accordingly to stand.

The arch angel Michael has a unique place in the destiny of God's people in the great tribulation. As a result of this future battle that is already evident in the earth, satan is excluded once and for all from access to the "third heaven" which we read about in 2 Corinthians 12:2.

"At that time Michael shall stand up, the great prince who stands watch over the sons of Your people; and there shall be a time of trouble, such as never was since there was a nation, even to that time. And at that time Your people shall be delivered, everyone who is found written in the Book"   *Daniel 12:1*

We are standing at the threshold of that time. God is speaking to the remnant church to prepare herself. Is your name written in the Book? Is God saying about you: *"this one is registered in heaven".* If you can sincerely answer "yes" to this, then prepare for war. The promise stands that we will be delivered, and we will have the victory. However, there is no victory without a fight!

"Now may the God of peace Himself sanctify you completely; and may your whole spirit, soul, and body be preserved blameless at the coming of our Lord Jesus Christ. He Who calls you is faithful, Who will also do it" 1 Thessalonians 5:23,24

All of us need to be sanctified. In other words, be set apart. Our bodies as a living sacrifice, holy and acceptable to God as our reasonable service. Our souls (minds) need to be renewed to be the mind of Christ, and the seven-fold Holy Spirit must. be the habitation of our souls. This way your thoughts and actions will be aligned with heaven to let His kingdom come on earth as it is in heaven. Our spirits sanctified by the Word. By this we will be preserved and ready to meet Christ in the clouds. Holy living is required in all three of these dimensions. Our members need to be slaves of righteousness and holiness. This is the command of the Lord so that we will be able to stand.

The church will come into a position of authority by the circumcision of our hearts, minds and tongues. Our minds and tongues as members of our body need to be sanctified through faith. Slandering one another and speaking against God's promises, as well as cursing the nets (ministries) of others will not be found amongst a holy remnant. Let us set aside all malice and prepare for the war that is at hand.

GOD'S LOVE IN ZION

The remnant in Zion will walk in strong covenant relationship with God and one another. They will be rooted and grounded in His love. His love will secure them. They will release God's love unconditionally, helping one another, supporting one another. They will be bond slaves for God, willingly executing His mandate irrespective of their own lives. The remnant will love God with all their hearts, strength, minds and souls. They will be committed to Christ to do His will. This is a statement that the angels in heaven made about the remnant:

They did not love their lives to death.

What a profound statement!

POWER OF MALCHIZEDEK - PRIESTHOOD AND MARKET PLACE IN ZION

There will be unity between the priesthood, those who serve full time at the altar and the kings serving full time in the marketplace. Zion will carry the revelation and answers for the business world. Kings will come to Zion for revelation and strategy on new business ideas as the marketplace is being brought into the church. God will prosper the marketplace to fund the priesthood and missions for the final harvest to be brought in.

There were two bronze pillars been made for the temple of Solomon.

"Then he (Solomon) set up the pillars by the vestibule of the temple, he set up the pillar on the right and called its name Jachin and he set up the pillar on the left and called its name Boaz"   1 Kings 7:21

These pillars carried great spiritual significance. The name Jachin means "he that strengthens and make steadfast". Boaz means "in him is strength". It is significant that both the meanings of these names are connected to strength. Boaz is the strength and Jachin is strengthening. These two pillars will come together in the end time church as Jachin represents the priesthood and Boaz the marketplace. The priesthood is those who have been called into full time ministry at the altar. The marketplace represents the kings who have been called to full time business. When they come together under the order of Melchizedek, Jachin will strengthen Boaz (the marketplace), as within Boaz there is strength and Jachin strengthens. The end time harvest will be funded by the kings.

There will be a hastening of the work of God. A transfer of wealth will take place to build God's house and to rebuild the tabernacle of David, to fund twenty-four seven worship.

"A good man leaves an inheritance for his children's children, but the wealth of the sinner is stored up for the righteous"   Proverbs 13:22

"Therefore your gates shall be open continually; they shall not be shut day or night, that men may bring to you the wealth of the Gentiles"   Isaiah 60:11

The spoils of war will be taken from the world to fund God's Kingdom. He will work it by His mighty right hand.

"Juda also will fight at Jerusalem and the wealth of all the surrounding nations shall be gathered together. Gold, silver and apparel in great abundance"

                                                               Zachariah 14:14

God will personally guide the remnant. The remnant will be dependent upon God for all that they need as in the days of the wilderness. Their expectancy will be from God only.

Provision for the remnant will be supernatural provision. Concerning the city of Zion, this is how it will be.

"He will dwell on high; His place of defense will be the fortress of rocks, bread will be given him. His water will be sur". Isaiah 33:16

The remnant will command water and food to come forth as they walk in the power of the age to come. "The elect of the Lord will say so." The remnant will carry the rod of authority.

"They will decree a thing and it will be established for them, and the light of His glory will shine on their pathways" Job 22:28

Decrees will go forth from Zion. The remnant will carry the authority of the Name of the Lord and operate in it. The Name above all other names, in this age and the age to come, the Name of Jesus Christ. The lamb of God will be in the midst of the remnant to perform their decrees.

WARFARE FROM ZION

The remnant will know how to war against the beast and the anti-Christ. The remnant will be matured to take up the sword themselves. The remnant will usher in the coming of the Lord by the spirit of Elijah, declaring war against the spirit of Leviathan, Jezebel and Python, the sea serpent spirits opposing the end time church. As the marine kingdom will come against the church in these last days and usher in and prepare the way for the anti-Christ and the beast, the remnant will counteract in the spirit and power of Elijah.

The remnant will rise as an end time army. Sanctified and set apart. Knowing their callings and positions in the army. Understanding how to use their weapons against the enemy. Therefore a lot of equipping of the saints is now at hand to prepare the remnant church. Their foundations will be strong in the Word of God and they will be yielded to the Spirit of the Lord. The remnant will carry the sword of the Word.

Spiritual warfare will become eminent. These are the times we have entered into now. Heaven is coming to war with the bride of Christ. The arch angel Michael has been appointed for this end time task and has already been positioned. A fully surrendered life is necessary. Holiness is key and a life fully yielded to the Spirit of God. The end time army will stand united in covenant with God and one another.

Revelation 12:7 - 11 depicts this final conflict.

"And war broke out in heaven: Michael and his angels fought with the dragon, and the dragon and his angels fought. But they did not prevail, nor was a place found for them in heaven any longer. So the great dragon was cast out, that serpent of old, called the devil and satan, who deceives the whole world, he was cast to the earth, and his angels were cast out with him, then I heard a loud voice in heaven, "now salvation and strength and the kingdom of our God, and the power of His Christ have come, for the accuser of our brethren, who accused them before our God day and night, has been cast down. And they overcame him by the blood of the lamb and by the word of their testimony, and they did not love their lives to the death."   Revelation 12:7 - 11

As the remnant will war together with Michael and his angels, maturity and fullness of Christ is required. Sonship, everyone walking in authority and holiness. The earth is crying out for the manifestation of the sons and daughters of God. As sons and daughters, we will command the elements to obey in these last days and to fight with us.

There will be order in Zion. Apostolic order and governance restored in Zion. Each one will know their place in the Joel 2 army. There will be no competition. All will be leaders, sanctified by God carrying the sword of the Word. Churches will gather and work together in unison. We are one global army. Everyone taking up their rightful place, matured and fully equipped to handle instruments of warfare.

Teamwork will be the signature of the remnant. We will all fight a common enemy. This army will stand together, loving one another, caring for one another and helping one another. With the Joel 2 final outpouring of the Spirit of God upon all flesh, the children, youths, elderly people, young people and leaders will all be empowered by the Spirit of God. The selfless and nameless will rise as the voice of the Lord will be everywhere. Fire will go before this army and fire will be behind this army. This is the face of the end time church, the remnant.

FALSE PROPHETS AND FALSE TEACHERS

False prophets and false teachers will rise in the end times. It was never God's intent for His sons and daughters to find their revelation from a prophet. God speaks to His children personally. There is nothing wrong to put a prophet on the test to get a word confirmed which the Lord have already spoken to you.

But to sit under prophetic gatherings to receive a word for your next season is wrong. To consult a prophet to speak into your life without you first receiving your own revelation from God is wrong. The main purpose of a prophet in office is to equip the body of Christ. This conduct teaches the church to be weak and may lead to division in the body of Christ.

A prophet needs to be part of a five-fold ministry team according to the Word in Ephesians 4:11, appointed by leadership. Prophets should not be lone rangers and need to be under covering of an apostolic mantle. Jesus warned against the false prophets when He said the following words: *"Beware of false prophets, who come to you in sheets clothing, but inwardly they are ravenous wolves". You will know them by their fruits.*
Matthew 7:15,16

So be careful, as the five-fold ministry offices have been set in the church by Jesus Christ Himself as the legislative governing body of the church. All outside of that is illegitimate authority. If there is a call upon your life to be a prophet, it will be recognized by the leaders of the five-fold ministry where you serve at the altar. Members in the congregation will also start to notice your call. Once the call has been confirmed an extensive period of training follows before you are being released into the call by the leadership of your church. Training and raising of a prophet take many years. God will shake and silence all illegitimate authority and self-appointed leaders in this end time move of God which has already begun. The hand of the Lord will be against these prophets.

Concerning that which is false, the Word declares:

"I appeal to you, brothers, to watch out for those who cause divisions and create obstacles contrary to the doctrine that you have been taught; avoid them for such persons do not serve our Lord Jesus Christ, but their own appetites, and by smooth talk and flattery they deceive the hearts of the naive" Romans 16:17,18

Many of these false prophets have torn churches apart and created havoc in God's sanctuary.

The remnant will not run after prophets. They will be led by the Spirit of God.

"My sheep hear My voice, and I know them, and they follow Me"   John 10:27

The matured will hear the voice of the Lord. God knows them and they will follow after Him only. Let us get rid of this sickness in the church of running after prophets.

POISON IN THE FOOD:

Be careful of poison in the food of the sons and daughters of God. This is also referred to as heresy within the church. We are warned that in the last days false doctrine will rise.

"For the time is coming when people will not endure sound teaching, but having itching ears they will accumulate for themselves teachers to suit their own passions, and will turn away from listening to the truth and wander off into myths"

2 Timothy 4:3,4

The end time revelation and teaching of the Word of God will be a hard word for many and be rejected by many. As everyone will have to choose now. God requires purity and holiness. God requires a sacrificial and complete surrendered life.

Many false teachers and prophets will prophecy from their soul dimension and teach heresy contradicting the Word of God, His ways and protocols, with the sole agenda to make money for themselves.

We were never supposed to trade using the Gospel. We received freely and freely we need to give it away.

Apostles are watch dogs over doctrine. Where are the real fathers and mothers to the church? Those apostles whom God appointed. They will rise now in much authority and the office of the apostle will once more be respected.

"See to it that no one take you captive by philosophy and empty deceit, according to human tradition, according to the elemental spirits of the world, and not according to Christ"
Colossians 2:8

Be careful of myths and any doctrine that deviates from the teaching of Christ Jesus. The remnant will be well undergirded in the Word of God and carry the Word as a sword to decree from Mount Zion.

"If anyone teaches a different doctrine and does not agree with the sound words of our Lord Jesus Christ and the teaching that accords with godliness, he is puffed up with conceit and understands nothing. He has an unhealthy craving for controversy and for quarrels about words, which produce envy, dissension, slander, evil suspicions, and constant friction among people who are deprived in mind and deprived of the truth, imagining that godliness is a means of gain" 1 Timothy 6:3 - 5

From the above it is clear that unsound doctrine is responsible for all sorts of evil entering the church. The remnant will know the Word of God. Pastors and preachers using the Gospel to make money for themselves will be shaken and see the judgment of God upon their evil works. This is the Word of the Lord:

"Woe to the shepherds who destroy and scatter the sheep of My pasture! says the Lord. Therefore, thus says the Lord God of Israel against the shepherds who feed My people: You have scattered My flock, driven them away, and not attended to them. Behold, I will attend to you for the evil of your doings, says the Lord. But I will gather the remnant of My flock out of all countries where I have driven them, and bring them back to their folds; and they shall be fruitful and increase. I will set up shepherds over them who will feed them, and they shall fear no more, nor be dismayed, nor shall they be lacking, says the Lord" Jeremiah 23:1-4

In the last days we will see a change of leadership as all self-appointed leaders will be removed by God, those who stand for their own gain. The remnant church will be pure and God-appointed leaders will prevail. Those who were hidden and rejected but prepared for a time such as this, they will be brought to the forefront by the Hand of God.

ZION'S FUTURE TRIUMPH

The lame will be assembled, and the outcast will be gathered. Those coming to Zion will be the ones that are rejected, drug addicts, prostitutes and all that are outcasts. The lame will be made a remnant. Youth will come. They will be equipped in Zion and stand as leaders for our God. All these will gather. The outcast will be made a strong nation in Zion.

Is the church ready to receive these people? This is what the end time harvest will look like. The Lord will reign over them in Zion. The former reign and dominion will come. The governmental position in the courts of heaven will go forth from Zion and be established.

Deliverance will take place in Zion. Many nations and people will look down on the remnant in Zion and say let her be defiled and let our eyes look upon Zion. But they do not know the thoughts of the Lord, neither do they understand His counsel. The enemies of Zion will be gathered like sheaves on the threshing floor by God Himself.

Intercession will go forth from Zion. He will make the remnant's horn like iron. A horn refers to authority. The remnant will rise in authority over the enemy. A fresh anointing for strength and stability will be poured out over the remnant. Iron is symbolic of strength and stability. The remnant's hooves will be made like bronze. Bronze refers to the suffering, testing and sanctification in the fire of trials. The remnant will be strong. The people being tested, tried and sanctified, set apart for God. They will reign and triumph. The remnant will break many nations into pieces and consecrate their gain to the Lord and their substance to the Lord of the whole earth. This transfer of wealth will be used to fund the end time harvest as mentioned before. We find an account of all the aforementioned in the Word of God in *Micah 4:6 - 13*.

CHAPTER 6

AUTHORITY, TRUE IDENTITY SONSHIP

The prophet Ezekiel was a member of the Zadok priesthood. He was trained in the priesthood and was deported to Babylon in 59 B.C. Ezekiel's call came to him four years before he was deported. He was exiled in the second siege of Jerusalem, and he wrote to those left in Jerusalem about its eminent and total destruction, including the departure of God's presence.

Ezekiel was a forerunner prophet in as much as his visions, his spiritual experiences and interaction with the Spirit of God anticipated the activity of the Holy Spirit in the New Testament.

Ezekiel's message was addressed to a demoralized remnant of Juda, exiled to Babylon. His message focused on the moral responsibility of each believer concerning his walk with God as opposed to a corporate responsibility shielding the believer. Every son and daughter of God needs to take personal responsibility to grow and mature in Christ and refrain from sin. In chapters 25 - 32 Ezekiel prophecies the future blessings for God's covenant people. The repentance of a faithful remnant will result in the recreation and restoration of God's people. That time is now. The Divine Spirit will quicken the remnant to a new life. Ezekiel depicted the sons and daughters of God as a kingdom of priests and a holy nation.

He depicted a restored sanctuary in the midst of a gathered people, who's head is the King Priest, kingly and priestly anointing joining and rising as the David generation. It foreshadowed the restored tabernacle of David, the church.

We need to look at this history, as Ezekiel anticipated the new covenant's "new birth" experience, which would be by the Spirit. We are living in the dispensation that Ezekiel prophesied, where man is coming forth as sons and daughters of God. Greater works are coming forth through the sons and daughters of God by the authority they carry in the Spirit. Authority leads to dominion. They will live righteously before God and as a result ask and receive. Blessings come forth in the end times for the true sons and daughters of God. God wants to speak and reveal to His sons and daughters in these last days.

FACE OF THE SONS

Ezekiel saw a vision of four living creatures and gave an account of what he saw as follows:

"Also from within it came the likeness of four living creatures. And this was their appearance: They had the likeness of man.

Each one had four faces, and each one had four wings. Their legs were straight, and the souls of their feet were like the souls of calves' feet, they sparkled like the color of burnished bronze. The hands of a man were under their wings on their four sides, and each of the four had faces and wings. Their wings touched one another. The creatures did not turn when they went, but each one went straight forward. As for the likeness of their face, each had the face of a man, each of the four had the face of a lion on the right side, each of the four had the face of an ox on the left side, and each had the face of an eagle. Thus were their faces."
Ezekiel 1:5 - 11

Why is this significant?

Remember, Ezekiel prophesied and pointed to the coming life in the Spirit of New Testament believers. This depicts a picture of the true sons and daughters of God walking in authority with prophetic foresight and hindsight.

Although these living creatures are represented at the throne of God, it also is symbolic of the sons and daughters of God and how they will exert authority and operate in the last days. These living creatures show us a picture of the image of Christ, and we have been created in this very same image.

- The ox is representative of servanthood and anointing
- The eagle is representative of prophetic sight
- The lion is representative of calling, apostolic governance and dominion
- The man is representative of sonship

These living creatures had the likeness of a man. Each one had four faces. They have 360 degrees sight. As sons and daughters, we also have 360 degrees sight. The souls of their feet were like the souls of calves' feet, representing the lamb that was slain and the end time harvest that will be brought in through the blood of the Lamb. They sparkle like the color of burnished bronze. These sons and daughters will shine as a result of God's glory being poured out upon the remnant. Bronze refers to suffering, testing and sanctification. The true sons and daughters of God, the remnant, will be tested in the fire by circumstances and trials and tribulations, sanctified, set apart by God in the last day army that is rising under this great move of God on the face of the earth.

The hands of a man were under their wings. The five-fold ministry will replace the five tentacles of the spirit of religion that held the church captive for years. The five-fold will arise as God's governing system in the remnant church. Each of the four faces had wings. This refers to the swift movement of the Spirit of God upon the earth in the last days. Their wings touched one another. This refers to the unity in the body of Christ. We will be locking shields and stand united in the Joel 2 army, with one common goal, to defeat the premature rising of the dragon and the beast, to allow God's kingdom to come. As it is in heaven, let it be on earth.

The creatures did not turn when they went, but each one went straight forward. The sons and daughters that makes out the remnant will have one focus. They will not retreat but march forward. Their ears will be turned to the Master, to look into His eyes and to do what He commands. They will focus and move in the Spirit. As for the likeness of their faces, each had the face of a man. They will walk in the fullness of Christ, fully matured in the LORD, and in full authority of their sonship and inheritance with much power.

Each of the four had the face of the lion on the right side. The right side is the dominant side and represents a place of ruling. The lion represents the apostolic rule and governance. God's sons and daughters will understand their authority and rule and reign from mount Zion, bringing heaven to earth through their prophetic decrees. They will regain dominion over the seven mountains of society. They will bring heaven to earth by their decrees. Apostolic rule will be re-established by their decrees. The will understand their callings.

Each of the four had the face of an ox on the left side. The left side is the determining side. They will take up their places in the end time army determined by their gifting and calls. Each one will know their call and area of gifting. They will take up their places and war. And each had the face of an eagle. They will have 360-degree prophetic sight. Hindsight and foresight. They will see from God's perspective all that He sees. They will receive by revelation and legislate from mount Zion and live and operate from a place in the Spirit. The eagle represents the prophetic. In the last days there will be an outpouring of the Spirit of God on all flesh. The children will prophecy. The youth will see visions. The elderly will dream dreams and the leaders will receive prophetic insight and revelation. The prophetic will be eminent and God's voice will be everywhere.

Looking at this picture and the present condition of the church, there is a lot of equipping to be done. All five-fold leaders now have to rise and equip the body whilst we bring in the harvest. It is the time of sanctification for these very purposes, as God's governance needs to be set up.

SONSHIP THROUGH THE SPIRIT

Now that we have a clear picture of the face of the sons and daughters of God, let us proceed to the life in the Spirit. Always remember that there is no gender concerning the things of the spirit. When the Word of God refers to "sons", it also includes the daughters of God. God awaits the consummation of His great plans for the church. *"For as many as are lead by the Spirit of God, theses are sons of God".*
                    Romans 8:14

Sonship calls for maturity in the Spirit. It is an apostolic/prophetic function in the body of Christ to bring God's sons and daughters to full maturity. They need to grow up and be mentored and groomed into a lifestyle of "seeing" and "hearing" in the Spirit and live in an atmosphere of God's revelation. Therefore, being *"lead by the Spirit of God"* involves progressively putting to death the sinful appetites of the lower nature. The more fully they are led by the Holy Spirit, the more completely will they be obedient to God and be conformed to holiness.

As sons and daughters, we received the Spirit of adoption by whom we cry out "Abba Father". Abba is the loving nature of our Father. Father encompasses our Father as a Judge.

"The Spirit Himself bares witness with our spirit that we are children of God, and if children then heirs of Christ, if indeed we suffer with Him, we may also be glorified together"
                    Romans 8:14 - 17

From this Scripture it is clear that there is an inheritance for each son and daughter of God. It is our responsibility to grow to full maturity in the Spirit, engage in the call upon our lives and receive our inheritance. As we are being glorified together with Christ, we ought to rule with Him from heavenly places. His glory shall be revealed in and through us, especially as the end time ecclesia. The church will carry His glory. His glory will be seen upon the church. Creation earnestly expects and await for the revealing of God's sons. God subjected the creation to futility, because of Him who subjected it in hope. Because God knew that the creation itself will be delivered from the bondage of consumption into the glorious liberty of the children of God.

The whole creation will be delivered back to God by the sons and daughters subduing it. We were called to do this. Jesus Christ will receive the glory. In hope, Jesus Christ subjected the creation as He knew that the sons and daughters of God will be instrumental in delivering the earth from bondage. We know that the whole creation groans and labors with birth pangs until now. The whole created universe has suffered the consequences of human sin, being subjected to decomposition, futility and corruption. However, this process is only temporarily, as God has provided hope for it to be restored and delivered. We as sons and daughters will be instrumental in this process. At the time of our final redemption, creation itself will be set free from enslavement to decay and will share in God's glory.

It is imperative for God's sons and daughters to arise as He has put His hope in us to carry His end time glory and be instrumental in His end time purposes.

Once again, in the book of Galatians 4, the Word refers to sonship.

"But when the fullness of time had come, God sent forth His son, born of a woman, born under the law. To redeem those who were under the law, that we might receive the adoption as sons. And because you are sons, God sent forth the Spirit of His Son into your heart, crying out "Abba Father". Therefore, you are no longer a slave, but a son, and if a son, then a heir of God through Christ"

Galatians 4:4 - 7

How many inheritances are laid up in heaven that has not been claimed through a lack of knowledge? How many destinies and inheritances are aborted in the earth? People die and they remained immature, or walked with the spirit of religion which withheld them from growing and reaching their God-given mandate and destiny. As sons, walking in true identity and heavenly authority, we have an inheritance laid up in heaven. We are not slaves that we should beg and have no access to the master. Our true identity is connected to the inheritance as God has mandated each son and daughter to build a part of His kingdom.

TRUE IDENTITY

It is important for us to agree with God in covenant relationship on who He says, we are. We need to flesh out the mandate and call upon our lives. Fleshing out the call and mandate requires provision which will be attracted to agreement and alignment of our true identities. The seed of the call is hidden in the identity.

As a son your inheritance is locked up and connected to your true identity. It is connected to your persona, the way you are known in heaven. As you were predestined and foreknown according to Romans 8, before you came into the earth. How you were known in heaven before you came to earth is for you to find out. Those are the mysteries that is hidden in the heart of man. Who does heaven and God say, that you are. As you need to flesh that out in the earth, all God's recourses can only be attracted to your true identity, your persona. It cannot come to your personality. It is all about what He wants to flesh out in the earth through your life. He provides for the mandate. It is about agreeing with heaven on who you are, as God will only relate to you the way He sees you, relating to your true persona.

There is a promise that Jesus spoke about connected to this matter on agreement. It is a kingdom principle.

"Again I say to you that if two of you agree on earth concerning anything they ask, it will be done for them by My Father in heaven"　　　　　　　　　　　Matthew 18:19

Agreement with God will cause you to move in the direction that God leads.

Stepping into inheritance is to step into your true identity. Stepping into your identity releases resources, stepping into your identity brings your inheritance forth. Therefore it is of paramount importance that your identity is established through the renewal of your mind.

"Do not be conformed to this world, but be transformed by the renewing of your mind, that you may prove what is the good and acceptable and perfect will of God"
　　　　　　　　　　　　　　　　　Romans 12:2

Your true identity is wrapped up in His perfect will. We can only agree to something that we have become aware of, and once we are aware of it, we have to believe and agree with it. That is the reason why we need to know His perfect will. As the perfect will of God is aligned to the call and purpose for your life. We are destined through identity to inherit and walk in the call.

The apostle Paul prayed for the Ephesians in the book of Ephesians 1 that the eyes of their understanding will be enlightened, that they may know what is the hope of His calling. He prayed that they would comprehend the riches of the glory of His inheritance in them.

There is an inheritance connected to sonship which heaven backs up. It calls for maturity in Christ to come to the fullness of the understanding of Christ, especially to be rooted and grounded in His love. No people's pleaser. It is about that which He wants to flesh out through our lives on the earth. A son is a matured believer, knowing who God is and knowing and walking in heavenly authority. It is only when we understand who He is that we can know who we are. Jesus asked His disciples: *"Who do you think I am?" (Matthew 16).* He wanted His disciples to understand His true identity, because that revelation of Him would shape the very nature of their own lives.

We first have to know the nature of God, what He is really like, before He can tell us how we are known in heaven. Why? Because we are made in His image. You can only understand your design if you know Who the Designer is and what His nature is like. As that resembles "who you are". He defines you.

Jesus said to His disciples: *"But who do you say that I am?"* Simon Peter answered and said *"You are the Christ, the Son of the living God."*

Jesus answered and said to Him, *"Blessed are you Simon Bar Jona, for flesh and blood has not revealed this to you, but My Father Who is In heaven." "And I also say to you that you are Peter, and on this rock I will build My church, and the gates of Hades shall not prevail against it". "And I will give you the keys of the kingdom of heaven, and whatever you bind on earth will be bound in heaven, and whatever you loose on earth will be loosed in heaven."* Matthew 16:15 - 19

Jesus tested His disciples to see whether they knew His true identity. Peter received revelation from heaven on how Jesus is known and has also. made Himself known on earth. It is your responsibility, once you have received revelation of whom heaven says that you are, to make your persona known on the earth. Our true identity is revealed to us through intimacy with God and through spending time in His word. As the DNA of the call is in the blood, your spiritual DNA will jump to attention as soon as you read the Word and your spirit man identifies with whom heaven says that you are.

The moment Peter received a revelation of who Jesus was, Jesus made known to him who he was called to be. This revelation could never have come without first knowing who the Designer is. The One who fabricated you knows the purpose for which he designed you to be.

What happened next? Authority was released to Peter. The keys of the kingdom was handed to him. The moment you know who Christ is and He reveals to you who you are, from that moment onwards you will walk in the authority of the call. Peter now realized his call and the authority bestowed upon him to bind on the earth and to loosen in heaven. Once this revelation and impartation came, Peter started his ministry and he preached. We will never know who we are without a revelation of who He is.

When I know who I am, then I know how to relate to others and how I am supposed to live. Right now there are many in the body of Christ who are saved, but have no idea who they truly are. Especially as a result of a fatherless society, this is a great consequence. Identity was transferred to Peter from his father in heaven. Should your earthly father neglected this, maybe because he did not even know who he himself was, and why he was born on the earth, then call upon your heavenly Father, the only true living God. He will reveal Himself to you and also make known unto you who you are and how you are known in heaven.

When the people around me know my identity, then they know how to relate to me. Calling me up to that place of authority in Him. That is why it is of utmost importance that you find your "tribe". Likeminded people who know you by your identity, not by your past. Let these people agree with heaven on who you are and treat you accordingly.

This will allow you to reach your destiny and be held accountable. It is very important whom you walk alongside with as it will usher you into destiny.

When we know each other's identity and relate to each other accordingly, it leads to honor in the body of Christ. We call others "up" to that place all the time - this becomes the real nature of accountability. This is what church is all about. This is the ministry of reconciliation. To view people the way God sees them and call out the greatness in them whilst holding them accountable for the call.

ACCOUNTABILITY CALLS UP TO:

- Another level of being
- Our true place in the heart and affection of the Father
- Our righteous place in Christ
- Our real relationship with the Holy Spirit

Who I am sets the tone for all my commitments in the earth.

EFFECTS OF TRUE IDENTITY

My true identity opens up the following to me:

- An elevated status above my enemy and circumstances. Saul enquired about David after he had victory over Goliath. David was appointed ruler and king over Juda and later Israel. Before David was never a factor to his enemy, Saul, until he had victory over Goliath. We read about this story in 1 Samuel 17:55 and 2 Samuel 5:2,3.

- Legal authority over the enemy and certain areas. David was prepared in the field, tested and learnt to overcome, and was mandated by God to be king over Israel when he was anointed in the field. Although he did not walk in all of that straight away. He first had to be prepared outside of the public arena. We learn about David's preparation in 1 Samuel 17:34 - 38.

- Permission to overcome every obstacle. Weapons were not a problem for David, as he was appointed with the only weapons he knew, a staff, sling bag and five stones. He knew who he was, he knew who God was on account of past history and he knew he was anointed by the Spirit of the LORD which came upon him. He also knew that the battle belonged to the LORD Who will fight. David understood covenant relationship.

- Right to rule and establish peace where you live. David established peace for Israel when he defeated Goliath and soon thereafter was appointed ruler over Israel by being appointed king. The evidence for this statement is found in 1 Samuel 17:46 - 47.

- Stepping into inheritance, releasing resources. It was declared by Goliath that whoever had victory will be enriched with great riches. David received the spoils of war on behalf of Israel, as all the riches of the Philistines came into the hands of David and Israel. 1 Samuel 17:25 refers.

- No fear. David said to Saul that no man should fear, as he would fight the Philistine. 1 Samuel 17:32 refers.

- Recognized and sought after. Saul enquired about who this youth was that killed Goliath, as he himself was a king and was afraid. 1 Samuel 17:55

- Your thinking about yourself changes and your self-esteem rises. Many a times we come across low self-esteem, only to realize it is as a result of a person not knowing who they are and the direction they should go. Lack of identity leads to low self-esteem. David's thinking about himself changed as he did not refer to himself as a shepherd boy but was explaining how he went about when trouble hits. 1 Samuel 17:34 refers.

- Your language about yourself changes. David was talking about the outcome of the war. In the face of adversity, he was talking about Who GOD is, calling out GOD's attributes. He also talked about how he himself was in the field during his testing that qualified him. 1 Samuel 17:34 - 38 refers.

- Elevated prayer taking you to a different plane. You hear things because of your identity in Christ. David could confidently talk about defeating Goliath, because he had history with GOD. You will start to pray from a perspective of sonship, with authority as the Holy Spirit makes known to you the things to come and the outcome over situations.

PROCESS OF ESTABLISHING TRUE IDENTITY

Your true identity is already imprinted into your spirit man. Even before you were born your true identity was known in heaven. Your spiritual persona, the way you are known in heaven, was already made known.

"The LORD has called me from the womb: from the matrix of my mother, He has made mention of my name. And He has made my mouth like a sword, in the

shadow of His hand He has hidden me, and made me a polished shaft: in His quiver He has hidden me"   Isaiah 49:1,2

We are being called from the womb. Mention has been made of our names in heaven. The name carries the very persona of the human being. He placed the prophetic in our mouths and hid us while we were prepared and until the time was ripe to expose the call to the world.

John the Baptist was announced by the angel Gabriel, to his father prior to his birth.

"But the angel said to him, do not be afraid Zacharias, for your prayer is heard; and your wife Elizabeth will bear a son, and you shall call his name John."

"And you will have joy and gladness, and many will rejoice at his birth. For he will be great in the sight of the LORD, and shall drink neither wine nor strong drink. He will also be filled with the Holy Spirit, even from his mother's womb. And he will turn many of the children of Israel to the LORD their GOD. He will also go before Him in the spirit and power of Elijah to turn the hearts of the fathers to the children, and the disobedient to the wisdom of the just, to make ready a people prepared for the LORD"   Luke 1:13 - 17

How intimate is your relationship with GOD? Do you know what you should name your children as the spiritual persona is hidden in the name of the child, or do you call your child any name that sounds good to the ear? It is the responsibility of every parent to enquire from GOD on "who" this child is that will come into the world which you will have custody over. You need to agree with GOD on the persona of your child and raise the child accordingly.

John the Baptist had a very distinctive call that was made known to his father, Zacharias. John was sanctified from the mother's womb. There were special instructions on how to raise such an anointed son. He was not to drink strong drink. The ministry of reconciliation rested upon his shoulders. He was to bring restitution between fathers and children, also spiritual fathers and spiritual sons and daughters. The anointing of Elijah was upon him to prepare the way for the LORD. His message was that of repentance to turn the disobedient to a just lifestyle. He made ready a people to receive Christ.

This is the same spirit of Elijah that will now again be released to the end time church to call people unto repentance and to prepare the way for the coming of our LORD Jesus Christ.

Even before we are born there are words and dreams being released over us by GOD through the Holy Spirit. Godly parents should enquire from GOD and raise their children in these dreams. These words are established in your spirit man. You can only know who heaven says you are if you engage and read His word, so that He can establish you in your true identity.

HOW CAN THIS HEAVENLY PERSONA BE ESTABLISHED?

There are eight points that need to be followed as part of the process.

- Blueprint. A blueprint of how heaven sees you is engrained in your spirit before you were born. By reading and encountering GOD's word, your spirit man will become alive when it meets with the Word of GOD. Certain parts of Scripture will speak and confirm to your spirit man by becoming a "rhema" word. When this happens, then you know that this is how you are known in heaven. The DNA engrained in your spirit man will respond to the "rhema" word of GOD. The "rhema" word of GOD means when the word becomes alive through revelation and it no longer is the letter of the word, only black on white.

- GOD speaking. GOD will speak to you from the secret place, or prophetically confirm to you how you are known in heaven. GOD will start to reveal Himself to you in a way that you can come to know His persona, the Holy Spirit's persona and also the persona and nature of Jesus Christ. You will mature into sonship from that place where you grow in the knowledge of Christ. Leaders and people around you will start recognizing the call on your life. The call will be confirmed. By two or more witnesses a word is established over your life, this is a kingdom principle referred to in 2 Corinthians 13:1. That is why it is very important to belong to the family of believers where there is proper apostolic cover and order, as sons and daughters are released from the altar of the church where they are committed, after serving at the altar. You have to find your tribe. Pray to GOD and ask Him who is your apostolic oversight that will be instrumental to lead you into your destiny. Don't go to just any church. Find your tribe, church and the appointed leadership where GOD has sent you to. As I have mentioned before, it is an apostolic and prophetic function to raise and release sons and daughters into their GOD given destinies.

- Agreement. Agreement is necessary with GOD and heaven on how you are known in heaven. How you are known in heaven needs to be fleshed out on the earth. Agreement is necessary as your negative self will start to rise the moment GOD tells you who you really are. Many before us questioned GOD and even laughed when their true identity was being made known. Your negative personality is expressed in a victim mentality, making you a victim thinker. When GOD tells you who you really are, the natural mind raises up and questions GOD. This makes you prone to deception and you become vulnerable to the evil one. You believe this worst of yourself. You live with a sense of unworthiness. We are entirely too self-conscious. Sometimes this is where we are stuck in the process. As the negative side of our personality's wars against the true identity of who GOD says that we are. It is the negative side of our personalities which make us slaves whilst we are called to be sons. This part needs deliverance and needs to be discarded of. It resembles the "old man" and needs to be put off.

"Do not lie to one another as you have put off the old man with his deeds, and have put on the new man who is renewed in knowledge according to the image of Him Who created him"   *Colossians 3:9 - 10*

We need to understand that the new man is matured and models after the image of Christ, understanding and knowing who he is in Christ.

Agreement is a very strong kingdom principle. The spirit world is governed by agreement, positive or negative. Even the enemy cannot have any hold on us unless we agree. How much more if we agree with our Father on the plans and purposes, He has for us on the earth. The very reason He saved us is because He called us to flesh out His kingdom purposes on the earth.

You need to answer the "call" upon your life in the same way you answered unto salvation. Agree and accept the call and start moving forward in your true identity towards your destiny. GOD will allow it all to work out for the good because you love Him and have been called according to His purposes. It, however, remains your responsibility to seek out His face and encounter His blueprint that is already implanted in your spirit man. When GOD tells you about your identity, your negativity about yourself will rise, it has to, in order for GOD to get rid of it as you don't need it anymore. GOD deals with the subconscious part of your personality, which plays the victim as we have already mentioned, by shredding it and getting rid of it through the process of demonstrating His goodness. It is His goodness that leads to repentance. Repentance means to turn away from evil towards GOD's ways and His thoughts. The only way to establish your true identity is to kill off the negative aspects of your personality. This is your assignment to put on the new man that is renewed in knowledge by Christ Who created him. When GOD shows you the negative aspects of your personality, a battle will take place on the inside of you. The series of steps that you can take from where you presently are to where GOD wants you to be is called a process.

-       Positioning. Once agreement has taken place, there is a definite positioning from your side. Now is the time that GOD will start to prepare you. In the same manner David was anointed in the field, he was being prepared and trained to steward GOD's people. By stewarding the flock in the field, protecting the sheep from the lion and the bear, David was building history with GOD which he was going to need in later years to fight Goliath. This is the time to be trained in which ever area that is needed for the call. This is the preparation phase. It is the time when you process through difficult sets of circumstances that you build history with GOD as you can always rely on the blood covenant and victory. There has to come a time when you need to exercise the way heaven sees you as you have already partnered with GOD's perception on "who you are".

- Practice. A time will come when you are trained and need to practice that which has been deposited into you through true identity, the Word, your history with GOD and the experience you have gained so far. You have to step out of the boat by faith. David stepped out of the boat by approaching Goliath on account of who he knew GOD was to him and on account with his history with GOD. David's spirit on the inside rose up when GOD's armies were defiled. His persona rose up. True identity will cause you to rise up and take action.

- Testing. There will come a time when your true identity will be publicly tested. Once, again just like David fighting Goliath. This is the time where the covenant relationship that you hold with GOD is tested. That is the reason why it is imperative that you truly know who GOD is, as at this point you will rely on His goodness and strength only, as you were tried and tested through a set of circumstances in the wilderness and came through victoriously.

During this time resentment from leaders and people in authority may rise. In 1 Samuel 18 Saul resented David. Persecution became part of the parcel. However, GOD raised up support for David in 1 Samuel 20 through the life of Jonathan. At this point GOD will send you destiny helpers.

- Stepping out. In 2 Samuel 2 David was anointed king of Juda. He had to overcome many battles, even on his way to destiny to become king over the whole of Israel. God gave him stewardship over sheep in the field, then over Juda and lastly, he was ushered into full destiny to become king over Israel.

"You shall shepherd My people Israel and be ruler over Israel".

2 Samuel 5:2

But he first had to show himself approved over Juda. David grew into deeper levels of authority. The giant is always at the gate of your promised land and destiny. Therefore, extensive training is necessary.

- Anointed and released into destiny.

"Therefore all the elders of Israel came to the king at Hebron, and David made a covenant with them at Hebron before the LORD. And they anointed king David over Israel."

2 Samuel 5:3

This is such an important and final step in the call where you are being re-leased and anointed by the elders or leadership of your church to step out in full authority into the call and destiny. GOD is a GOD of order and will always anoint and release you through leaders in the five-fold ministry from the altar of the house where you served. Any other way of being released is illegitimate authority.

TRUE IDENTITY WILL BE TESTED

David's son, king Solomon's true identity was tested once GOD made known unto him who he was. Let us look to see what happened here.

At Gibeon the LORD appeared to Solomon in a dream by night and GOD said to him *"ask! What shall I give you?"* Already GOD was testing the condition of king Solomon's heart by allowing Solomon to choose. And Solomon said: *"You have shown great mercy to Your servant David, my father, because he walked before You in truth, righteousness, and in uprightness of heart with You; You have continued this great kindness for him, and You gave Him a son to sit on his throne as it is this day. Therefore, give your servant an understanding heart to judge Your people, that I may discern good and evil. For who is able to judge the great people of Yours? The speech pleased the LORD, that Solomon asked this thing"*

1 Kings 3:5 - 7

This is the kind of prayer that pleases the heart of GOD. When we acknowledge our own limitations, but at the same time understands our true position and identity in Him and ask accordingly. This is a prayer of agreement. Our heavenly Father will respond to that.

Then GOD said to him, *"because you have asked this thing, and have not asked a long life for yourself, nor asked riches, nor have asked the life of your enemies, but have asked for yourself understanding to discern justice, behold I have done according to your words; see I have given you a wise and understanding heart"*

1 Kings 3:10-12

Both riches and honor were also given to Solomon. Here is a perfect example of a heart being tested by GOD and the heavenly call and persona being agreed upon by Solomon. As sons and daughters of GOD our prayer life has to change to reflect and agree with the calling upon our lives. GOD will always honor such a prayer that is in agreement with heaven's purposes.

Now that wisdom and understanding was bestowed upon Solomon during this night vision at Gibeon, GOD also immediately tested that which He anointed Solomon with.

Too harlots approached king Solomon regarding one of their sons that died because one of them laid on the son during the night and consequently the child died. At this point in time they were contending over whose son the remaining son was, as they each had a son. Both claimed that the living son was theirs. They started to fight over the son as they both wanted the son. So, they went to king Solomon straight after he agreed with GOD on his heavenly persona and asked from GOD all that is needed for the call upon his life. GOD gave Solomon wisdom and understanding which was now, through this incident, being tested.

And the king said, *"the one says, this is my son, who lives, and your son is the dead one; and the other says, "no, but your son is the dead son, and my son is the living one."*

The king said, *"bring me a sword".* So, they brought a sword before the king. And the king said, *"divide the living child in two, and give half to one, and half to the other."* Then the woman whose son was living spoke to the king, for she yearned with compassion for her son; and she said, *"O my lord, give her the living child, and by no means kill him!"* But the other said, *"let him be neither mine nor yours, but divide him."* So the king answered and said: *"Give the first woman the living child and by no means kill him; she is the mother."* And all Israel heard of the judgment which the king had rendered; and they feared the king, for they saw that the wisdom of GOD was in him to administer justice"   1 *Kings 3:23 - 28*

That which GOD bestowed upon king Solomon was publicly tested and Solomon came through victoriously to such an extent that the nation of Israel had reverence for his judgment and acknowledged his wisdom. The anointing that GOD has placed on all of His sons and daughters will publicly be tested. GOD will give the victory and those whom you lead will know that GOD is with you.

How great is our GOD to allow our hearts to be tested. To bless us with His anointing and grace gifting and then publicly give us the victory. Victory and honor always follow public testing. GOD know what He has invested in each of His children, however, it is for the son or daughter to believe it, agree with it and allow it to be tested. This is how we build history with GOD. Heaven backs up who He says we are, and His name is glorified throughout the earth by that. All for His glory!

In the process we are also being elevated by walking in our heavenly authority gaining dominion over the domain GOD has given authority over. After that day king Solomon was feared and reverenced, the whole nation knew that he had understanding and wisdom upon his life. They knew he could be trusted as a king. This process established his identity and caused him to be elevated in the eyes of the nation.

PRAYING FROM YOUR IDENTITY

Your personality will produce fear-filled prayers and worry-filled prayers emanating from the subconscious/conscious mind. We were never called to pray from our soul (mind) dimension.

Jesus said the following: *"Most assuredly, I say to you, the Son can do nothing of Himself, but what He sees the Father do; for whatever He does, the Son also does in like manner. For the Father loves the Son, and shows Him all things that He Himself does, and He will show Him greater works than these, that you may marvel".*
John 5:10,20

This is how we ought to treat prayer. Because our Father loves us, He will show us what He does. We need to "see" in the spirit realm to see what our Father is busy doing. For if Jesus did not do anything out of Himself, why will we. Mature sons and daughters "see" in the spirit and do in a like manner

Faith-filled prayers come from the heart (spirit man). From a deep place of agreement with heaven's agenda. From a place of understanding sonship. That we are co-laborers in letting God's kingdom come on the earth in every situation.

Prayer needs to come from a place of understanding the heart of the Father and Jesus and the Holy Spirit. Understanding your call, understanding the riches of His glory of our inheritance in Him, and understanding the great power that is available to those who believe. It is different positioning producing different results when we pray as matured sons and daughters, no longer begging, but declaring and decreeing God's purposes.

As our Father is sovereign and allows everything to work out according to the counsel of His will, we can have full confidence to agree with heaven.

"In Him we have obtained an inheritance, being predestined according to the purpose of Him, Who works out all things according to the counsel of His will."

Ephesians 1:11

We cannot pray against His will or counsel that already has been pre-determined. We need to agree in order to see manifestation. Heaven backs us up and we agree with Him and pull down our inheritance and destiny that is pre-destined, by agreement and by voicing it. The church needs to learn this positioning and operate from this elevated place in Him. However, if you do not know who you are or what your purpose is on the earth, how can you then agree with heaven. How can two walk together unless they agree?

Praying from identity as a son of God will lead to the following:

- Legal authority over the enemy in certain areas.
- Overcoming every obstacle.
- The breakers anointing to break through barriers is being released when we agree with heaven on God's purposes in the earth.

"The one who breaks open will come up before them; they will break out, pass through the gate and go out by it; their King will pass before them, with the LORD at their head."   *Micah 2:13*

This is "Perez" - the breakers anointing. Praying from your identity will bring about breakthrough.

- The right to rule and establish peace where you live.
- Producing spirit filled prayers. Praying in tongues and worship releases the atmosphere of heaven whereupon revelation starts to trickle through. As the end time ecclesia, or remnant church, we will decree what we have seen in the Spirit and God will establish it on the earth. As a result of His presence there will be light on our pathways.

-     Confidence will arise.

"Now this is the confidence that we have in Him, that if we ask anything according to His will, He hears us. And if we know that He hears us, whatever we ask, we know that we have the petitions that we have asked of Him"
    1 John 5:14,15

He answers prayer that is in agreement with His will. A hundred percent answering of prayer is possible. As we mature as sons and daughters, we leave the childish things behind and become selfless. Lives laid down on the altar as our reasonable service. We sacrifice our lives to fulfill His purposes. As a result, our prayers no longer centers around ourselves, but around His purposes and call.

All of this calls for maturity. As matured sons and daughters we have an inheritance as we are co-heirs of our Father through Christ. We are no longer slaves. As a slave does not know about the plans and purposes of his master, we are sons who have full access to our Father and can come with boldness to the throne of Grace at any time to be able to know His plans and purposes for human mankind. Because we are sons, He sent out His Spirit into our hearts, crying out "Abba Father." Our Father responds to the cry of His children to fulfill His purposes through us. One man truly walking with God is always majority!

HOW IS THE GODLY TRI-UNE KNOWN IN HEAVEN?

As sons it is very important to know the nature and persona of our Father, of Jesus Christ, and also of the Holy Spirit. As this knowing will lead us to full maturity. We will no longer be swayed by false doctrine or any behavior that is not congruent to the nature of our Father, and Jesus and the Holy Spirit. We will know them and walk with them. Therefore we need to, individually, look at each of the deity separately.

GOD, THE FATHER

Why is it important at this stage to mention the personas or nature and function of the godly triune? A mature son and daughter walks in divine revelation of who the Father is, who Jesus Christ is and whom the Holy Spirit is. This brings forth much needed maturity to be able to discern in these last days. If I know my Father, then I also know how He will deal with me through all circumstances. It is about knowing each other, about true relationship and revelation from another realm to be able to bring heaven to earth. As it is in heaven, let it be on the earth. This was Jesus' model prayer in Matthew 6.

Moses asked God to show him His glory for it to come into his conscious state. In response God proclaimed how He is known in heaven. He made His persona and nature known to Moses as Who He is, is wrapped up in His glory - His manifested presence. And He (Moses) said: *"Please show me your glory"* Exodus 33:18

Now the LORD descended in the cloud and stood with Him there, and proclaimed the name of the LORD. And the LORD passed before him and proclaimed, *"The LORD, the LORD God, merciful and gracious, long suffering and abounding in goodness and Truth, keeping mercy for thousands, forgiving iniquity and transgression and sin, by no means clearing the guilty, visiting the iniquity of the fathers upon the children and the children's children to the third and fourth gene-ration."* Exodus 34:5 - 7

It is astounding to come to the realization that God the Father's persona is wrapped up in His glory. The way He manifests Himself in the earth tells the story of "Who" He is. All of that is connected to His name. He is Who He says He is. His nature is merciful, gracious, slow to anger as to always allow a window period for repentance before He judges. He is abundant in loving kindness and Truth, not dealing with us according to our wrongdoings. Forgiving our trespasses and rebellion and sin. Should we come to Him as a loving Father, His arms always open to forgive and wipe away all transgressions, inequity and sin.

"I will betroth you unto Me, yes I will betroth you to Me in righteousness and justice, in loving kindness and mercy. I will betroth you to Me in faithfulness, and you shall know the LORD" Hosea 2:19

Here are five guarantees of the persona and nature of the LORD God. This is His character and the way He deals with His children in covenant relationship. If we can know "Whom" He is, then it defines "Who" we are. That brings a security to the believer that results in an authority upon a life that emanates from Him only as it secures the soul of man as He defines us.

Connected to that is the call, purpose and destiny. We are mandated by a loving heavenly Father to participate in letting His kingdom come on earth and building His kingdom as co-laborers.

JESUS, THE SON OF GOD

Jesus was baptized, being filled with the Holy Spirit, returned from the Jordan and was led by the Spirit into the wilderness, where He was tempted by satan and in final preparation of His call.

"Then Jesus returned from the desert to Galilee in the power of the Spirit and begins His ministry by teaching in the synagogues in the surrounding regions. So He came to Nazareth, where He had been brought up. And as His custom was, He went into the synagogue on the sabbath day and stood up to read. And He was handed the book of the prophet Isaiah. And when He had opened the book, He found the place where it was written: "the Spirit of the LORD is upon Me, because He has anointed Me to preach the gospel to the poor, He has sent Me to heal the brokenhearted, to proclaim liberty to the captives and recovery of sight to the blind, to set at liberty those who are oppressed; to reclaim the acceptable year of the LORD." Luke 4:14 - 19

During those years before the ministry of Jesus there was no prophetic voice being released for a period of four hundred years. There was deep spiritual death and hunger in the region. No revelation. The voice of God was afar off. Jesus came to release a Spirit dimension over them and to bring life. By reading from the book of Isaiah, Jesus made His very purpose, call and persona known. He went to Nazareth where He was rejected before to bring a Spirit dimension and to release a revelation of Who He was. Jesus stood up to make known how He is known in heaven. He made known His persona and nature. He made known part of His assignment on earth. He brought to the attention of everyone present what His mandate was whilst walking on the earth, fulfilling His heavenly mandate.

This was totally irrefutable. Your true identity will always astonish others. Their eyes were fixed on Him as they could not argue with Him. He spoke with such authority as He knew exactly who His Father was who sent Him, and emanated His exact radiance and character.

"If you have seen the Father, you have seen me." John 14:19

This He often told His disciples. The sad dimension is that He was once again rejected in Nazareth. The crowd did not recognize the Spirit dimension He was releasing. Their re-

sponse on Jesus making known His call was: *"And they said: "Is this not Joseph's son?"* They looked down on Him as a carpenter's Son as apposed to look at Him the way heaven sees Him. They did not accept the call upon His life and rejected His mantle. Then Jesus replied and said: *"Assuredly I say to you, no prophet is accepted in his own country"*
Luke 4:24

All those in the synagogue were filled with wrath and they rose up and thrust Him out of the city, wanting to throw Him over the cliff. Then He left and went His way.

Why are we dealing with these matters?

In the last days many of God's sons will be rejected and persecuted for making their true identities known. However, God will lead us out to where there is honor for the mantle and to those who are hungry for what we are carrying in order for the anointing to flow. The anointing is costly, therefore do not waste it on a group of people that would not accept God's chosen vessel. Go where the anointing flows and the people are hungry for what you carry. Serve your metron where you have been assigned to reign, pray and find out from God by revelation through the Holy Spirit which area and group of people He has assigned you over.

So we see the heart and nature of Jesus on display to preach the kingdom, heal the sick and the broken hearted, to release the captives, to proclaim the acceptable year of the Lord and the day of the vengeance of our God. To comfort all who mourn. To give to them the oil of gladness for morning and beauty for ashes. He gives a garment of praise for a spirit of heaviness. Jesus is our Healer and Advocate.

HOLY SPIRIT

Jesus revealed the Holy Spirit's persona whilst He was on earth, before His Spirit was sent to the earth. This is how He revealed the Holy Spirit to His disciples before He went to be with His Father, in order for His disciples to recognize the Holy Spirit when He is released upon the earth and also in an effort to comfort them.

"However, when He, the Spirit of Truth, has come, He will guide you into all truth; for He will not speak on His own authority, but whatever He hears He will speak; and He will tell you things to come."

"He will glorify Me, for He will take of what is Mine and declare it to you."

John 16:13 - 14

Here the true character of the Holy Spirit is clearly depicted. He is the Spirit of Truth guiding us into all Truth. He is a person Who speaks. He does not speak on His own authority, but only speaks that which He has heard from the Father. He will prophetically tell us things to come. He is the Administrator of the will and affairs of heaven.

He will always point to Jesus and glorify Him as He will take and administrate that which belongs to Jesus and declare it to us. Should we, in return, declare what the Spirit said, it will manifest on the earth. This is the realm that the end time church will walk in.

"But the Advocate, the Holy Spirit, whom the Father will send in My name, will teach you all things and will remind you of everything I have said to you"

John 14:26

The Holy Spirit is our defender and our helper, our Advocate who knows every detail of our lives. He reminds us of all kingdom principles and of the Word of God, so that there will be light on our pathways.

However, there are seven aspects to the Holy Spirit that we as sons need to know, as we come to know the Spirit of God intimately in every situation. As the situation presents itself on the earth the Holy Spirit will also present the aspect of His character that is necessary to deal with the situation. The seven-fold Holy Spirit has to be the habitation of our souls. We draw from the Holy Spirit feeding into our souls His very being of Who He is. We need to know Him in these aspects in order to draw upon His Spirit.

"The Spirit of the Lord shall rest upon Him, the Spirit of wisdom and understanding, the Spirit of counsel and might, the Spirit of knowledge and of the fear of the Lord."

Isaiah 11:2

Here we see the seven aspects clearly spelt out:

- Spirit of the Lord which is connected to His power,

- Spirit of wisdom which is connected to His direction concerning matters,

- Spirit of understanding which is connected to comprehending His Word.

- The Spirit of counsel which connected to His strategies and problem solving.

- The Spirit of might which is connected to His boldness displayed through us in the face of adversity.

- Spirit of knowledge which is connected to revelation knowledge from His throne by the Holy Spirit telling us about things to come. Revealing knowledge that we could not otherwise have known.

- The Spirit of the fear of the Lord is connected to His glory and reverential fear of the Lord. It is connected to holiness.

These are the attributes of how the Holy Spirit is known in heaven and on earth as the Holy Spirit is the third person of the godly triune in heaven and the first person of the Godly triune on earth.

The moment when we grasp "who the Holy Spirit really is, our identities are being established. He defines us. All that He is, is continually available to us in every situation. We should never be defeated unless we walk outside of His will and guidance. Jesus Christ emanates the exact radiance, and glory of the Father of glory. We are to emanate the exact character of Christ wearing the persona and image of Christ. Even the angels know how they are known in heaven.

ANGELS

"And the angel said to Him, I am Gabriel, who stands in the presence of God, and was sent to speak to you and bring you these good tidings."   Luke 1:19

The angel Gabriel was announcing how he was known in heaven. An announcement was sent forth of how John the Baptist was known in heaven, by the angel Gabriel, before John was born.

Remember when the angel Gabriel visited Zacharias to announce the birth of John the Baptist, the angel made John's persona known. He said that John will be great in the sight of the Lord. He will also be filled with the Holy Spirit from the mother's womb. He will turn many children of Israel to their God. He will go before them in the spirit and power of Elijah to bring reconciliation. He had to prepare the way for the Lord's coming. Here we see clearly how the heavenly persona of the angel Gabriel was demonstrated and made known. The assignment and heavenly persona of John the Baptist was also made known and established.

It is in the exact same way that our assignments and true identity is being established on the earth. It needs to be released over your life and agreement with heaven needs to flow.

When agreement comes, and you start to walk and flesh out the call, purpose or assignment of your life, everything falls into place. However, for this to be established, you first need to have an understanding of "Who" God is, "Who" Jesus Christ is and "Who" the Holy Spirit is, and be rooted and grounded in His love for you. As your true identity lies in who heaven says that you are.

Find your Elizabeth, the one who prays with you for your destiny to be fulfilled. Find people that are like minded and treat you according to who heaven says that you are. This will all be instrumental in establishing your true identity over your life.

CHAPTER 7

HABITATION OF THE SOUL AND THE SEVEN-FOLD HOLY SPIRIT

HABITATION OF THE SOUL AND THE SEVEN-FOLD HOLY SPIRIT

For a very long time God was absent through His Holy Spirit in many churches as He was not welcomed and acknowledged. The church entertained the spirit of religion which is a Babylonian practice. They offered their own agendas and man made programs and inhibited the flow of the Spirit. Whereas God's desire was and still is to have a habitation amongst His people. A dwelling place for Him in the Spirit where all believers are being built together, growing into a holy temple in the Lord. His original intent was that the fullness of Him would fill all in all. Now we found that the church has deviated from the original plan and intent and will be restored in this final phase and showdown of God's power and glory before the rapture of the remnant church. Those who have laid down their lives for Him. Those who will love Him first and have their ears turned to the Master. Those who move in the Spirit and look into the Master's eyes and do what He shows them to do. Those who walk in purity, unity and holiness. Those who are set apart for Him. We can all be part of the remnant if we are prepared to pay the price. Therefore, this study is necessary to finally prepare the remnant for the second coming of the Lord Jesus Christ.

As matured sons and daughters, we will be very dependent upon the Holy Spirit in these last days. We will be led by the Spirit in obedience to the Master, our Lord Jesus Christ.

For this very purpose our wounded souls need to be healed and delivered from all past hurts and any demon oppression of the soul. Understanding the soul dimension and understanding that the soul feeds off a spiritual habitation that surrounds it, either being the Holy Spirit or the demonic realm, becomes eminent.

A transition must take place from being a "church" generation to becoming "kingdom" orientated generation. When the seven-fold Holy Spirit (the mind of Christ) feeds our soul, it will result in the kingdom of God continually being released. You will always release that which you carry, positive or negative. This is the very reason why sometimes you enter a room or sit next to someone and suddenly start to feel depressed. If the person sitting next to you suffers from depression, that spirit is being released into the atmosphere. Whereas we are called to be carriers of heaven's atmosphere and shift circumstances and atmospheres around us, releasing His kingdom. Your spirit and God's Spirit connecting becomes the Mind of Christ.

"But he who is joined to the LORD is one spirit with Him".   1 Corinthians 6:17

To be kingdom minded means to be functioning in a hundred percent effectivity. The structure over your soul will determine the fruit you express.

The soul was created to live in a spiritual habitation as it feeds off the "spiritual". We have been created as a triune being. Spirit, soul and body. We are spirits living in a human body who has a soul. Our spirits are a higher dimension than the soul.

We are created in the likeness and image of God the Father, Jesus Christ and the Holy Spirit. We were created to have dominion over the earth, not the devil. The enemy is contending to take dominion, but the church needs to position and take back dominion through understanding our authority and drawing on the Holy Spirit that will lead us into all truth and victory. It is time to arise.

In Genesis 2:7 man was formed from the dust of the earth and the breath of Life (Spirit) of God was breathed into the nostrils of man and man became a living

being. When the body was created from the dust of the earth, a dimension that comes from below combined with a dimension that comes from above, God's ruach breath, which is eternal, the soul of man was formed.

In Genesis 2:17 the Lord instructed man not to eat from the tree of knowledge of good and evil. He said: *"If you eat you shall surely die".* Man rebelled against God, they ate and from that moment the life-giving Spirit of God was severed from their souls. Sin separated spirit and soul. When spirit and soul was separated man fell. The soul became corrupted and inhabited by evil. This rebellion leads to spiritual death and corruption.

Before they ate from the tree of good and evil, Adam ruled in the garden. He walked with God and heard His voice. His soul was fed by the Spirit of God unto everlasting life. Adam had dominion but lost it. Adam is referred to as the first Adam and had his spirit "joined" with God. Jesus as the second Adam came to restore this habitation of the soul and accomplished the joining or fusing of the spirit and the soul. For those who are joined with Christ is one spirit with Him. Jesus took rulership and dominion back and handed it over to us as sons and daughters.

HABITATION OF THE SOUL

Habitation in this context refers to "dwelling place" of the soul. The soul was created to live in a spiritual habitation. The soul is surrounded by a spiritual dimension, either demonic or by the Holy Spirit. Either you are connected to God and a rebirth took place which results in ruling through your spirit man, as a result of the seven-fold Holy Spirit nourishing your soul continuously. Therefore, the soul needs to be delivered of whatever else rules over it. The remnant will be pure in heart, soul and spirit.

"I will give you a new heart and put the new Spirit within you, I will take the heart of stone out of your flesh and give you a heart of flesh. I will put My Spirit within you and cause you to walk in My statues, and you will keep My judgments and do them"
Ezekiel 36:26,27

Ezekiel was prophesying the process and consequence of a new birth that will take place in the New Testament under the blood covenant of Jesus Christ. The spirit of man becomes reborn and at that moment is connected to the spirit of Christ.

Another state of man is being reborn and the Spirit of Christ living inside a person, in other words, you are connected to the Spirit of Christ, but the soul can still be under demonic influence. The soul of man needs to be healed and delivered. Adam walked in perfect unity with God in body, soul and spirit in the garden of Eden before they sinned. Adam had the mind of Christ, the seven-fold Holy Spirit of God hovering over his soul. That was all he knew before he sinned.

Jesus is formed in us by the seven-fold Holy Spirit. It is a fusion between two spirits, the spirit of man and the Holy Spirit. This produces His character and fruit within us.

"He who is joined to the LORD is one spirit with Him."   *1 Corinthians 6:17*

DWELLING PLACE OF THE SPIRIT

Our hearts become the dwelling place of the Holy Spirit when we are reborn and therefore our bodies become the temple of the Holy Spirit. But there is more.

As explained, there is a deeper work as the Spirit of Christ can be "inside" without the habitation of His Spirit over your soul. The soul needs to be saved or redeemed. That is your responsibility to free the soul from old soul wounds, allow the Holy Spirit to heal you and get your soul delivered from all demon infiltration over the soul. Once this is done, it is time to invite the seven-fold Spirit of Christ to inhabit your soul area.

Paul made mention of this in Ephesians. We are corporately the church of Jesus Christ, all sons and daughters purchased by the blood.

"Having been built on the foundation of the apostles and prophets, Jesus Christ Himself being the chief cornerstone. In whom the whole building, being fitted together, grows into a holy temple in the LORD. In whom you are also being built together for a dwelling place of God in the Spirit."   Ephesians 2:20 - 22

This is the aim of Jesus for His church. That He would be formed in all of His sons and daughters by having our souls as a habitation for His Spirit. This way the church will be a dwelling place for God in the Spirit. The church will be a hundred percent effective and rule and have dominion. The church will be in unity and in Zion, the end time remnant church, He will command a blessing and life forever more.

FUNCTION OF THE CHURCH

"But now the manifold wisdom of God might be made known by the church to the principalities and powers in the heavenly places."   Ephesians 3:10

We are aware that a great war is raging in heaven right now over rulership, dominion and the preparation of the remnant to be raptured. Satan was thrown out of heaven and now wants dominion in the earth. However, dominion is part of the inheritance of the sons and daughters of God. Hence the war that the book of Revelations is referring to between the arch angel Michael and the bride of Christ. Heaven and earth will culminate in this war and fight together. This is the reason why we need to be prepared, healed and delivered to fight the good fight. Engage and take up our places in the body of Christ. That time has arrived, and is upon us now.

This is the function of the church, if we want to rule in this dispensation just before the coming of Jesus Christ to meet His remnant bride in the clouds, we need to prepare and be sanctified. He is coming for a ruling, spotless bride carrying full authority by the ruling of His Spirit. We will be united in Spirit. We need this manifold wisdom now more than ever before. God is restoring His church and the latter glory of the church will be greater than the former. God's wisdom will be on display in this final showdown of His glory and power.

HOW ARE STRONGHOLDS BUILT?

We need to get rid of strongholds molding the soul. Let us look at how a stronghold is built.

We have all been given a free will - you decide. Neither God nor satan can overrule your will and thereby take your mind. Your will is seated in the soul dimension. Your soul dimension represents the will, intellect and emotions. The devil can and will attempt to lie to you, but he cannot control your will. Satan wants you to yield your will and agree with his lies.

Once you have yielded, satan gains ground and gains control over your mind and thoughts. Now a stronghold of the enemy has been built by lies. Strongholds prevent us from hearing God's voice.

When the seven-fold Holy Spirit molds the soul, it allows you to hear God's voice and keep you to govern as you only hear His voice. The Holy Spirit feeds into your soul His mind, the mind of Christ. The mold of your soul determines your fruit.

"For though we walk in the flesh, we do not war according to the flesh. For the weapons of our warfare are not carnal, but mighty in God for pulling down of strongholds; casting down arguments and every high thing that exalts itself against the knowledge of God, bringing every thought into captivity to the obedience of Christ."
    2 Corinthians 10:3 - 5

It is our responsibility to replace thoughts and lies with the truth of the Spirit and God's word, which is Spirit. Connecting and listening to what God has to say and agree with that only. Also decreeing the truth, for it to be established by God. The moment you agree with satan, a stronghold is built.

KEY TO CHANGE

Exercise your free will. Decide to get your soul healed of all wounds and bloodline iniquities. As demons will attach themselves to wounds. Get deliverance and build a new habitation or mold around your soul. Ask the Holy Spirit to be the habitation of your freed soul. Feed on the Word of God. Find your tribe and walk alongside likeminded people, who will hold you accountable.

HOW TO BREAK THE OLD MOULD

After your soul is healed of wounds and has been delivered of its unrighteous mold, the mold has to be replaced with a new surrounding.

- Rebirth:

"Jesus answered and said to him, most assuredly I say unto you, unless one is born again, he cannot see the kingdom of God".　　　　　　　　　　　　　　*John 3:3*

To see in the spirit and in the heavenly realms your spirit needs to be reborn.

"Jesus answered, most assuredly I say to you, unless one is born of water and the Spirit, he cannot enter the kingdom of God"　　　　　　　　　　*John 3:5*

Rebirth requires repentance of old ways and thoughts. A turning away from wickedness to turn wholeheartedly to God, His word, and His ways. I believe there are many believers in the church that has never been reborn.

- Worship:

God wants to be worshipped in Spirit and in Truth. Build the tabernacle of David. Worship until revelation comes and then declare the revelation as a decree and God will establish it on the earth. Walk in your heavenly authority. Raise up your walls of intercession. Build a wall before the throne of God on behalf of others.

- Intimacy:

"The LORD has given me the tongue of the learned, that I should know how to speak a word in season to him who is weary. He awakens me morning by morning. He awakens my ear to hear as the learned"   Isaiah 50:4

Know Christ and the heavenly realms. It is your inheritance.

- Word:

"You will declare a thing, and it will be established for you; so light will shine on your ways."   Job 22:28

We need to know the Word of God in order to make declarations and decrees over situations. Thereby we reign and rule with Him in heavenly places as His word is the final authority in heaven and on earth.

We are living in the final hours of this dispensation prior to the return of Jesus Christ for His remnant bride. He is coming back for a victorious and pure bride walking in full authority of heavens' purposes. Prepare yourself. Be sanctified. Examine yourself and repent. Turn away from all wickedness.

"And I heard another voice from heaven saying, "Come out of her, My people, lest you share in her sins, and lest you receive of her plagues."   Revelations 18:4

Here the scripture is referring to mystery Babylon, the current world system and all its demon influences and wickedness. We need to come out of Babylon and be separate and consecrated for the work of the LORD.

"Behold, the fear of the LORD, that is wisdom, and to depart from evil is understanding."   Job 28:28

THE SEVEN SPIRITS OF GOD

"And the angel of the church in Sardis write, these things says He who has he seven Spirit of God and the seven stars"

Revelations `3:1

It is important to notice that the seven Spirits of God originates from God, but was given to Jesus Christ. Hence the Word states that He (Jesus) has the seven Spirits of God. These are the seven attributes of the Spirit of Christ.

"And from the throne proceeded lightnings, thundering and voices. Seven lamps of fire were burning before the throne, which are the seven Spirits of God"

Revelations 4:5

From the above scripture it is noted that the seven Spirits of God is also represented in heaven.

"And I looked, and behold, in the midst of the throne and of the four living creatures, and in the midst of the elders, stood a lamb as though it had been slain, having seven horns and seven eyes, which are the seven Spirits of God sent out into all the earth"
Revelations 5:6

From this passage we learn that the seven Spirits of God is also represented on earth.

It is written : *"There shall come forth a Rod (Jesus predicted by the prophet Isaiah) from the stem of Jesse (His lineage) and a Branch shall grow out of his roots (Jesse, David's father) roots"* Isaiah 11:1

Jesus was from the lineage of David, who was Jesse's son.

"The Spirit of the LORD shall rest upon Him, the Spirit of wisdom and understanding, the Spirit of counsel and might, the Spirit of knowledge and of the fear of the LORD"
Isaiah 11:2

From this verse we notice that the word "Spirit" was over time written with a capital letter "S" which tells us this is Jesus' Spirit. The Holy Spirit, the Spirit of Christ.

"His delight is in the fear of the LORD, and he shall not judge by the sight of His eyes, nor decide by the hearing of His ears; but with righteousness He shall judge the poor, and decide with equity for the weak of the earth. He shall strike the earth with the Rod of His mouth, and with the breath of His lips He shall slay the wicked. Righteousness shall be the belt of His loins, and faithfulness the belt of His waist"
Isaiah 11:3 - 5

From the above scripture it is clear that Jesus legislated and governed by the seven Spirits of God upon Him. These verses speak about the outcome and effect of the seven-fold Holy Spirit upon Jesus. He was operating in the fullness as a result of what He carried.

Fullness of spirit leads to quick understanding, insight and fear of the LORD. It is also clear that the seven Spirits of God are seven manifestations of the Holy Spirit that rested upon Jesus and now ought to rest upon us in order to legislate from mount Zion, govern and have dominion on the earth and in heavenly realms. We rule and reign with him. For the Spirit to rest upon you, it requires a holy lifestyle totally surrendered to Christ and yielded to His Spirit. Purity and holiness are the key to hosting His presence.

MANIFESTATIONS OF THE SEVEN SPIRITS OF GOD

- Spirit of the LORD:

"And the Spirit of the LORD rest upon Him". *Isaiah 11:2*

The Spirit of the LORD can be described as the Spirit of lordship, dominion and power.

FUNCTIONS OF THE SPIRIT OF THE LORD

The seven-fold Holy Spirit descends from above and becomes the Spirit upon, He rests upon a son or daughter of God for the purposes of:

Dominion, to rule over a God given domain as part of an assignment from God. The Spirit of the LORD puts you in charge of situations to declare and decree. The Spirit of the LORD establishes.

"You will declare a thing and it will be established for you, so light will shine on your ways."
Job 22:28

Where the Spirit of the Lord is, His manifested presence, His light and glory will also be eminent. The Spirit of the LORD is for empowerment to speak God's truth into a situation.

"Therefore, prepare yourself and arise, and speak to them all the I command you. Do not be dismayed before their faces, lest I dismay you before them. For behold, I have made you this day a fortified city, and an iron pillar, and bronze walls against the whole city"
Jeremiah 1:17,18

By the Spirit of the LORD, we are able to arise as sons and become strong in His power to stand and declare. His power brings forth strength in us as we have been tested in the fire. We stand by the Spirit of the LORD that comes upon us in a given situation.

"No man shall be able to stand against you all the days of your life, as I was with Moses, so I will be with you, I will not leave you nor forsake you. Have I not commanded you? Be strong and of good courage, do not be afraid, nor be dismayed, for the LORD your God is with you wherever you go" Joshua 1:5,9

It is by the Spirit of the LORD that the army of the LORD is led. By this aspect of the Holy Spirit, we become fierceless even in the face of adversity. Boldness results. We are enabled by the Spirit of the LORD to war and stand in difficult circumstances. As sons and daughters, we need to learn to pull on this aspect of the Holy Spirit and ask the Spirit of the LORD to come upon us and inhabit our souls.

OPERATION OF THE SPIRIT OF THE LORD

A special anointing (an ability from God) is released when the Spirit of the LORD is in operation.

"So when I saw it, I fell on my face, and I heard a voice of One speaking. And He said to me, son of man, stand on your feet, and I will speak to you, then the Spirit entered me when He spoke to me and set me on my feet, and I heard Him who spoke to me"

Ezekiel 2:1,2

It was by the Spirit of the LORD that Ezekiel was set on his feet. This aspect of the Holy Spirit will cause you to stand when you become weak to pray or to war. The Spirit will be upright in you. It is by the Spirit of the LORD that we are enabled to overcome extreme difficulty. An a anointing is released by the Spirit of the LORD to be strengthened, to activate and to mobilize. This is especially significant in the end times the as sons and daughters we will be cognizant of all the different aspects of the Holy Spirit, as to draw upon those aspects as the circumstances of severe persecution and even martyrdom is approaching.

"Now when they came out of the water, the Spirit of the LORD caught Philip away, so that the eunuch saw him no more, and he went on his way rejoicing"

Acts 8:9

It is by the Spirit of the LORD that we encounter God and explore heavenly realms. It is by the Spirit of the LORD that we are transported from one place to another, which will be a common phenomena in the end times when severe persecution takes place.

This is New Testament revelation. In other words Philip was born again and consequently the Holy Spirit resided inside of him. However, the Spirit of the LORD that came upon was an exterior manifestation of the Spirit and he was caught up by the Spirit of the LORD.

The Spirit of the LORD empowers.

'You shall receive power'. *Acts 1:8*

"Behold I sent the promise of my Father upon you, but tarry in the city of Jerusalem until you are endued with Power from on high" *Luke 24:49*

The Spirit of the LORD "empowered" them to be witnesses, to teach and preach the truth of the kingdom under difficult circumstances. We need to walk cognizant of the Holy Spirit, recognize Him, host Him well as the Spirit "upon" and know that we have power, the same power that raised Jesus Christ from the dead is available unto us who believe.

It was the Spirit upon that enabled Jesus. We need to live a life style that welcomes the Holy Spirit and carry His Spirit upon us in order to release a Spirit dimension into situations around us. Releasing His power. This, however, requires a clean and pure heart, a yielded spirit and a surrendered life and soul. Jesus is the chief cornerstone, we are the living stones and should carry the Spirit without measure in the same dimension upon us.

The kingdom of God is demonstrated in power. We cannot only do church, pray, preach and teach without a demonstration of the power of God.

"For the kingdom of God is not in word, but in power'.   1 Corinthians 4:20

MIRACLES BY THE SPIRIT OF GOD

The end time church will be a supernatural church. By the Spirit of the LORD we command the elements of nature. Miracles happen by the Spirit of the LORD.

"But truly I am full of power by the Spirit of the LORD, and of justice and of might, to declare to Jacob his transgressions and to Israel his sin"   Micah 3:8

The Spirit of the LORD allows you to see and declare boldly.
PREPARE YOURSELF

It is all about how hungry you are for the LORD. God will not entrust that which is precious to those who are not hungry and will not steward well. God always requires stewardship over His kingdom matters. Sons are matured and know how to steward well.

If you hunger for the things of the Spirit, cleanse yourself, be sanctified by the washing of the Word of God. Those who steward God's Word well will be undergirded in the things of the Spirit as God's Word is Spirit and it brings life. Ask God in the Name of Jesus to pour out His Spirit upon you in His fullness. Ask with a humble heart and expect the Spirit to come upon you. Prepare to receive Him, invite Him and recognize Him when He descends and come upon you. Recognize His presence, yield to Him and be lead by Him in all ministry.

THE SPIRIT OF WISDOM

It is the function of the church that the manifold wisdom of God will be on display to the powers and principalities in the heavenlies, by the church. In other words, we need to take authority and dominion over the domain that God has entrusted to us.

We will strike the earth with the rod of our mouths and nullify the plans of the enemy. This is our birthright as sons. We have entered these times. The church is rising by a move of God to no longer be powerless and an onlooker over evil, but to be powerful and move supernaturally to override the schemes of the evil one. A new church era has arrived. The same Spirit that rests on Jesus Christ without measure, will rest upon the true sons and daughters of God. The end time church will carry His fullness.

Wisdom is applied knowledge. It means to know exactly what to do and which direction to take when at a crossroad. Wisdom will help you to rightly judge as you will "know" certain things that are not visible to the eyes, nor can be heard by the ears. God's wisdom will direct the true remnant. Wisdom will reign over the Father's business. The true remnant's feet will be prepared and directed by the Holy Spirit of Wisdom, revealing true hope. Brokenness with understanding of the Spirit brings hope and anchors the soul. The remnant's mind will be anchored by hope despite of all the chaos in the world around us. Wisdom will usher in the harvest. Wisdom comes from the altar of God when you access heavenly realms. The remnant will be skilled in accessing the heavenly realms in the end time move of God on the earth, which has now arrived. As a result the church needs to be prepared and sanctified by the Word and by the Spirit of the LORD to receive and carry the weight of His glory.

Wisdom is insight. Wisdom will move and propel you towards executing God's purposes in the earth. Wisdom mobilizes. It is "knowing what" to do and to do it.

Wisdom directs.

"Wisdom is the fear of the LORD and to depart from evil is understanding."

Job 28:28

Wisdom and understanding goes hand in glove. Wisdom leads to understanding. It is by the Spirit of the fear of the LORD that His glory will be ushered in. His glory can only fall on a person or on a congregation where the fear of the LORD is eminent and present.

Wisdom will direct your mind and your mind becomes anointed with an ability from God to legislate and execute on the earth. An ability from God is released through His wisdom to direct your thoughts and decisions. Your mind becomes "one" with His mind, the mind of Christ. Sound judgment follows as a result.

"And all Israel heard about the judgment which the king has rendered, and they feared the king, for they saw the Wisdom of God was in him to administer justice"
1 Kings 3:28

Wisdom will allow you to do God's will and to administer justice in the courts of heaven.

WHERE IS WISDOM FOUND?

"From where then does wisdom come? And where is the place of understanding? It is hidden from the eyes of all living, and concealed from the birds of the air."

"God understands its way and He knows its place."   *Job 28:20,21,21*

Wisdom cannot be seen with the naked eye as we have already mentioned. Wisdom comes from God; it is hidden and needs to be searched out.

"It is the glory of God to conceal a thing, but the honor of kings, to search out a matter."
Proverbs 25:2

Wisdom is also concealed from the eyes of the birds of the air, this is indicative of demons. Wisdom is hidden from all demon activity. They do not have access to the deep things of God. However, His wisdom is available to His sons and daughters.

HOW CAN WISDOM BE FOUND?

Wisdom comes from the secret place where you search and seek God's face and ask for His Spirit of Wisdom to come upon you. This is where you enter the heavenly realms through fasting and prayer and a life that is totally surrendered to Christ and yielded to His Holy Spirit to guide and lead you in all truth. The fullness of His Spirit comes upon a life like this.

"That path that no bird knows, nor has the falcon's eye seen it, the proud lions have not trodden it, nor has the fierce lion passed over it. He puts his hand to the flint; and overturns the mountains at the roots. He cuts out channels in the rocks, and his eyes sees every precious thing. He dams up the streams from trickling; what is hidden he brings forth to the light, but where can wisdom be found, and where is the place of understanding? Man does not know its value, nor is it found in the land of the living. The deep says, it is not in me; the sea says it is not with me; it cannot be purchased for gold, nor can silver be weighed for its price. It cannot be valued in the gold of Opher, in precious onyx or saphire. Neither gold nor crystal can equal it, nor can it be exchanged for jewelry of fine gold. No mention shall be made of coral or quarts, for the price of Wisdom is above rubies."
                          Job 28:7 - 18

What does all of this mean from the book of Job?

Job knew God personally and never rejected Him when he was tested in the furnace of affliction. Job had a platform to voice these deep insights. There is a path that no bird knows. Birds, the flacon's eyes, proud lions and a fierce lion which is mentioned in *Job 28:7 - 8*, refers to the ranking of demons in the spirit realm. The fierce lion being satan himself. Birds and falcons are lower ranking demons. Proud lions refer to principalities. The point that Job is making is to proof that demons and principalities as well as satan has no access to the secret place, neither to our spirit man when it is reborn.

In the secret place we call out to God, pray in tongues, fast and seek His face. Satan has no business here. He has no access to the wisdom of God that comes forth from this place. Jesus, in *Matthew 6,* taught on the secret place where God hears us in secret and rewards us in public. This is the place where mountains (problems) are overturned and uprooted by the seven-fold Spirit of God. This is the place where you legislate and make declarations from heavenly realms, and God will establish it on the earth.

Job said that, from this place, your spiritual senses and eyes will start to "see" precious things. Streams of spiritual revelation are dammed up. Revelations flow from the wisdom and throne of God. Secret things are revealed. That which is hidden comes to the light. You will know the secret things of God. That which people are hiding from you will be revealed in order for it to be dealt with. All by the Spirit of Wisdom.

We have continuous access to this place by the blood of Jesus Christ and through the Holy Spirit. God will release His Wisdom over those who steward His word well and who hosts the presence of His Spirit well. Those who value His presence and the deep things of God. Those who are prepared to search Him out and seek His face. Those who spend time with Him and puts Him first. Those who call upon His Name.

'Happy is the man who finds wisdom, and the man who gains understanding; for her proceeds are better than the profits of silver, and her gain than fine gold. She is more precious than rubies, and all the things you may desire cannot compare with her. Length of days are in her right hand, in her left-hand riches and honor. Her ways are ways of pleasantness, and all her paths are peace. She is a tree of life to those who take hold of her."
Proverbs 3:13 - 18

These are all the attributes that wisdom will bestow upon your life. It is the wisdom of God that makes rich, brings happiness, peace, honor, a long life and makes you a tree where people can come and eat the fruit, be blessed and receive life. People will find shelter under the tree and healing will come forth from its leaves. A life in the Spirit opens these realms to the sons and daughters of God. The true remnant will walk in this in the days to come as God is restoring the church to its original intent. With restoration multiplication comes. The latter will be far greater than the former.

SPIRIT OF UNDERSTANDING

By the Spirit of Understanding we understand or comprehend the mysteries of God. Wisdom speaks to the spirit of man, understanding interprets the things of the Spirit to make it understandable and palatable.

"And He opened their understanding that they might comprehend the scriptures".
Luke 24:45

This is a special anointing released by the Spirit of the Lord to receive revelation and to be able to make sense of it. The Spirit of Wisdom "reveals" and the Spirit of Understanding brings "comprehension". Our understanding needs to be activated and opened.

Paul prayed the following prayer to the church in Ephesus as he understood the realm of the Spirit. This is how he prayed.

"That the God of our LORD Jesus Christ, the Father of glory, may give you the Spirit of Wisdom in the knowledge of Him. That the eyes of your understanding being enlightened "opened" that you may know what is the hope of your calling."
Ephesians 1:17,18

It is the Spirit of wisdom that will lead you to know Christ and thereby your spiritual senses and eyes will be opened to understand your call. These spiritual senses need to be opened and activated even by the laying on of hands by your spiritual oversight at the altar where you serve.

EFFECTS OF THE OUTWORKING OF THE SPIRIT OF UNDERSTANDING

You will know what is the hope of your calling. You will know what is the riches of His inheritance. You will know what is the greatness of His power that is available to those who believe. You will understand and comprehend the width, length, depth and height of the love of Christ that passes all knowledge. This will lead you to be filled with the fullness of God.

"That Christ may dwell in your hearts through faith, that you, being rooted and grounded in love, may be able to comprehend with all the saints what is the width and length and depth and height, to know the love of Christ which possess knowledge, that you may be filled with all the fullness of God"   *Ephesians 3~:17 - 19*

It is by the operation of the Spirit of understanding which leads us to comprehend His love and the fullness of Him. Every aspect of the Holy Spirit has been given for a reason. We as sons and daughters in these last days need to learn to draw on the Spirit of God.

HOW IS THE SPIRIT IMPARTED?

"So Jesus said to them again! As the Father has sent Me, I also send you." And When He had said this, He breathed on them, "receive the Holy Spirit"

John 20;21,22

We are sent and equipped by the Holy Spirit.

The Greek word "emphusao" means to "blow at or on". Jesus blew on them and said to them, *"receive the Holy Spirit"*.

In exactly the same manner, God breathed the breath of life into Adam and he became a living being with the Spirit of God as the habitation of his soul. Jesus as the second Adam came to restore this for us.

Jesus baptizes us in the Holy Spirit and with fire. The Spirit upon a believer is a dimension that comes from above after rebirth has taken place. In other words, there are two dimensions of the Spirit. God's ruach breath that He breathes into a believer at rebirth. And then another dimension of being baptized in the Holy Spirit when the Spirit of the LORD comes upon a believer who lives a pure and holy life. The seven-fold Holy Spirit then becomes the habitation of a healed and delivered soul and directs the believer from that place. The spirit man rules, the soul follows and directs the body into action.

"When anyone hears the Word of the kingdom, and does not understand it, then the wicked one comes and snatches it away"   Matthew 13:19

We cannot comprehend the scriptures without the measure of the Spirit of God residing over our souls.

Satan wants to steal the Word of God from your heart as all life comes from the Word which is Spirit and it brings life.

HOW DOES UNDERSTANDING COME?

Understanding comes by revelation. Paul explains in *Ephesians 3:1 - 4 that God made the mystery of Christ known to him by revelation. Remember that revelation comes by the Spirit of Wisdom. The Spirit of Wisdom and Understanding works together. It is our inheritance to understand God's kingdom and to know the mysteries of the kingdom of God.*

SPIRIT OF COUNSEL

"The Spirit of the LORD shall rest upon Him, the Spirit of Wisdom and Understanding, the Spirit of Counsel and Might"   Isaiah 11:2

The Spirit of Counsel will guide you from within directing your path. Your ears shall hear a word behind you saying, *"this is the way, walk in it"*. You hear with your heart, however from within you are directed.

The Spirit of Counsel is a strategist. By the Spirit of Counsel God will release to you strategy against the viles of the enemy. You will hear and know which direction to take.

FUNCTIONS OF THE SPIRIT OF COUNSEL

"Unto us a Son is born, and the government will be upon His shoulder. And His name will be called wonderful, counselor, mighty God, everlasting Father, prince of peace"
                                                                                                              Isaiah 9:6

The Hebrew meaning of "wonderful counselor" means "extraordinary strategist". This aspect of the Spirit of the LORD will allow you to receive supernatural strategy to move forward in times of trouble, following instructions from above. It will also be instrumental in fulfilling the mandate of God upon your life as you will be instructed by the LORD.

EXAMPLES OF THE SPIRIT OF COUNSEL AT WORK

"Moses and the crossing of the Red Sea. God delivered His people from the hand of Pharaoh and the Egyptians by Moses, the deliverer. Moses was instructed by God and given the strategy to lift up his rod (symbol of authority), and stretch out his hand over the sea to divide it.

God said to Moses to stop crying out and lead the people forward. Moses followed the instruction by the Spirit of Counsel and Israel was delivered. Only by God's counsel you will move forward into victory. There is always a battle strategy. This account of affairs is found in *Exodus 14:15 and 16*.

Jehoshaphat and the Ammonites, Moabites and Mount Seir. Jehoshaphat seeked God's face as he feared the Ammonites, Moabites and Mount Seir. They were enemies of God mobilizing against God's people (Juda) whom Jehoshaphat was leading. Jehoshaphat proclaimed a fast. The entire nation of Juda sought God's face. Prophecy broke out. The Spirit of the LORD came upon Jehaziel, a Levite, and he released to the king and the nation the strategy, as the strategy to win the battle was revealed to him prophetically. The strategy was to place singers in front of the army. The battle belonged to God. They never fought; they only followed the instruction from heaven.

As they sang, the angels of God were activated, and they slayed the enemy. The enemy was panic stricken and started to fight amongst one another and everyone in the enemy's camp was killed. The weapons of warfare were on display. We found an account of this in *2 Chronicles 20:1 - 17*

Isaac and the famine in Gerar. In the midst of famine, when everyone departed to Egypt where Joseph had a storehouse during the time of famine, Isaac was counseled by God to remain in Gerar where the famine was. Doesn't make sense, does it? God's counsel will never make sense to the natural mind, as we are not to live by what we see, but what we *"see and hear from God"*. Isaac dug wells for water in the land where there was famine and was very successful and blessed in the land that God had sworn to Abraham and his descendants. Elsewhere in the land water dried up, but Isaac had water and food and was very prosperous against all odds. All by following God's counsel and following instruction in times of crisis. This is the Spirit of Counsel at work. The account of the above is found in *Genesis 26:2,3*

SPIRIT OF KNOWLEDGE

"My people are destroyed for a lack of knowledge, because you have rejected knowledge, I will also reject you from being priest for Me; because you have forgotten the law of your God, I will also forget your children"   Hosea 4;6

The knowledge that the Word of God refers to in this scripture is "revelation knowledge". The Greek word for revelation knowledge is "ginosko". The Word declares that this knowledge is God's law as it is knowledge that no man could know, it is revealed through the Spirit of knowledge. It forms part of the governing system that heaven operates from. It is by revelation that the just will live and have their being. Without revelation knowledge from God we will perish as the spiritual realm is more real than the worldly realm of our everyday life. God wants to reveal Himself and wants to reveal His plans and purposes for individuals, families, nations and generations. Therefore, we cannot reject it, as it will have an effect on our ministering before God as priests and also on our children. God is a generational God and will reveal that which needs to be imparted to the next generation.

The definition of knowledge according to the dictionary is "being aware of something or knowing something with familiarity gained through experience or association or theory." This type of knowledge is "head" knowledge and the Greek word for this type of knowledge is "gnosis".

However, revelation knowledge (ginosko) is exact knowledge, specific knowledge, knowledge that is removed from the mind and is knowledge that supersedes the mind. It is a higher knowledge as it comes from above.

There is gnosis, head knowledge available in the earthly realm and ginosko, knowledge available from the heavenly realm, which is knowledge downloaded into the heart of man.

What is the difference then? The source where it comes from differentiates between the two worlds of knowledge. Head/mind knowledge is found on earth as you read, expose yourself to written knowledge and do research. It is knowledge that is readily available.

Revelation knowledge comes from heaven by the Holy Spirit of Knowledge and is revealed to us in our hearts. Because of the Source it is coming from, it supersedes all other knowledge and has a far-reaching effect in the earthly realm. This knowledge, that, when it is made known to you, you will know that you know that you know, and it will be confirmed by witnesses as the Kingdom of God represents a judicial system.

"By the mouth of two or three witnesses every word shall be established'

2 Corinthians 13:1

By this revelation knowledge becomes established knowledge, which is irrefutable. This kind of knowledge turns on the light.

FUNCTION OF THE SPIRIT OF KNOWLEDGE

The Spirit of Knowledge brings understanding and direction together with wisdom which is applied knowledge. We have already discussed *Ephesians 3:17 - 19* where Paul explains the depth, length, breadth and width of the love of God and how this is a mystery that supersedes all knowledge. He then states that we need to be rooted and grounded in the love of God.

Paul was talking about to know (ginosko)concerning the love of Christ. In other words, he is talking about having a revelation on how much Christ loves us. This is a mystery. You cannot know His love and be grounded in it should you not have had a revelation about his love. A revelation by The Spirit of Knowledge from the throne of God.

This love surpasses knowledge (gnosis) which is head knowledge. Our minds cannot comprehend it. For as long as you do not have revelation knowledge in your heart to understand the love of Christ for you, it will be very difficult for you to walk as a son or daughter of God. We are in end times now. The church needs to arise and be secured in His love. It is His love that will usher in His glory which will bring in the end time harvest. Those who will come into the kingdom of God will be broken people, wounded people, addicted people who might not look and smell nice. How are we going to love them with the love of Christ if we ourselves do not understand and are not filled with the mystery of His love. During the end times it will cost you something to love and bring in the harvest. Only love and faith pleases God. We need to know by revelation the place that we hold in the heart of the Father as it will take us through. This is a knowledge that goes beyond.

WHY DO WE NEED THIS REVELATION ON THE LOVE OF GOD?

- The purpose is for your soul (mind, will and emotions) to be rooted and grounded in the love of Christ and to walk in His fullness. This anchors the soul. We are entering a time of severe persecution and even martyrdom. Only His love will take us through as to not walk away from Him. The natural mind cannot comprehend this type of love unless it is revealed to the heart of man, head knowledge is not going to help the end time church to bring in the harvest. His true sons and daughters will be secured in Him and willing to give up their lives for the Master.

- Revelation knowledge affects your mentality. This is when you're thinking process is being affected by what you "know" (revelation).

"But is written: "Eye has not seen, ear has not heard, nor have entered into the heart of man the things which God has prepared for those who love Him, but God has revealed them to us through His Spirit. For the Spirit searches all things, yes, the deep things of God"
1 Corinthians 2:9,10

Here we read about an example of this kind of knowledge. This brings so much comfort and security to the heart of man.

THE SPIRIT OF MIGHT

The Spirit of Might is connected to God's supernatural, overcoming strength and miraculous power. By the Spirit of Might an overcoming strength and power comes forth and takes a hold of you to enable you to do extraordinary exploits for God in boldness.

The Spirit of Might leads us to the book of Judges, as well as 1 Samuel, as both Samson, who was a judge, and David who was a king, operated in this Spirit.

At Timnath Samson was tearing a lion apart by the Spirit of Might. Refer to *Judges 14:5,6*. At Lehi Samson slew a thousand men by himself by the Spirit of Might. *Judges 15:14,15* refers. Samson took vengeance on the Philistines by pulling down the pillars of the temple of their god Dagon and killed more men on that day than in his entire life. *Judges 16:28* refers.

David slayed Goliath with a stone from his sling in 1 Samuel 17 by the same Spirit at work.

The Spirit of Might enabled them with extraordinary power and might to overcome. This is how the end time church will overcome by the same Spirit.

FUNCTIONS OF THE SPIRIT OF MIGHT

The Spirit of Might makes you bold. The Spirit of Might is an overpowering human force that overcomes human strength and takes over human senses. By the Spirit of Might supernatural dynamic power is on display.

Paul explained this in his prayer to the Ephesians.

"For this reason I bow my knees to the Father of our LORD Jesus Christ, from whom the whole family in heaven and earth is named, that He would grant you, according to the riches of His glory, to be strengthened with might through His Spirit in the inner man"
Ephesians 3:14 - 16

From this scripture it is certain that this is a "working" in the "inner" man and is spontaneous and exceeds the natural. It coms over you as a cloak when the circumstance calls for it. The end time ecclesia will be exposed to many trials and tribulations where we will have to count upon this aspect of the Holy Spirit.

SPIRIT OF THE FEAR OF THE LORD

The Spirit of the Fear of the LORD is connected to the reverential fear of the LORD. Where the fear of the LORD is present, the following will be eminent:

-   Prevailing prayer and fasting as this Spirit is connected to priesthood. Look at the life of the prophet Samuel, who was called as a priest to minister before God on behalf of Israel:

"He has made us kings and priests before his God and Father"   *Revelations 1:6*

This is our first call, to minister before God and reign with Him in heavenly places. Without the reverential Fear of the LORD this command will certainly be neglected. The Spirit of the Fear of the LORD focusses on that which has eternal value. We have to partner with God and have the same mindset.

- Godly order. Reverence for God will allow you to submit to godly ordained leadership, as these leaders need to guard over your soul and are accountable to God.

"Obey those who rule over you, and be submissive. for they watch out for your souls, as those who must give an account. Let them do so with joy and not with grief, for that would be unprofitable to you"   Hebrews 13:17

This is God's kingdom order. Leaders must pray for their members and guard over their souls as to give an account to God concerning them. Members must make it easy for the leaders as to have respect and show honor as godly appointed leadership does not come without accountability before God.

- Godly discipline. Obeying God's instructions and commandments according to His Word. This happens by the Spirit of the Fear of the LORD who leads us into obedience. The altar of giving and tithings will be restored.

"Will a man rob God? Yet you have robbed Me! But you say, in what way have we robbed You? In tithings and offerings. You are cursed with a curse"

Malachi 3:8 - 9

Only by the fear of the LORD will these altars be restored once again. God will not be mocked. Those who do not fear God, will not give head to His commandments.

- Unity. Where the Fear of the LORD is, the church will stand in unity and God will command a blessing over the ecclesia. The mountain of Zion (God's governing) will be restored and blessed by the effect of His Spirit.

- Humbleness.

"He has shown you, oh man, what is good; and what does the LORD require of you, but to do justly, to love mercy, and to walk humbly with your God"

Micah 6:8

CONCLUSION

"As many as I love, I rebuke and chasten. Therefore be zealous and repent "

Revelations 3:19

The church has to repent and restore God's altar for the end time harvest and revival to be gathered. Godly order and governance need to be restored back to the altar for God's fire to come down on the altar and for the latter rains of Joel 2, the final outpouring of his Spirit upon all flesh to come down from heaven. This is where we are in this final hour.

By the Spirit of the Fear of the LORD and the Reverential Fear of the LORD coming upon the church, this Spirit will bring about change. The Spirit of the Fear of the LORD will be instrumental in ushering in the final move of God's glory upon His church. The church is in a window period of grace to prepare and to sanctify herself for this outpouring. Let us prepare and be ready.

"Behold I am coming as a thief. Blessed is he who watches, and keeps his garments, lest he walks naked and they see his shame" *Revelations 16:15*

CHATER 8

PROCESS OF BEING MADE READY

THE PROCESS OF BEING MADE READY

The process of preparing the remnant to gather the final harvest, to prepare the way for the LORD, as well as to be ready when Jesus will appear in the clouds to rapture His remnant bride, is a detailed process that will require teamwork. Ministries need to join forces to make preparation, stand in unity and each son and daughter needs to find their place and assignment in the body of Christ. Apostolic order needs to return to the church. Too many movements and ministries are alienated from the body of Christ as lone rangers. This is not God's order. Apostolic order was demonstrated to us by the early church and implemented by Jesus Christ through the five-fold ministry. We all need to be part of a five-fold ministry team and under spiritual covering of an apostolic prophetic mantle. There are several matters that will be shaken and removed in this end time season. Every foundation that is not laid according to the Word in Ephesians 4, and every organization and ministry and movement that was not birthed by God will be shaken in this end time movement of God. All that is man-made has to be removed when God will finally, once more, shake the works of men's hands. All illegitimate authority will be shaken. The church is now returning to its original intent and will fulfill its mandate on the earth. The gates of hades will not prevail against the church as heaven is preparing to work with the sons and daughters of God. However, order needs to be restored. Apostolic order.

In this preparation and sanctification phase God will do a quick work. Here are some of the matters that need to be addressed during this process of preparation:

-    Jesus will sanctify, cleanse and purify His church with the washing of water by the Word. The church is defiled and many abominations before God are being overlooked by leaders who are compromising themselves and thereby are weakened to stand up to the truth. We cannot love our lives more so that we will not speak up. This is not the hour to be popular, but it is the hour to please God in every way. The Word of God is lying dormant on the shelves of believers' homes. How will we declare a thing in the earth for God to establish it on the earth should we not know the truth of His Word. Many false teachers, prophets and apostles will arise now that the anti-Christ is ready to come to the forefront. Be aware of their fruits. Are they adhering to God's apostolic order and original design, or do they want to do their own thing. Prophets are to be part of a five-fold ministry team and not operate on their own. Accountability needs to return to the body of Christ. As many young Christians who are still babies in the faith are being lead astray by prophecy and heresy. We need to be filled with the truth of the Word and carry the Sword of the Spirit, ready to war and decree from mount Zion.

"That He might sanctify and cleanse her with the washing of water by the Word, that He might present her to Himself as a glorious church, not having spot or wrinkle or any such thing, but that she should be holy and without blemish."

Ephesians 5:25 - 27

This is a picture of the remnant church being made ready. Do we at all care that Jesus Christ paid the price and is interceding for His blood purchased children. But we have lowered the standard. If you reject the design (God's way of doing things), you reject the Designer; if you reject the Designer, there is no purpose anymore; where there is no purpose deceit steps in. To ignore and defile His original plan, intent and design, has become acceptable in the church. No longer to be married, but to live together, became an acceptable practice, even within the church. God's judgment is coming upon the church and the leaders for compromising and accepting this lifestyle and keeping a blind eye. Have we reached the point where we should rather ask people to leave the altar than joining them to the altar. God wants to see purity within the church. Let them all come to the altar to be healed and delivered. But do not come to the altar and remain in your old ways. The altar is the place from where God's love and mercy flows, from where healing and deliverance flows. Therefore, we need to allow ourselves to be cleansed and purified.

"Now the works of the flesh are evident, which are: adultery, fornication, uncleanness, lewdness, idolatry, sorcery, hatred, contentions, jealousies, outbursts of wrath, selfish ambitions, dissensions, heresies, envy, murders, drunkenness, revelries, and the like; of which I tell you beforehand, just as I also told you in time past, that those who practice such things will not inherit the kingdom of God"
Galatians 5:19 - 21

This is the Word of God on it. God is sovereign over His Word to perform it, as He cannot be divided against Himself. God will judge these things. It is now the time of separation, the vile from the precious. These fleshly conducts can and will no longer be tolerated in the church. We need to stand up for what is right and share the truth. Engaging in these things without repentance will cause a person certainly to end up in hell. Turning away from all wickedness is required. There is still time to repent and choose Life.

Who is prepared to build the house of the LORD?

The house of the LORD is lying in ruins currently.

"Is it time for you yourselves to dwell in your paneled houses, and this temple to lie in ruins? Now therefore, says the LORD of hosts: "Consider your ways!" You have sown much and bring it little; you eat but do not have enough; you drink but you are not filled with drink; you clothe yourselves but no one is warm; and he who earns wages, earns wages to put into a bag with holes." Thus says the LORD of hosts: consider your ways! Go up to the mountains and bring wood and build the temple, that I may take pleasure in it and be glorified, says the LORD. You looked for much, but indeed it came to little; and when you brought it home, I blew it away." "Why?", says the LORD of hosts. "Because of My house that is in ruins, while everyone of you runs to his own house"   Haggai 1: 4 - 9

This is an example of the present situation. Everyone runs for their own interests whilst the house of the LORD is not being built, neither financed. God will choose for Himself a selfless, true remnant that will build His house. His house will be victorious and glorious. Anything that does not glorify God needs to be discarded of. God will not share His glory. All the earth will glorify Him in these days as it is the days of Elijah. So the Truth of His Word will be taught and will prevail. The Truth of the Word will wash us clean and align us to His end time purposes.

-    Repentance and Restoration. *"Repent"* does not mean to turn to more dedicated efforts to please God by keeping the law or performing better works. The plea is to simply turn to God Himself - to allow Him to cleanse and restore. To turn away from old ways and wickedness and to turn to God and walk in the ways of God as stipulated in His Word.

After pronouncing judgment on the people because of their apostasy, God presents the promise of restoration. He says He will bring forth their righteousness as the noon day should they turn to Him with all their heart. He also says He will make them as a garden that is well watered, as a fountain from which the water never fails.

-    Truth and Unity restored. The Truth of the Word will reveal heresy as God's people are rooted and grounded in the truth of His Word and in His love. God is raising up leaders who will bring the unprecedented truth of the Word. First Peter teaches us that there is an important purpose for our unity. We as believers are as living stones being built together as a spiritual house, a holy priesthood, to offer up spiritual sacrifices, acceptable to God through Jesus Christ. God is seeking a spiritual habitation amongst His people where His glory can come down and fill the temple. The end time church and the earth will be filled with the glory of the LORD. This is unity. Where there is unity, the Spirit of the LORD is welcomed. The Spirit of Truth will prevail, and much revelation will come forth.

- Priesthood restored. It is important to realize that the priestly function is part of the ongoing ministry of Jesus. He is our great High Priest who forever lives to make intercession for us according to the will of the Father. The blood of Jesus Christ must be applied by us in the secret place to cleanse us every day and to receive fresh revelation daily. We must receive His Presence and turn away from sin. The enemy wants to keep the church from its priestly function to intercede and lead the way to build a wall before the throne of God on behalf of our families, nations, individuals and cities. A righteous remnant, interceding, can cause God's mercy to come down on the undeserving. We must never underestimate the power that is released when united believers intercede in humility.

Humility and genuine brokenness releases God's favor, for He resists the proud, but gives grace to the humble. The Spirit of intercession still seeks those who will stand before God in prayer on behalf of those who either cannot or do not know how to or will not pray for themselves. This is our priestly function as we have been appointed priests and kings by Jesus before God our Father. To pray effectively we need to understand the levels of anointing in prayer, which we will discuss shortly.

- **Ministry of Reconciliation restored.**

"And He died for all, that those who live should no longer live for themselves, but for Him Who died for them and rose again. Therefore, from now on, we regard no one according to the flesh. Even though we have known Christ according to the flesh, yet now we know Him thus no longer. Therefore, if anyone is in Christ, he is a new creation, old things have passed away, behold, all things have become new. Now, all things are of God Who has reconciled us to Himself through Jesus Christ and has given us the ministry of reconciliation. That is, that God was in Christ reconciling the world to Himself, not imputing their trespasses to them, and has committed to us the Word of reconciliation"   *2 Corinthians 5:15 - 19*

What does all this mean? Reconciliation is the process by which God and man are brought together again. We were once estranged from Him, but we have been brought to God and restored to relationship through the shed blood of Christ. We are encouraged to follow the standard He left for us - to be reconciled to God first and with each other as He reconciled us to Himself. As we model His ministry of reconciliation, the world will be impacted. However, Paul admonished us not to live for ourselves, but for Him Who reconciled us. Furthermore, we are not to regard no one according to the flesh. This is key. The way we look at one another and relate to one another, especially strangers and those who are poor and downcast, has to be through His eyes. All people were predestined and foreknown according to *Romans 8*. They each were known already in heaven before they came to earth. We need to relate to every person we come across according to who heaven says that they are, to their true identity in Christ, their heavenly persona. Not by what we see in the flesh.

This will allow us to look and relate the way Christ relates to all creation. We now know Christ no longer by the flesh, but by the Spirit. Therefore, we need to relate to people around us according to the revelation we receive of them in the Spirit. This will allow honor to return to the church and will also be a strong weapon to gather the harvest. This is done prophetically by the Spirit through the blood of Jesus. The moment we relate to people according to who they really are, their self-value returns, and they are elevated to their true identity in Christ. This is the ministry of reconciliation in action and is what real church is all about. We cannot consider their trespasses and treat them accordingly, as Christ wants to reconcile them to Him, not imputing their trespasses to them. He has committed to us, His children, the ministry of reconciliation, in other words the prophetic word spoken by us revealing someone's true identity and relating to them that way in all honor. That is true love and will cause the unsaved to have hope and to be reconciled to Christ. The old things will pass away for them and they will become new creations in Christ.

If the church fails in the ministry of reconciliation, we will proceed in religion. The true remnant church will carry His unprecedented love to a wounded and broken world. Loving and seeing through the lenses of reconciliation, the way Christ sees them and love them accordingly. With the outpouring of His Spirit in Joel 2, His voice will be everywhere, even the children will prophecy. Prophecy and the ministry of reconciliation is connected to make known true identity and to look in the Spirit and not by what the eye can see in the natural.

THERE ARE THREE LEVELS OF ANOINTING

Anointing can also be described as "an ability from God to do something".

- **Lepers Anointing.**

"You have an anointing from the holy One, you know all things"   1 John 2:20

This anointing represents an ability from God to the sinner to be saved.

"For by grace you have been saved through faith and not of yourselves, it is the Gift of God"
Ephesians 2:8

The pre-requisite for this anointing is "faith" unto salvation. When you are saved, the Holy Spirit resides in you for the purpose of eternal security. It is a once-off anointing and cannot be lost unless the believer intentionally and willfully renounces and walk away from the covenant relationship with God. Your spirit is now connected to the Holy Spirit and that enables you to come before the throne of Grace boldly. Now the door for prayer is opened.

- **Priestly Anointing.**

The prerequisite for priestly anointing is salvation. This anointing is for ministering before the LORD in prayer and intercession. This anointing calls for a "yielded" life before the Spirit of God and a "surrendered" life to our LORD Jesus Christ. In much prayer and pondering on the Word of God, the existing anointing in us increases and we become continually filled with more of the Spirit of God until we are saturated to carry the fullness of His Spirit. Overflowing with His Presence. *The "fullness" of the Holy Spirit is measured in overflow. The fruits of the Holy Spirit will become very evident at this stage in the believer's life. This anointing is for Presence, power and service. Presence is evident in power. His Presence comes upon us for shifting the atmosphere wherever we go, to enable us for the call upon our lives, for healing the sick, to deliver those who are in bondage and to preach the gospel with power.*

This anointing can be lost when sin enters the heart, and the Holy Spirit is grieved. Then it takes time again after repentance for the Spirit to return and remain. As matured sons and daughters we need to learn to host the Holy Spirit through a life of continual prayer and intercession, as well as through our daily devotion. We need a fresh anointing daily from the holy One.

- **Kingly Anointing.**

"To Him who loved us and washed us from our sins in His own blood, and has made us kings and priests to His God and Father"   Revelations 1:5

This anointing is for authority over the power of the enemy.

"All authority has been given to Me in heaven and on earth"   Matthew 28:18

The same authority has been delegated to the sons and daughters of God.

The prerequisite for this level of anointing is ministering before the LORD, combined with total surrender and obedience. It is about hearing and obeying. Obedience to the Word of God. It requires that your body is a living sacrifice, holy and acceptable to the Father, as your reasonable service, according to *Romans 12:1*. It requires a death to your own desires and will. It calls for a life totally surrendered to the will of God at all times. A life that is laid down on the altar only for the Master's purpose. Radical obedience brings about a level of authority. This will earmark the end time ecclesia. It will be a people sold out to the purposes and counsel of His Will walking in purity and holiness. They will see and hear and obey the Master's voice at all cost. This is the highest level of anointing.

It is sad to say that most of the church still sits at the first level of anointing where they are saved but operates from the outer courts. Matured sons and daughters know God intimately and walk in the kingly anointing where they will have full authority and dominion over the domain of the kingdom assigned to them. Each in their sphere of influence, pleasing the Father. Understanding heavenly realms and decreeing from mount Zion.

FUNCTION AND ROLE OF THE FIE-FOLD MINISTRY

"To each one of us grace was given to a measure of Christ's gift "and He Himself gave some to be apostles, some prophets, some evangelists and some pastors and teachers. For the equipping of the saints for the work of the ministry, for the edifying of the body of Christ"
Ephesians 4:11 - 12

PURPOSE OF THE FIVE-FOLD MINISTRY

"Till we all come to the unity of the faith and of the knowledge of the Son of God to a perfect man, to the measure of the stature of the fullness of Christ. That we would no longer be children tossed to and fro and carried about with every wind of doctrine, by the trickery of men, in the cunning craftiness of deceitful plotting"
Ephesians 4: 13 - 14

So we see that the purpose of the five-fold ministry, which was partly omitted as the blue print for the church, is being restored in the end time church. The purpose of the five-fold ministry is to:

- For all to come to the unity of faith. Without extreme faith we will not be able to navigate the last days.

- For all to come to the full knowledge of Jesus Christ. To be rooted and grounded in His love, to know Him and for our souls to be anchored in Him.

- For all to become "perfected" in Him and to mature into the fullness of who He is.

- So that we will all not be tossed and turned by heresy and unsound doctrine. The ecclesia will know the truth of the Word and will carry the Word and the Spirit as a sword.

There will be much poisoning of the food and false doctrine as well as false teachers rising in these last days. We need to be well undergirded in the Word of God.

RESULTS OF THE FIVE-FOLD MINISTRY BEING RESTORED

"But, speaking the Truth in love, may grow up in all things into Him who is the Head - Christ. From Whom the whole body, joined and knit together by what every joint supplies, according to the effective working by which every part does its' share causes growth of the body for the edifying of itself in love"

Ephesians 4:15 - 16

- We will speak the Truth in love as the Word of God will be in our hearts and we will be anchored.

- We will grow up in Him and acknowledge Him as the Head, leading the church becoming matured sons and daughters, obeying Him only.

- Every joint or member of the body of Christ supplies something, and each does it's part. By that way we will be joined and knitted together, and this will cause the growth of the body.

- By functioning in this ordained order of God, the body will edify itself in love.

We have already explained that the spirit of religion has five tentacles and invaded the church over many centuries. As the result the church is far from maturity, far from its inheritance, deviated from God's original plan and intent for the church. It is also the reason, together with witchcraft, that many sons and daughters never reached maturity and to not know or understand their callings and positioning in the body of Christ. Man-made programs and agendas were the order of the day.

By the Spirit of the LORD these tentacles will now be removed. The spirit and power of Elijah is rising up in the end times against Jezebel and her witchcraft to demolish the plans of the enemy. The church will no longer be held captive and be powerless. It will rise and be victorious. The five-fold ministry will replace the spirit of religion, and the church will be governed from mount Zion. Apostolic order is returning to the church. An apostolic team effort will mark the end time church. Therefore, a proper understanding of the function and role of the five-fold ministry is needed as the body of Christ, and especially those who will be added to the church as the end time harvest is upon us, will be properly equipped. Leaders will be equipped to usher in the harvest. That time is now.

"Five" is the number of the cross, for atonement and for grace. Paul talks about the grace gifting that Jesus Christ has given to the church as leadership gifts in *Ephesians 4*. In this context "grace gifting" refers to an ability that Christ has put on individuals to do that which He called them to do. The church is His body, He is the chief cornerstone, and He takes full responsibility for the establishing and future growth of the church. He has been appointed Head over His church. Christ sacrificed His life for His church!

We are focusing on the five-fold ministry as the model that Jesus demonstrated to the church as the blueprint for the governing and full functioning of the body of Christ. Jesus Christ was the ultimate leader and operated in all five offices to a full measure during His time of ministry on the earth.

He was fully anointed and carried the Spirit without measure to operate in the full five-fold ministry role in order to demonstrate and equip His disciples. He never left them alone. He equipped them and duplicated Himself in man for the church to proceed in power. The purpose of His ministry was to establish the church as a whole and to ensure that the mandate that was given to Him by His Father will continue through every believer on the earth until He returns to take those who belong to Him by covenant, to where He is. Without this model, the mandate which is the great commission in *Matthew 28:16 - 20* and *Mark 16:15 - 18,* cannot be fulfilled.

It is not a choice but a command for us to go into all the world and preach the gospel to every creature, make disciples (followers) of all nations, teaching them and baptize them in the Name of the Father and of the Son and of the Holy Spirit.

The 21st century church has deviated from this mandate for several reasons. For a very long time several offices were not acknowledged in the church, especially that of the apostle and the prophet. As a result, the structure and governing as well as the foundation of the church was not in order. This resulted in the church being weak and unable to function in its full capacity. The church was rendered powerless and members unfulfilled, without knowledge, broken and some have even fell by the way. It also resulted in the great commission not being fulfilled. The church missed the mark and her mandate to fulfill God's original intent.

Now is the appointed time and season whereupon the Father is restoring the end time church to its full glory - for the purpose of the mandate to be fulfilled on the earth before the coming of our Lord. We are honored to be part of this restoration process and therefore we need to take heed and prepare ourselves, be sanctified and set apart as the true remnant.

Through all of this it is very clear that our ministry, call and area of gifting as well as the five-fold ministry is not only meant for the environment of the church, but it is also to be applied in the marketplace. There can be a call to full-time ministry at the altar or a call to the marketplace or both. The same principles apply for the church as well as for the marketplace. The church and marketplace were never to be separated from one another as God blessed both arenas. It was separated under the Levitical priestly order. When Christ died and restored man unto Himself as He became the second Adam, the order of Melchizedek was also restored. This will be covered in full in the next chapter.

HEADSHIP OF CHRIST AND THE GOVERNING OF THE CHURCH

The church is entering a new era where we will see several changes in an effort to bring her back to God's original intent and to align to end time purposes.

"When He raised Him from the dead and seated Him at His right hand in the heavenly places, far above all principalities and power and might and dominion, and every name that is named, not only in this age but the age to come. And He put all things under His feet, and gave Him to be Head over all things to the church, which is His body, the fullness of Him who fills all in all"   Ephesians 1:20 - 23

Jesus Christ is the Head of His church and will see her through to the end. The church needs to repent and turn back to the original blueprint that Jesus Christ prescribed for the church before He ascended to heaven.

All power and dominion have been given unto Him by His Father. He is the Ruler over the kings of this world and reigns from on high. He is seated far above all principalities, power, might and dominion. We are seated with Him in heavenly places and rule with Him from heavenly realms that are above the second heaven where these principalities and powers are operating from. Everything has been set underneath His feet and also our feet as He has transferred dominion and power to us. However, the church became weak and is not manifesting this dominion. This will be set right by God when He shakes all man made things on the earth. We as sons and daughters need to understand our authority and place in Him and take dominion. We can, however, only do this if we are matured into the fullness of Christ. Therefore, the five-fold ministry needs to be fully operative in the church to equip and bring the body to full maturity in Him. His fullness of all in all. He raised us up together and made us sit together in heavenly places in Christ Jesus according to the Word in *Ephesians 2:6.*

From this scripture it is clear that, although our physical bodies are on the earth, our spirit man is seated together with Christ Jesus in heavenly places from where we ought to rule, reign and legislate. In heaven all is in agreement. It is our responsibility to press into the heavenly realms and seek his face. To come to know His heart and mind on matters, to agree and govern over the domain He signed to us. Much equipping is necessary as a result of the church being governed incorrectly according to man's agendas for such a long time. Alignment has to take place to the Word of God.

It is no longer all about "your church", however, it is about kingdom building and impacting your sphere of influence. Apostles are to be founding churches, not Pastors as this is not a pastoral function. Apostolic hubs need to be established where the saints can be equipped and sent out. Members are not to be retained in the church but need to be released to accomplish their mandates and reign over their sphere of influence.

"Having been built on the foundation of the apostles and the prophets, Jesus Christ Himself, the chief corner stone in whom the whole building, being fitted together, rose into a holy temple in the Lord in whom you are also being built together for a dwelling place of God in the Spirit"   Ephesians 2:20 - 22

Jesus Christ is the Head of the church, but He is also the chief corner stone. Should the corner stone be removed the whole building will fall. The church is being held together by our Lord Jesus Christ. His model for the foundation of the church is the apostle and the prophet together with Himself as the chief corner stone. The rest of the building is being built upon this foundation. Any other foundation will not stand in the shaking that will take place in the end times. The end time ecclesia will model after Christ's original plan. The foundation will be secure.

Jesus Christ is the Rock; His Word is foundational. The unprecedented truth of His Word needs to return and be taught and preached. Truth will expose heresy. Heresy is false doctrine.

The apostle is a watch dog over doctrine and therefore forms part of the foundation of any planting. The prophet hears God's mind and heart and directs the church and provides oil to the lamp stand. As far as the destinies of God's sons and daughters are concerned, it is the prophet that sees and directs them to destiny. It is the apostle that teaches and trains them up for their destinies by setting the five-fold in order and watch continually over doctrine.

That is the reason why they work together, and together with the chief corner stone, Jesus Christ Who is the Word Himself, the foundation upon which all else is built. We ought not to deviate from the truth of the Word.

When this building is being built upon and rises into a holy temple in the Lord, it will be a dwelling place for the Spirit of the Lord amongst His people. When this happens and the church stands in unity, purified, sanctified, walking on the highway of holiness and each member finds its place in the body, then the Spirit of the Lord will descend upon the church and His glory will be seen. We need to make ready the way for the Lord to rapture a glorified and pure bride for Himself. That time is now! It is a total new dispensation, and we will never have church the way we knew it before. The church will be powerful, loving one another, sacrificing their lives for one another and for the call.

The book of Ephesians speaks on more than one occasion about the Headship of Christ and Ephesians 4 speaks about how the church should be governed by leadership offices through the grace gifting bestowed upon each leader in the five-fold. A leader is not being chosen by man but appointed by Jesus Christ. All legitimate authority comes from Jesus Christ. We are all leaders in our sphere of influence, but some have been called by Jesus Christ to office as a five-fold leader in office to equip the body of Christ. They are full time altar workers.

The five-fold leadership is the only leadership model that Jesus demonstrated and gave to the church for both business and church. The marketplace operates on the exact same leadership principles. He appointed apostles, prophets, teachers, evangelists and pastors and grace gifted them to a full measure of that which is upon Himself. When Jesus walked the earth, He operated as an apostle, prophet, teacher, evangelist and pastor. Before He ascended on high, He put gifts (grace giftings) on all people to a measure. Your measure fits your call. These are the five aspects of Himself that He gave. Now the church can grow and expand by means of Christ inside us and His persona and abilities being bestowed to each one of us according to the measure of Christ's gift. You need to know and understand the measure of your grace gifting. The five-fold ministry gifts are ministry gifts and are leadership offices to equip the body.

He was given to be head over all things to the church, which is His body. His fullness fills all in all. The purpose is for us to know Him in His fullness and reign with Him. Fullness equals full maturity in Christ. Knowing Jesus Christ. Without the fullness the body cannot fulfill its mandate.

Jesus carried a full measure of the Spirit of God, in the same way we are called to this fullness, in order to fulfill and complete that which He started on the earth, His church, and when He left He gave orders to His disciples and left them with the blueprint of how the church should function, in order for us to complete that which He started. What a great responsibility this is. Jesus knew that He left the blueprint in His Word and that He sent the Holy Spirit to help and lead the church. Who are we as man to make it something else to suit our programs and agendas and there by render the church dysfunctional and powerless to a point where generations are no longer interested in the church.

The church is subject to Christ. It is about His principles and ways. We cannot make it other than how it is prescribed in the Word of God. We need to stick to these principles and the original blueprint for the governing of the church in *Ephesians 4.*

FUNCTION OF THE CHURCH

"That now the manifold wisdom of God might be made known by the church to the principalities and powers in heavenly places"   *Ephesians 3:10*

God's manifold wisdom comes from the secret place according to the book of Job 28, which we have already discussed. These strategies and mysteries, the secret things, are made known to the church through intimacy with Jesus Christ. This is part of the overcoming and ruling of the church over principalities and powers in heavenly places. This is definite function of the church, and the gates of Hades will not prevail against the church as a result of continual revelation from the throne of God. It is the responsibility of the church to make known to the principalities in the second heaven, the Wisdom of God. Strategies to overcome and be victorious over the enemy are released by God's Wisdom to the church. He makes known to us that which is to come by His Spirit. The church needs to be equipped to understand the spiritual realm and understand how to receive revelation and agree with God's plans and purposes. They need to learn to change their prayers from begging and asking to authoritative prayers of decreeing and declaring His will in order for Him to establish our decrees on the earth.

"Let the redeemed of the Lord say so, whom He has redeemed from the hand of the enemy"
Psalms 107:2

The great commissioning of *Mark 16:15 - 18 and Matthew 28:16* talks about three distinct functions that need to be performed by the church. We have entered the era of extensive equipping on the one hand whilst we warfare, and on the other hand the gathering of the final harvest. These are the three distinct areas of function:

- Preach the gospel to every creature.

- Make disciples of all nations.

- Teaching them. A disciple is a learner and needs to be taught God's ways when they are saved.

- Baptize them in the Name of the Father and of the Son and of the Holy Spirit.

We all have an evangelistic call, but the office of the evangelist has been appointed for this purpose specifically as well as to equip and train us on "how to" reach the unsaved. The evangelist in office receives a strategy from God for the region that needs to be evangelized. He teaches and trains those to go with him and gather the harvest, although we all have the responsibility to bring in the harvest. Evangelists work outside of the local church; however, they are part of a five-fold ministry team.

To disciple nations means to teach and train them in the mysteries of the Word of God. According to *Isaiah 50:4* He gives us an instructed tongue as that of a learner. He wakes our ears in the morning to hear as the learned.

The church needs to be instructed and taught in the Wisdom of God.

"Let the Word of Christ dwell in you richly in all wisdom, teaching and admonishing one another"
Colossians 3:16

"My people are destroyed for a lack of knowledge (revelation knowledge), Because you have rejected knowledge, I will also reject you from being a priest for Me"
Hosea 4:6

This is a very serious warning to the church. We have full access through the blood of Jesus to access the throne of God, to know the heavenly secrets and strategies and to navigate heavenly realms. We are to live from heavenly revelation that is available to us continually through the blood of Jesus by the Holy Spirit. Should we not participate in this, we will be rejected as priests, as this is the very function of each believer to minister before God as a priest and a king.

If the five-fold ministry is not administered well in the church and the apostle who is the watch dog over sound doctrine is dismissed, and the prophet is not directing making sure the church is moving in the right direction, how will the building be built and be functional? In fact, we are destroyed by a lack of knowledge, revelation knowledge and stripped of our priesthood and inheritance in the process, should we neglect this important function. This is serious considering that Christ paid the price and laid down His life for His church.

"He loved us, purged us by His blood and made us priests and kings to His God and Father"
Revelation 1:5

Each born again child of God must be baptized. It forms part of the foundation of the believers life and serves as confirmation of that which has already been established - salvation. When you are baptized in the Name of the Father and of the Son and of the Holy Spirit, immersed under water, you openly confirm that you are part of Jesus Christ and belong to Him and is raised with Him to a new life in the Spirit that comes from Him. However, the way this ordinance was demonstrated to the church by Jesus being baptized, was twisted to make it something else. It will be restored back to the church. Water baptism is a step of obedience and a public declaration that you have died to yourself and have been risen with Christ. This is a command and not a choice. An ordinance is a set way in which somethings need to be done. This is the way it was ordained in the Word of God from the beginning. God requires truth and obedience.

Should the five-fold ministry not be in place, the above areas will lack, and this results in the church not fulfilling her mandate.

FUNCTION OF THE FIVE-FOLD LEADERSHIP GIFTS

These gifts are from the Son, Jesus Christ, to facilitate and equip the body of Christ. A leader in the five-fold ministry is appointed by the sovereign will of Jesus and not appointed by man. The office is recognized by man but not given by man.

"But to each one of us grace was given according to the measure of Christ's gift"
Ephesians 4:7

"And He Himself gave some to be apostles, some prophets, some evangelists, and some pastors and teachers, for the equipping of the body of the saints for the work of the ministry, for the edifying of the body of Christ, till we all come to the unity of the faith and of the knowledge of the Son of God, to a perfect man, to the measure of the stature of the fullness of Christ"   Ephesians 4:11 - 13

- The body of Christ needs to be equipped.

This means they need to be taught and trained in their specific areas of gifting and callings. To teach them refer to theoretical teaching. To train them refers to practical application of what was taught. This can only happen through a proper leadership development plan and personal mentoring. Nowadays we find little mentoring of the sons and daughters of God within the church. As spiritual mothers and fathers to those whom we are discipling, it is our responsibility to mentor them until they reach full maturity in Christ.

Equipping also means to bring the body to wholeness in body, soul and spirit. The church needs to be healed and delivered through proper Holy Spirit ministry from the effects of the past life of sin and iniquity. Iniquity are sins that were passed down from the bloodline.

Equipping also entails the proper laying of the foundation of the believer's walk in Christ. Teaching of the truth of the Word of God, water baptism and baptism in the Holy Spirit with the evidence of speaking in tongues.

We cannot attend church on Sundays, listen to a service and walk out. Every son and daughter of God has a calling, a mandate to be fulfilled in the earth and a destiny in Him that is connected to their inheritance in Christ Jesus. Therefore, the apostolic and prophetic needs to return for God's people to be equipped through the five-fold. No more religion. Each one has a significant part to play and needs to find their place in the end time *Joel 2* army. As a result, the church will become an apostolic hub to equip and sent out.

- The edifying of the body means that the body of Christ needs to be built up in the faith and through the Word of God. New thought patterns need to be established according to Romans 12. It is a total new lifestyle and way of doing church that is coming forth. The sons and daughters of God need to understand and walk in their heavenly personas, their true identity. It needs to be made known to them, prophesied over their lives and they need to be established in their true identities by the laying on of hands of the apostles and prophets. These destinies need to be fathered or mothered until they walk in it.

- Unity of the faith refers to every believer being filled and baptized in the Holy Spirit. Believers need to learn to host His presence and release His power on the earth.

- Knowledge of the Son of God refers to the resurrected Spirit of Christ inside of the believer. We have to be cognizant, aware and knowledgeable about the "person" of the Holy Spirit, the Father and the Son. We need to understand their different natures and areas of gifting bestowed upon mankind. We can only walk in authority and discern the lies of the enemy if we know "who" He is on the inside of us. Then we can know who we are, as who we are, is an extension of who He is. He defines us. We are who He says we are. This leads the believer into true identity (sonship). Without this authority and the true sons and daughters of God fleshing out their true identities and dominion over the evil one, the church cannot conquer. However, the apostolic/prophetic is being restored and in the end time army every son and daughter will demonstrate their true identities and authority. The earth is eagerly waiting for the manifestation of the sons and daughters of God in order for the earth to be subdued to Christ's dominion.

- A perfect man refers to the stature of Christ inside of us, His image portrayed through us. Our faith needs to be perfected through trials and tribulations.

- *James 1.* His image and character are being formed in us through difficult circumstances when the blood covenant is being tested. He comes through for us and we build history with Him on order for us to know that we can trust Him fully. Once we have been tested in the furnace of affliction His image is being displayed through our lives as we proceed from glory to glory in Him. Maturing and fully trusting and dependent on Him alone.

- The fullness of Christ refers to His full image and power, His raw love being on display through our lives to a dying and broken world. Through a lifestyle of total surrender and the Holy Spirit demonstrating and administrating His power through us, a supernatural lifestyle results. Walking in obedience in the kingly anointing. Believers receive the power to move beyond to extend the kingdom for the fulfillment of *Ephesians 1:10: "that in the dispensation of the fullness of the times He might gather together in one all things in Christ, both which are in heaven and which are on earth in Him."* We have entered the phase.

- The fulfillment of the great commission. It is the function of the five-fold ministry leaders as a team to ensure that the harvest is being brought in through the church. In this end time movement of God, we will see a team effort. No one is supposed to be a loner and not be under spiritual covering. As five-fold ministry teams we will work together to gather the final harvest.

- The five-fold ministry leadership gifts have been given as gifts to the body to direct the other groups of giftings, as they are underpinning to the core. Also to make sure that the other two groups of giftings - *Romans 12* giftings, which are redemptive gifts that the Father gave to mankind as well as the *1 Corinthians 12* gifting of the Holy Spirit, is exercised and applied in the church. This will be corrected as part of the restoration process of the church.

FIVE-FOLD MINISTRY OFFICES AND THEIR FUNCTIONS

"And He gave some to be apostles, some prophets, some evangelists and some pastors and teachers" *Ephesians 4:11*

APOSTLE DEFINED

The Greek word apostello is a verb and refers to the "act of sending". The Greek word Apostolos is a noun and refers to "the sent one".

An apostle is one who is sent as a representative of another and bears the full authority of the sender.

The apostle has a heart for the overall vision and is a vision carrier. He receives a vision from God and is then mandated and sent to execute the vision in the earth. An apostle is a master builder. In the same way a CEO is positioned in a company, the same way an apostle is positioned to govern the church and put it in order. An apostle is sent by Christ to be His spokesperson. The apostle lays the foundation of the Word and is a watchdog over doctrine. Others build upon the foundation that has been laid by the apostle.

"Now the wall of the city had twelve foundations, and on them were the names of the twelve apostles of the land" *Revelations 21:14*

It is Jesus Christ who appoints and mandates the apostle with delegated authority for the mandate.

THE CALL OF THE APOSTLE

It is Christ who calls - Jesus calls someone into office. Man cannot appoint an apostle. Leadership only confirms the call. Christ calls ordinary men by simply saying *"follow Me"*, but to the one called this has a powerful impact.

ATTRIBUTES OF THE APOSTLE

- Strong and forceful personality by means of consistent assertiveness of one's own person, ideas and presence. They cannot be ignored. Examples in the New Testament is Paul, an apostle to the Gentiles, and Peter, an apostle to the Jews.

- Great authority. An apostle is an officer of Christ and bears full authority of the One who sent him, Jesus Christ. His accountability is directly to Christ as his authority and mandate comes from Christ.

- A true apostle. The Lord Jesus Christ is behind what they do and say, as they are commissioned for a task. Their authorization is linked to the person of Jesus Christ.

- It is a commissioning rather than an office and comes with much humiliation as to carry the nature of Christ.

- Apostles proclaim the Word and therefore their time should be spent in the Word of God and prayer.

- Full and obedient dedication to the task is demanded.

- Thus, we see that the apostle is an officer of Christ who's primary function is to found (plant) churches or schools.

- Jesus' authority is extended through the apostle.

- Apostles bring the saints to full maturity.

"Therefore I write these things, lest being present I should use sharpness, according to the authority which the Lord has given me for edification (building up) and not for destruction" (Paul speaking) 2 Corinthians 13:10

- The authority of the apostle is limited and extends only to those he has birthed and formed in the churches he planted. Relinquishing authority over other churches whom he did not found or plant.

LEADERSHIP SKILLS OF THE APOSTLE

- Leadership is the ability to inspire others into action, this mantle is upon the apostle.

- Leadership entails vision, confidence, ability and grace. These are all resting upon the shoulders of the apostle as the governing of the church is laid upon the shoulders of the apostle.

- Leadership motivates mass human effort to a common goal. Apostles do this with ease.

- Leadership reads people, determine their strengths and weaknesses and place them in the exact organizational position to best use their strengths. An apostle knows the destinies of their sons and daughters.

- Since apostles are tasked with founding and building up churches, the above grace gifting is significant upon the apostle.

- Apostles possess intimate knowledge of the Lord since he mandated them, and their accountability is directly to Him.

- Apostles have a closeness as they have full power to speak and act as Jesus does.

- They are being directed by the Holy Spirit continually in an effort to lead the church.

- Intimate knowledge comes to the apostle by the Word of God, much prayer and studying of the Word and being led by the Holy Spirit.

- Apostles spend the majority of their time in studying the Word, prayer and fasting. By hearing God's voice and obeying, the apostle knows exactly how to build the church up and lay the foundation through the Holy Spirit's instruction.

SIGNS AND WONDERS

Paul talks about the trademarks of the apostle in *2 Corinthians 12:12*. *"Truly the signs of an apostle were accomplished among you with all perseverance, in signs, wonders and mighty deeds."* With true apostles these signs, wonders and mighty deeds will follow them.

MATURITY AND VERSATILITY OF THE APOSTLE

Apostles need to be matured in character, teaching, training, experience, hardships, trials and tribulations, endurance and humility.

A true apostle needs to be underpinned in all five aspects of the five-fold ministry functions, with qualifications and the necessary ministry experience before they are ordained and released into office by their spiritual oversight. This process can take up to forty years. The apostle must do whatever is needed to find and build up the church at any moment in time until matured leaders are fully equipped to take over and maintain.

FUNCTIONS OF THE APOSTLE

- Evangelism. The apostle evangelizes an area and then plant a church with the new converts. They often stay in one region until the church is established.

- Apostles lay the spiritual foundation. *"For no one can lay any foundation other than the one that is already laid, which is Jesus Christ"*
1 Corinthians 3:9

"Having been built on the foundation of the apostles and prophets, Jesus Christ Himself, being the chief cornerstone." Ephesians 2:20

The apostle becomes the watch dog over doctrine in the church and has the responsibility to make sure that the food of the sheep is not poisoned by heresy and false doctrines of devils.

- Build churches. They edify and build the church up into a living temple and a dwelling place for God in the Spirit. And then they continue to supervise the church in material, as well as spiritual needs.
- Ordains elders (leaders). *"Paul and Barnabas appointed elders for them in each church and with prayer and fasting, committed them to the Lord, in whom they had put their trust."* Acts 14:23

Once the apostle has laid the foundation, ordained the elders, he moves on to a new territory or a new region and starts all over again. He returns from time to time to the established churches to make corrections, check their progress and encourage them.

HARDSHIPS OF THE APOSTLE

Apostles suffer many hardships connected to the nature and call of their function. In the book of Revelations, the apostle John was exiled to the island of Patmos as part of persecution against him for establishing the gospel.

Both Paul and Peter made reference in the Word about their hardships, shipwreck, trials at governmental level and imprisonment. In *2 Corinthians: 11: 22- 28* Paul was mentioning some of the hardships as *"weariness and toil, in sleepless often, in hunger and thirst, in fasting often, in cold and nakedness besides other things, what comes upon me daily: my deep concern for all the churches."*

These are only but a few that he mentioned. True apostles are concerned over the church day and night and has a travail for the body of Christ.

Satan stands up against the apostle. *"For we wanted to come to you - certainly I, Paul, did again and again but satan stopped us"*   *1 Thessalonians 2:18*

I had personal experience of this when I had to attend an important international prophetic round table with apostle Surprise Sithole in Nelspruit and fell sick to the point of being hospitalized for ten days. The spirit of Jezebel wants to attach herself to the apostles to strip them naked of their authority. This is the spirit that we apostles will, especially, encounter in the end time church. However, God is rising up the spirit of Elijah to come against her evil forces.

PROPHET DEFINED

A prophet is a man or woman who is called by Jesus Christ to operate in the office of a prophet as a spokesperson to release the mind of the Father. A prophet is one sent by God to speak the Word of the Lord to:

- A direct word to a person.
- A direct word to a group of people.
- A direct word to a nation.
- A direct word to a church.

The prophet brings a direct word to a specific person or group of people. This is not prophesying in general. A prophet is called by Jesus Christ, they are God trained individuals whom God has molded and shaped through a very difficult process of hardship to be a spokesperson for Himself. A prophet does not belong to himself, but belongs to God first, then to the church and then to himself. The prophet is a gift to the body of Christ. The prophet is the oil to the lamp stand, who is the church, which allows it to burn bright and to give direction and bring correction. The prophet is also a watch dog through intercessory prayer between the enemy and the church. This is the reason why prophets need to be part of a five-fold ministry team within the church.

THE CALL OF THE PROPHET

Isaiah's call: *"Also I heard the voice of the Lord saying: whom shall I send, and who will go for Us?" Then I said, "Here am I! Send me."*   *Isaiah 6:8*

Take note that "Us" is spelt with a capital letter, in other words, heaven was asking this question. God Himself, Jesus Christ and the Holy Spirit. The counsel of God was looking for someone to send.

This was the hour of Isaiah's call. Isaiah answered the call by saying *"Here I am, send me."* Prophets are called and will have a personal encounter with the Lord as part of their testimony of being called.

Jeremiah's call: *"Then the Word of the Lord came to me, saying: "Before I formed you in the womb I knew you; before you were born, I sanctified you: I ordained you as a prophet to the nations."*

"Then I said: "Ah Lord God! Behold I cannot speak, for I am a youth. But the Lord said to me: "Do not say, I am a youth, for you shall go to all whom I send you, and whatever I command you, you shall speak. Do not be afraid of their faces, for I am with you to deliver you, says the Lord. Then the Lord put forth His hand and touched my mouth, and the Lord said to me: Behold I have put My words in your mouth. See, I have this day set you over the nations and over the kingdoms, to root out and to pull down, to destroy and to throw down to build and to plant."
Jeremiah 1:4 - 10

The prophet is called

What we notice concerning the call of the prophet is the encounter God has with the chosen prophet and also a specific mandate released to the prophet as well as a specific metron of influence that only God determines through His sovereign will.

Persons called and matured to this office are endowed with the necessary grace gifting from above. Prophets need to be matured through a process of hardship. The prophet's character needs to be established and be above reproach.

CHARACTERISTICS/ATTRIBUTES OF A PROPHET

- Strong personality. Prophets are intense about their walk with God and intense about atmospheres surrounding them. They are sensitive to the spiritual realm and pick up atmospheres. It is hard for a true prophet to understand how people cannot be a hundred percent committed to God. Prophets have to deliver strong messages with authority, hence the strong personality.

- Direct issue orientated. Prophets see things in either black or white. There are no gray areas with a true prophet. Either right or wrong. The prophet is low on compassion and mercy over people who do not measure up to the way God sees them. However, the matured prophet loves and cares about God's people to the extent that they often mother/father their destinies. Matured prophets do not compromise.

- Strong in prayer. The prophet is given to much prayer and is ushered into the secret place by God. There is a definite pull towards the secret place and times of solitude. The true prophet carries a burden for God's will and His people. The prophet is intense, and this flows over into his prayer life. Prophets engage in intercession as they are mandated by God to pray and fast and often carry a burden for a nation, church, individual or circumstance that God has mandated them with. They are often in travail for that which God wants to establish in the earth.

- Outward life in order. The prophet has his outward life in order as he sees things either right or wrong. The prophet is not easily ensnared into sin as he continually ministers before the throne. However, the prophet may easily be ensnared to pride and judgmentalism. These two are satan's snares against the prophet.

- Authority and power. Prophets move with great authority and power in the prophetic gift. This authority and power are delegated authority and power on display as the prophet is only the conduit.

- Poor long-term counsellors. Prophets lack the mercy and patience for this long-term counseling. The prophet delivers a direct message and then moves on.

- Spiritual gifts accompany a prophetic call. All the *1 Corinthians 12* gifts of the Holy Spirit flow through the prophet as a result of an intensive prayer life and purity. However, the prophet is most skilled in the revelatory gifts of the Holy Spirit. Word of wisdom, word of knowledge and discernment. The prophet easily discerns demonic influence and knows how to deal with it.

LEADERSHIP SKILLS

The prophet serves as a leader on the five-fold ministry team appointed to the church. Therefore, the prophet also has to learn to submit to other leadership offices, especially the pastor of the local church. The pastor and the prophet serve two very different functions. The pastor has a heart for the flock and sometimes oversees and allows wrongs to creep in as his heart is focused on the people and not on issues. He is people orientated whereas the prophet is issue orientated.

The prophet's concern is God's will only. He places the mandate of the Lord above his own concern for individuals in the church. The prophet has a long-range vision for God's will whereas the pastor deals with the immediate. The prophet delivers a word from God to the pastor or the church and then his work is done. He moves on. Prophets travel continuously and also work outside of the church to deliver God's Word. God stirs up the prophet to bring error and hidden sin to the light to be dealt with. As a result, prophets are normally not popular. The pastor shows mercy whereas the prophet deals directly, willing to accept consequences. Prophets are not without honor except in their hometown and among his relatives and in his own household.

FUNCTIONS OF THE PROPHET

- They are intercessors as previously mentioned and position against the viles and the plans of the enemy wanting to attack the church.

- Prophets teach and equip the body of Christ.

- They are the oil to the lamp stand, the church and leads and give direction.

- Prophets point out sin and error in the church as they are strong in the Word and discernment

- They edify the body of Christ, building it up through the Word of God.

- They are part of the foundation of the church and walk closely alongside the apostle in laying the foundation.

- Prophets directs people's destinies in Christ and establish their identities in Him.
- Prophets belong to God first and secondly to the church.

HARDSHIPS OF THE PROPHET

God Himself trains and calls the prophet. They go through many trials and tribulations and are tested in the furnace of fire to become matured. Prophets are many times being misunderstood. Prophets are loners and do not have many friends. Prophets are ridiculed and it is many a time the church who kills the prophet.

SIGNS OF A MATURE PROPHET

- Mature prophets identify and love God's people.

- They are humble.

- A mature prophet esteems other prophets and are not jealous of them.

- Mature prophets submit to leadership and spiritual authority.

- Mature prophets realize that their office is a hard place.

- Mature prophets have great discernment and understanding regarding the spiritual realm and the manifestations of God's glory.

- Mature prophets realize that there are times when God speaks words to them that are to be kept confidential or to be released only on God's timing.

- Mature prophets are not lone rangers. They realize that they belong to the church.

EVANGELIST DEFINED

The evangelist is called by Christ and anointed to preach the gospel, the kingdom of God and to bring salvation to lost sinners. The evangelist's primary function is to proclaim the "good news" of salvation through the blood of Jesus to the lost. Evangelists have a heart for the lost and the harvest and wants to see souls saved. Evangelists carry a burden and travail for souls. Evangelists bring in the lost and moves on. They also baptize the new recruits and work outside of the church although they are also part of a five-fold ministry team of the local church.

CALL OF THE EVANGELIST AND HIS BURDEN

The evangelist has an intense understanding of the fate of the unsaved. His heart aches for the lost and he has a cry on the inside for the lost. His continual prayer is for the lost. It is the harvest field that drives him and therefore he often forgets about the rest, leaving saved people uncared for. When the evangelist has made new converts, he quickly wants to move on whereas these new converts need to be sent to local churches, or the apostle moves in to plant a church should there be no church. The evangelist, when called, does not have a long incubation period of training as their message is always the same - salvation and kingdom. However, the evangelist normally carries a very strong personal testimony. They equip the body of Christ and teach and train other evangelists in the field. They often operate strongly in gifts of healing, signs and wonders.

ATTRIBUTES OF THE EVANGELIST

- Evangelists often have great communication skills and strong voices that carry authority

- They have a convincing personality and nature and are compassionate.

- They are driven and energetic.

- They enjoy talking.

- The carry a travail for the lost and are not shy to approach anyone on the street.

- They are focused on salvation only and carry a strong testimony.

LEADERSHIP SKILLS OF THE EVANGELIST

Although they form part of the five-fold ministry team of the church, they often get out from under authority and want to run on their own. They are continually traveling as they work outside of the church. The local church sends out the evangelist and on his return he ought to report back to the leadership team and the church on a regular basis. Submission to leadership is of utmost importance in order for the evangelist to have the necessary prayer covering, as many a times they enter places where there is witchcraft or where it may even be dangerous to go. Accountability is of the essence.

FUNCTIONS OF THE EVANGELIST

- Gathering in of the harvest.

- Equipping other evangelists in the body of Christ.

- There are two types of evangelists: corporate evangelism, preaching to large crowds, carrying a corporate anointing and personal evangelism, evangelizing one on one.

- Baptizing new converts.

- Preaching the kingdom with a demonstration of healing, signs and wonders.

HARDSHIPS OF THE EVANGELIST

Evangelists travel a lot and have to adapt to all sorts of circumstances. They are not always accepted, as they are bold in their personalities. They need to guard against taking glory for themselves as it is God Who empowers them to perform miracles and wonders and especially healing powers. These powers come from the only true living God and the glory belongs to Him alone. The evangelist needs maturing in the field. Pride and ego can be inflated, and they continually need to guard against it. If new converts are not being discipled by the church after they have been saved, they can fall by the wayside which weighs heavily on the evangelist.

PASTOR DEFINED

A pastor is a shepherd and carries a heart that is directed to the flock and their needs. Pastors nurture the flock. *"Shepherd the flock of God the is among you, serving as overseers."*
1 Peter 5:2

The shepherd goes before the flock to protect them, guide, feed and care for them. God calls shepherds after His own heart.

THE FUNCTION OF THE PASTOR

- Every pastor must have a call of Christ to the office. The call needs to be confirmed by the leadership after the individual has received confirmation by God.

- The office of a pastor is a sacred position.

- The pastor is in charge and responsible for the congregation and the correct functioning of the house of the Lord he/she was entrusted to him by the apostle who planted the church.

- The pastor carries authority over the congregation which is an extension of God's authority.

- The pastor builds and nurtures the sheep.

- The pastor teaches and is instrumental in counseling to bring the body to full maturity as part of the five-fold function.

- The pastor has an administrative role and oversees the congregation.

ATTRIBUTES AND CHARACTER OF THE PASTOR

The book of Titus and especially Titus 1 deals with this aspect.

- The pastor identifies with the people.

- Loves the church and the people of God.

- Flows in great mercy.

- Cares more about the people than the issues.

- Focusses on the sinner and not the sin.

- The character of the pastor needs to be above reproach, above any action that opens him/her up to blame. A blameless character.

- One wife.

- Sober, not given to drunkenness.

- Self-controlled, to be in control of emotions, words and desires.

- Respectable, solicitous to guests and kind in seeing to their needs.

- Not violent, not to act with strong physical feeling or emotion.

- Gentle, patient, kind and sincere.

- Not quarrelsome or verbal strife marked by anger.

- Not a lover of money.

- Manage his own family well, especially those under his roof. Grownups have their own choices.

- His children to obey him with proper respect.

- Not a recent convert, but someone who has studied and shown himself approved.

- Good reputation with outside, respected in the community.

LEADERSHIP SKILLS OF THE PASTOR

He is part of the five-fold ministry team and is directly accountable to the apostle who appointed him over the congregation. He has to have an administrative skill. Influential with people. Good leadership skills. Earn love and respect of the community.

FUNCTIONS OF THE PASTOR

- Preaching and teaching the Word of God and activating the congregation to the action of the Word.

- Teaching, whereas preaching motivates to act, teaching tells us how to act. Pastors need to equip the body of Christ and bring them to maturity.

- Mentoring. Pastors are to be wise advisors in the counsels of God and release God's wisdom into personal problems and matters concerning the congregation's families.

- Managing and administrating, they manage the affairs of the church. They officiate marriages.

- Pastors manage and appoint trustworthy officials to manage the finances of the church.

- Pastors guard the flock against anything that can harm them.

- Pastors discipline and admonish according to the instructions given in the Word of God.

HARDSHIPS OF THE PASTOR

- Not always liked and many times gossiped over.

- Improper use of the pulpit to discipline members. This can be a downside to the pastor's call.

- Financial abuse can easily happen. Therefore, there has to be a proper church administration and financial board in place.

- Sometimes families run churches, this is called Nepotism and is not congruent to the Word of God.

- Not disciplining and overlooking sexual and other sins in the church.

- Fear of man and rejection may arise.

- Fear of losing pastorate or financial support.

- Looses vision easily.

- Undue political involvement can also be a problem.

TEACHER DEFINED

A teacher is someone called by Christ to steward the Word of God and to make the Word palatable for everyone to gain an understanding to a point where they start to change. To nourish and equip the body of Christ to grow to full understanding and the knowledge of Christ. There rests a double responsibility on the teacher of the Word. *"Not many of you should presume to be teachers, my brothers, because you know that we who teach will be judged more strictly."*
James 3:1

CALL OF THE TEACHER

- The teacher makes the Word palatable.

- Easily sees Biblical truths.

- Teacher has the ability to break doctrine open so that it can be easily understood.

- The teacher touches the heart with the Word to bring change about.

- The teacher equips the body of Christ, nourishes it and brings it to full maturity in Christ.

- Teachers do a lot of research.

- Teachers hold degrees and studies to show themselves approved as they need to be well undergirded in the Word of God.

- Teachers carries underpinning knowledge and revelation.

- Teachers have a natural speaking ability.

- Has a burden for the church and heart for Truth.

- They often travel.

There are two types of teachers:

- A reproductive teacher who teaches a syllabus that is already written and approved. They tend to work inside the church and are stationed.

- On the other hand, there are revelatory teachers. They receive revelation regarding the Word of God and teach a fresh revelation on God's Word. They mostly work outside of the church and travels a lot.

ATTRIBUTES OF A TEACHER

- Heart for the Truth.

- Well-spoken and articulated.

- Fond of research.

- Carry authority over the Word of God.

- Speaks with authority that comes from Christ Who called them.

- Black and white orientated.

- Structured in their approach and to the point.

LEADERSHIP SKILLS OF THE TEACHER

Teachers submit as part of the five-fold ministry team in- and outside of the church. The apostles are the watch dogs over the doctrine and should scrutinize all syllabuses and study materials before it is taught.

FUNCTIONS OF THE TEACHER

- Compiling syllabus.

- Travels to teach in regions elsewhere.

- Do research gathering of information.

- Study continually.

HARDSHIPS OF THE TEACHER

- Teachers are judged strictly according to *James 3:1*.

- They can be impatient to there who differ from them.

- Reluctant to receive correction.

- Has a casual interest in evangelism.

- Cannot accept error.

INTERACTION OF THE FIVE-FOLD MINISTRY WITHIN THE CHURCH AND THE MARKET PLACE

In the end times the church and the marketplace will become one. It should never have been divorced from one another. The marketplace will find it's strategies and revelation within the ecclesia and the ecclesia will be funded by the marketplace to bring in the end time harvest and to equip. God is restoring the combining of the priestly and kingly anointing as to accomplish His end time mission for the church. There is an enormous harvest that will come in through revival as a result of the shaking of all things. This will have to be funded. Furthermore, the body of Christ must be prepared and equipped to gather in the harvest and make them ready to meet the Lord in the clouds. This takes time and is costly.

Whether applicable to the church or the marketplace, God's principles for leadership and the model Jesus left behind remains the same for both arenas.

The apostle to the church fulfills the same function as the CEO to a business or organization. The prophet to the church fulfills the same function as a director of company. The evangelist to the church fulfills the same function as the marketing person to an organization. The pastor to the church fulfills the same function as the public relations and human resources officer to a company. The teacher of the church can be likened to a trainer and consultant in a company. Governed by the same principles and biblical leadership model based on *Ephesians 4:11*.

In the church environment the evangelist goes out to bring in the lost, baptizes them and gather the new converts into the church. The local pastor then takes over and makes sure that the new converts are nurtured, healed and delivered. They are being counseled by the pastoral team. The pastor makes sure that the church acts as a green house where these new converts can grow spiritually to full maturity in Christ. The teacher then comes along and teaches them all the mysteries of the Word of God. The prophet directs them towards their destinies and equips them. They lay foundation alongside the apostle who is the mother/father of the house. Their destinies are being fathered/mothered as they are mentored. The apostle will make sure that the house is well structured and set in order. The apostle will oversee the five-fold ministry offices in specific functions and roles, to make sure the church functions well. They keep a close eye over sound doctrine as to make sure that heresy does not enter into the church. The apostle makes sure that the saints are equipped thoroughly and grow to the fullness of maturity as sons and daughter of Christ.

When the church is well structured and the five-fold ministry is in place, then the church will fulfill its mandate, taking into account that these leaders are not man appointed, but are appointed by Christ, the Head of the church. By the time these leaders are recognized by man, it is only a confirmation after much fasting and prayer.

CHAPTER 9
THE ORDER OF MELCHIZEDEK

THE ORDER OF MELCHIZEDEK

There are many mysteries in the Word of God that need to be searched out.

"It is the glory of God to conceal a matter, but the glory of kings is to search out a matter."
Proverbs 25:2

Paul was speaking about these mysteries to the Corinthians when he was saying *"let a man so account of us as to the mysteries of Christ, and stewards of the mysteries of God."*

It is God's requirement that His mysteries be stewarded well. These mysteries are the secret things of God that must be "revealed" to be understood. A mystery is not something that cannot be understood, but it is something that is hidden to the sight of man. However, it is the purposes of God that He will reveal to us His mysteries when we are ready to receive the revelation and be trusted with it. The mysteries of God and stewardship goes hand in glove. God will never give us stewardship over anything if we are not ready and prepared to receive it. His revelation requires maturity in the Spirit, as He needs to trust us with it.

"To make all see what is the fellowship of the mystery, which from the beginning of the ages has been hidden in God Who created all things through Jesus Christ."
Ephesians 3:9

The church is sitting in a place of spiritual immaturity and needs to be equipped to full maturity by the five-fold ministry in these last days. Christ is coming for a victorious, holy and mature church.

"For though by this time you ought to be teachers, you need someone to teach you again the first principles of the oracles of God; And you have come to need milk and not solid food. For everyone who only partakes of milk is unskilled in the Word of righteousness, for he is a babe. But solid food belongs to those that are of full age, that is, those who by reason of use, have their senses exercised to discern both good and evil."
Hebrews 5:12 - 14

Paul admonished the church as all believers need to come to the fullness of Christ, full maturity to understand the end time mysteries of God and also to discern in these last days that which is false and that which is true. Paul explains the importance of being skilled in righteousness and encourages the Hebrews to grow and learn deeper things.

It is the time for the mysteries of God to be manifested. The bride must mature before Christ returns. When you are unskilled it causes the spiritual senses to be dull and there will be a lack of discernment. The body of Christ will not survive the end times without proper discernment. We are now preparing the way for the second coming of our Lord Jesus Christ and we are preparing the church to make herself ready. If your sword, the Sword of the Word, is sharp, you will discern and God will entrust you with the deeper things of His kingdom, His mysteries. Someone who is immature cannot steward God's Word well and mysteries need to be stewarded according to the Word.

These end times which we have approached now, will be earmarked also by false teachers and doctrines of devils, false prophets and false apostles. Jesus is coming for a matured and pure remnant.

The subject on the order of Melchizedek is one of God's mysteries that is revealed now and the corporate destiny of the end time ecclesia is wrapped up in the order of Melchizedek being restored and understood in the church. Individual destiny is wrapped up in true identity. Both need to be restored.

In the last days concerning the end time remnant church, this order must rise and be restored. The word "order' in this biblical context means that God has ordered the world and His kingdom ways and principles into a state of "order". It refers to a company of people, His true church, His priests and kings to walk in the order or ways that He has established it to be. The remnant needs to be equipped to walk in God's ways and honor His "order" and ordinances throughout the Word. His kingdom is a kingdom of *"righteousness and peace and joy in the Holy Spirit."*

Romans 14:17

WHO IS MELCHIZEDEK

In the light of *Romans 14:17* stating that the kingdom of God is a kingdom of *"righteousness, peace and joy in the Holy Spirit"* let us now have a look as to whom Melchizedek is according to the Word.

- Melchizedek was the king of Salem.   *Genesis 14:18*
- Melchizedek was the priest of God most high.   *Genesis 14:18*
- Melchizedek was king of righteousness and king of peace.   *Hebrews 7:1 - 3*
- Melchizedek was without father, without mother and without genealogy having neither beginning of days nor end of life.   *Hebrews 7:3*
- Melchizedek was made "like" the son of God. (Jesus Christ)   *Hebrews 7:3*
- Melchizedek remains a priest continually.   *Hebrews 7:3*

"For this Melchizedek, king of Salem, priest of the most high God who met Abraham returning from the slaughter of the kings and blessed him, to whom also Abraham gave a tenth part of all, first being translated "king of righteousness" and then also king of Salem, meaning king of peace, without father, without mother, without genealogy, having neither beginning of days nor end of life, but made like the Son of God, remains a priest continually." Hebrews 7:1 - 3

With all the above in. Mind let us unfold the mystery of Melchizedek as the end time church's corporate destiny is embedded in this order. It has become significant times that that we are living in. For the purposes of this book we will look into this `" order", but as this book will also be a syllabus, this will be taught in full detail in the School of Ministry regarding the end times and the preparing of the remnant church.

In the Old Testament the Levitical priesthood offered animal sacrifices. With the death and resurrection of Jesus Christ the Levitical priesthood was replaced by a new priesthood that images after the order of the priesthood of Melchizedek.

"Christ was designated as High Priest by the order of Melchizedek". Hebrews 8:10

Jesus is our High Priest after the order of Melchizedek. The book of Hebrews deals with the priesthood and offerings of Jesus modeling after this new "order" - the "order" of Melchizedek.

The name Melchizedek can be divided into two parts. "Melchi" meaning royal king, someone who has ascended to the throne of God. King of righteousness who brings righteous judgment. An upright king in whom there is no partiality.

"Zedek" meaning righteousness. Someone who has an upright spirit.

Melchizedek was the king of Salem according to Genesis 14:18. *"Salem"* meaning peace. Salem is also the ancient word for "Jerusalem". Jerusalem is a city of peace.

"In Salem is also His tabernacle and His dwelling place in Zion".   Psalm 76:2

Salem is a peaceful city as a result of a righteous king ruling and His presence abiding. This is what God is restoring now. A dwelling place for Himself in the Spirit - mount Zion where there will be peace and righteous ruling.

Melchizedek was a king of a peaceful city. A city where God's rule reigned. Righteousness leads to peace and joy in the Holy Spirit, which is the kingdom of God. The scepter of His throne is righteousness. The city of Salem and His dwelling place that He will now establish by the restoration of this kingly order and rule on the earth through the restoration of the "order" of Melchizedek and of His sons and daughters walking in this kingly rule in the end times, will cause righteousness, peace and kingly ruling from heavenly places to return to the remnant church.

The city of Salem is a description of heaven. Heaven and the rule of heaven is being established on the earth in the end times. The "order" of Melchizedek combined the priestly and kingly offices that were divided by the Levital priesthood. As we have stated, the priesthood under the law separated the kingly and the priestly. This is being restored in the church as the marketplace (kingly) and the church (priestly) joins forces for the final harvest to be gathered. This will be explained later.

Melchizedek is a priest of the most high God. The Hebrew word for the priest of Israel is "kohen", which means chief ruling priest. A priest of a company of priests or many priests.

The most high God lives in lofty mountains. - the only true living God "Elohim". Melchizedek is a representation of one of the aspects of the only true living God.

"I will ascend above the heights of the clouds, I will be like the most high."

Isaiah 14:14

So, we learn that Melchizedek is like the true living God. He is not the true living God, but he is like Him. In the same way we are created in the likeness and image of God. It is a representation. Looking at the attributes of Melchizedek's name and the meaning of the city that he was king over "Salem", gives us an indication of the righteous rule of God and the peace of His kingdom that will be restored before the coming of Jesus Christ.

God lives on lofty mountains. Concerning the fall of Lucifer the Word declares: *"For you have said in your heart: I will ascend into heaven, I will exalt my throne above the stars of God; I will also sit on the mount of the congregation on the farthest side of the north."*
Isaiah 14:13

There is also a temple in heaven. *"He who overcomes, I will make him a pillar in the temple of My God, and he shall go out no more. I will write on him the name of My God and the name of the city of my God, the new Jerusalem, which comes down out of heaven from My God. And I will write on him My new Name."*

Revelations 3;12

A temple means a sacred place of worship. Melchizedek is the kingly priest of the temple in heaven. He is the chief high priest of the temple in heaven. Melchizedek was represented in the earth and in heaven. The Father is represented in heaven and earth as He is omnipotent and omnipresent. Jesus Christ is represented in heaven and earth simultaneously as He is seated at the right hand of God on His throne and His Word was made flesh and His Spirit which is still with us on earth. The Holy Spirit is also represented both on earth and in heaven at the same time.

"For there are three that bear witness in heaven; The Father, the Word (Jesus is the Word that was made flesh when He came to the earth), and the Holy Spirit, and these three are One. And there are three that bear witness on the earth; the Spirit, the Water and the Blood, and these three agree as one." 1 John 5:7 - 8

The Holy Spirit is the third person of the godly triune in heaven and the first person of the godly triune on earth.

We are also represented both in heaven and earth as we are seated with Him in heavenly places. *"He raised us up together and made us sit together in the heavenly places in Christ Jesus."*   *Ephesians 2:6*

In the culmination of all of this we need to rule and reign as priests and kings and bring heaven to earth. As we are priests and kings at the same time, the end time remnant church will corporately decree and legislate with authority from heaven to establish God's end time purposes on the earth. That is the reason for this order to be understood and restored. The church is mostly sitting in the outer court, not taking up their priestly mantle and kingly authority.

"Without father, without mother, without genealogy, having neither beginning of days nor end of life, but made like the Son of God, remains a priest continually."
                              Hebrews 7:3

Melchizedek has always been existing in the same way in the same way we existed already before the foundation of the earth, as we were predestined and foreknown by God. We existed before we were sent to the earth to complete the assignments God gave us.

Melchizedek is like the Son of God and has been from eternity. He took on the image of the Son of God. The exact copy of Jesus Christ just as Jesus is the exact image and copy of His Father.

"Who being the brightness of His gory and the express image of His Person."
                              Hebrews 1:3

The Word of God speaks about our adversary, the devil, who walks around "like" a roaring lion, seeking whom he may devour according to *1 Peter 5:8*

This does not mean that the devil is a lion. No, he only presents himself as a lion.

Jesus also does not have an earthly Father, neither a beginning nor an end. He is eternal and comes from eternity. He manifests Himself as a priest and a king, "order" of Melchizedek, as it is only one of the seven manifestations of him on earth and in heaven. He makes intercession for us continually before the throne of God.

"Now He (Jesus) Who searches the hearts and knows what the mind of the Spirit is, because He makes intercession for the saints according to the Will of God."
Romans 8:27

He is our great High Priest according to the "order" of Melchizedek. A righteous Priest and a King that rules. He is the Prince of peace. *"This hope we have as an anchor for the soul, both sure and steadfast, and which enters the Presence behind the veil, where the forerunner has entered for us, even Jesus having become High Priest forever according to the "order" of Melchizedek." Hebrews 6:19 - 20*

As a righteous king he will judge his people, not according to what he sees, nor decide by the hearing of his ears, but with righteousness he shall judge. This same order of judgments, righteous rulership and priestly intercession was written about Jesus in Isaiah 11:4. We will discuss this rule and reign later.

PURPOSE OF THE ORDER OF MALCHIZEDEK

The purpose of the order of Melchizedek can be summed up in the following explanation:

- His Name is "Branch". *"There shall come forth a Rod (His authority) from the stem of Jesse, and a Branch (Jesus) shall grow out of His roots. The seven-fold Holy Spirit will rest upon Him, the Spirit of the Lord, the Spirit of wisdom and understanding, the Spirit of counsel and might, the Spirit of knowledge and the Spirit of the fear of the Lord."* Isaiah 11:1,2

- He (Jesus) is the forerunner for the saints and intercedes. *"Therefore, He is also able to save to the uttermost those who come to God through him, since He always lives to make intercession for them."* Hebrews 7:25

- He will build the temple. *"Therefore, they are before the throne of God and serve Him day and night in His temple. And He who sits on the throne will dwell among them."*
Revelation 7:15

And again, in the book of Revelation, *"Then the temple of God was open in heaven, the Arc of His Covenant was seen in His temple. And there were lightnings noises, thundering and earthquake and great hail."*

Revelation 11:19

> *"And another angel came out of the temple, crying with a loud voice to Him who sat on the cloud, thrust in Your sickle and reap, for the time has come for You to reap, for the harvest of the earth is ripe."*
>
> Revelation 14:15

Another scripture in the book of Revelation mentioning the temple in heaven is *Revelation 16:1*. This is ample proof that there is a temple in heaven. He is building His temple. We are His temple on earth, and we need to be made ready as there will come a day when the new Jerusalem will descend from heaven and we as the temple of Christ will be joined to the temple in heaven when Christ will reign eternally.

- He bears the glory. *"Who being the brightness of His glory and the express image of His person and upholding all things by the Word of His power, when He had by Himself purged our sins, sat down at the right hand of the Majesty on high."*
Hebrews 1:3

In the same manner the end time church will be carrying His glory.

> *"Arise, shine; for your light has come. And the glory of the Lord is risen upon you. For behold, the darkness shall cover the earth, and deep darkness the people, but the Lord will arise over you, and His glory will be seen upon you."*
>
> Isaiah 60:1,2

This is a true picture of the end time glorious church that Christ will be returning for. Now we can see the real purpose and need for the order of Melchizedek to be restored in the end times. The purpose is for all of the aforementioned to manifest. The Hebrew word for "glory" is "kabod". The Hebrew word "kabod" refers to the weight of His glory. The church needs to be prepared to carry the weight of His glory. When the glory of the Lord had filled the house of God, it was so heavy that the priests could not stand. The weight of His glory cannot be measured by man, as it is working for us a far more exceeding and eternal weight of glory. No man can stand in the weight of His glory. Nothing that is defiled or sick, neither any demon spirit can stand in His glory. Through His glory He sovereignly does what He wills. His glory expressed His honor and majesty. His glory is His manifested presence.

Everyone who is called by His name, whom He has created for His glory, He has formed and made to be glory carriers and to live in the light of His glory continually. All of this was discussed in Chapter One but still remains part of the order of Melchizedek fulfilled in Christ.

- Rule on His throne. *"A scepter of righteousness is the scepter of Your kingdom. You have loved righteousness and hated lawlessness; therefore God, Your God, has anointed You with the oil of gladness more than Your companions."*
    Hebrews 1:8,9

This is what God the Father voiced over Jesus Christ. This is the way that Jesus Christ will rule and judge from His throne.

"His delight is in the fear of the Lord, and He shall not judge by the sight of His eyes, nor decide by the hearing of His ears; but with righteousness He shall judge the poor (poor in Spirit) and decide with equity for the meek of the earth; He shall strike the earth with a rod of His mouth, and with the breath of His lips He shall slay the wicked. Righteousness shall be the belt of His loins, and faithfulness the belt of His waist.   Isaiah 11:3 - 5

Should you continue to read from these verses you will notice that peace followed His judgment. It is well with the city, nation or temple where the righteousness of God reigns as the inhabitants will live in peace. What really is important to realize is that He judges from a spiritual point of view, not by the natural, over what He sees or hears with the naked ear. In the same way we need to rule from mount Zion and discern in the Spirit to hear and see, so that we will be in right standing with God and know how to rule and reign without prejudice. We need to learn this in the present dispensensation as we will be judging with Him in the age to come. If we cannot get it right now, how will we know how to judge righteously with Him in the age to come.

"Do you not know that the saints will judge the world? And if the world will be judged by you, are you unworthy to judge the smallest matters? Do you not know that we shall judge angels? How much more, things that pertain to this life? If then you have judgments concerning things pertaining to this life, do you appoint those who are at least esteemed by the church to judge? I say this to your shame. Is it so, that there is not a wise

man   among you, not even one, who will be able to judge between his brethren?"
1 Corinthians 6:2 - 5

Paul admonishing and warning the church to be wise. This needs to be restored as righteous judgment is part of the order of Melchizedek and we are being prepared for an end time war and for eternity as God's perspective is an eternal perspective.

- A priest. *"The Lord has sworn and will not change His mind, You are a priest forever according to the order of Melchizedek."   Psalms 110:4*

There was a need for a new priesthood. "Therefore, if perfection were through the Levitical priesthood (Old Testament), what further need was there that another priest should rise according to the order of Melchizedek, and not be called according to the order of Aaron? For the priesthood being changed, of necessity there is also a change of the law. For He of Whom these things are spoken belongs to another tribe, from which no man has officiated at the altar. For it is evident that our Lord arose from Juda, of which tribe Moses spoke nothing concerning priesthood. And it is yet far more evident, if, in the likeness of Melchizedek, there arises another priest who has come, not according to the law of a fleshly commandment, but according to the power of an endless life (eternal priest) for He testifies: "You are a priest forever according to the order of   Melchizedek." For on the one hand there is an annulling of the former commandment because of its weakness and unprofitableness, for the law made nothing perfect; on the other hand, there is the bringing in of a beter hope, through which we draw near to God."   Hebrews 7:11 - 19

Jesus Christ is our eternal High Priest and as a forerunner ushered in a new "order" by which Jesus became our surety of a better and eternal covenant. Therefore, He is also able to save to the uttermost those who come to God through Him, since He always lives to make intercession for them. The old was being made absolute and we now have a High Priest seated at the right hand of the throne of the Majesty of heavens, a Minister of the sanctuary and of the true tabernacle which the Lord erected and not man. Before Jesus took on the role of Messiah, He took on the manifestation of Melchizedek.

- Peace between both the priestly and the kingly. *"Then he (king Solomon) set up the pillars by the vestibule of the temple; he set up the pillar on the right and called its name Jachin, and he set up the pillar on the left and called its name Boaz."*
1 Kings 7:21

This is a very interesting thing that king Solomon did as he received the design of the temple from God. These two pillars on both sides of the temple are representative of the priestly and kingly functions of the order of Melchizedek. The pillar on the left was called "Jachin". The Hebrew meaning of the name "Jachin" means "He establishes". This directly refers to the priestly function which is a function of establishing God's people in His ways.

On the right-hand side was another pillar at the entrance of the temple,   called "Boaz". The name "Boaz" means "in him is strength". Boaz is a biblical figure appearing in the book of Ruth in the Hebrew Bible, and in the genealogies of Jesus in the New Testament. Boaz was a biblical figure that represented the marketplace and kingly anointing to rule and provide. We now see that the kingly and priestly order of Melchizedek was already represented in the temple of Solomon and had both a prominent place at the entrance of the temple. In the end time move of God the priestly and kingly order of Melchizedek will also be prominent and be represented within the remnant church. There will be no more separation between these two realms as we find it now, but there will be peace between the priestly and the kingly. Peace will reign between these two offices of priest and king.

The kingly is an interpretation of the marketplace, as Boaz and Abraham were wealthy men. A fusion of peace will be in-between the priesthood serving full time at the altar and the kingly which also represents the marketplace. Kings will receive their revelation and strategies within the ecclesia in the last days from the priests and the priests will receive provision to fund the end time harvest that is at hand. Right from the beginning there was blessing and peace between these two functions as priests and kings. Remember it was separated from one another by the Old Testament priesthood of Levi. This will be restored in the end times. Here is the proof that there was peace and blessing between these two functions. Look at the interaction between these two offices from the book of Genesis.

> *"Then Melchizedek, king of Salem (peace), brought out bread and wine (priestly function to serve communion) he was priest of the Most High only living God". "And he blessed him (Abram) and said: "Blessed be Abram of God Most High possessor of heaven and earth; and blessed be God Most High, Who has delivered your enemies into your hand." "And He (Abram) gave him (Melchizedek) a tithe of all."*   Genesis 14:18 - 20

Look at the interaction here. The priesthood, Melchizedek, served the Covenant, bread and wine to Abram. Melchizedek served Abram the bread of life and the wine from heaven which a symbol of life in the Spirit. Melchizedek ministered to Abram true life and counsel from heaven. The kings (marketplace) will not be able to function in these last days without the counsel of heaven which will be found in the true remnant church. The priest needs to bless the destinies of the kings in order for them to be established as the kingdom of God is a judicial system that functions on agreement. This is a kingdom principle.

Jesus said: *"Again I say to you that if two of you agree on the earth concerning anything that they ask, it will be done for them by My Father in heaven."*
Matthew 18:19

Then Melchizedek blessed Abram and prophesied and decreed over him that he will be a possessor of the blessings of Heaven and Earth. Abram will be blessed both in heaven and on the earth. I thoroughly believe that it was this decree that Melchizedek made over Abram which caused him to be supernaturally blessed to have a son when him and his wife were over the age of childbearing. Melchizedek brought heaven's purposes down to the earth in making a declaration over Abram. God honored it and established it in the earth. This is how the priesthood will decree a thing from heavenly places, as we are seated with Christ in heavenly places, on the earth in these last days and God will establish it. This is exactly how God's purposes on the earth will be established in these last days. Melchizedek also declared that God delivered Abram from his enemies on the earth and that was also established for Abram. Melchizedek also blessed God Most High. Look at this powerful priestly function on display empowering the kingly office that Abram walked in.

Abram was so thankful that he gave Melchizedek a tithe of all he had. This order is returning and restored in the end times. The kings funding the ecclesia which represents the priestly, and the priestly decreeing God's purposes over the kings for it to be fulfilled in the earth. Peace and blessing between these two offices restored.

Furthermore, again repeated in the New Testament. *"For this Melchizedek, king of Salem, priest of the Most High God, who met Abraham returning from the slaughter of the kings and blessed him, to whom also Abraham gave a tenth part of all, first being translated "king of righteousness" and then also king of Salem, meaning "king of peace".*
Hebrews 7:1,2

Be cognizant that Abraham's name was changed from Abram to Abraham, after the promise of God and the fulfillment of the promise. Now the priest Melchizedek again met Abraham after the promise was established and fulfilled and also after that which

Melchizedek prophesied over Abraham concerning both the promise and his enemies being fulfilled. How do we know that? Melchizedek met Abraham after his name was changed and also met Abraham when he was returning from the slaughter of his enemies. Again, Melchizedek blessed Abraham and Abraham tithed a tenth part of all. This is full circle. The priest blessing God, blessing and decreeing over the king and the king tithing to fund the priesthood. Apart from a transfer of wealth that will take place in these days to fund the end time harvest, this is also how the end time harvest and the full time five-fold ministry offices will be funded to proceed to equip the armies of God in these last days. This is God's order and forms part of the order of Melchizedek being restored.

I can assure you that in the shaking that is coming, God will shake all things that is not built on His foundation and that does not function according to His order. This is the very reason why the church became a man-made thing in deviating from God's order, ordinances and commandments. Jesus Christ is the Chief Cornerstone in the foundation of the church. He has been appointed Head over all things to His body, the church. His fullness of all in all. He is preparing and restoring His church for the purpose of His second coming. I believe that the rapture will be the reward for the remnant as they will be greatly spared from the great hour of trial that will come upon the whole world to test them.

These seven points sum up the entire purpose of the order of Melchizedek and how it is fulfilled in Christ and will be further fulfilled by the end time church in these last days. As we are made in the likeness of Christ and Christ is our High Priest in the likeness of the order of Melchizedek.

Furthermore, this is preparation for the last days ministry. We are also priests according to the order of Melchizedek to bring the rule and God's worship of His kingdom to this world. We need to bring heaven to earth. Allowing His kingdom as priests and kings to be released into every situation in the earth. Ruling and reigning from heavenly realms with Him. So that the kingdom of God will rule before the second coming of Jesus Christ. The Lord's prayer becomes significant in this age. Jesus taught his disciples how to pray to release heaven to earth and allow His kingdom to invade earth. This is how He taught:

"In this manner, therefore, pray: "Our Father in heaven, Hallowed by Your Name, Your kingdom come, Your will be done, on earth as it is in heaven."

Matthew 6:9 - 10

"All authority has been given to Me in heaven and on earth."   *Matthew 18*

The same authority was delegated to us as a kingly anointing to fulfill the great commission in the earth which is now upon us. The final gathering of the harvest of all nations.

"Go therefore and make disciples of all nations, baptizing them in the Name of the Father and of the Son and of the Holy Spirit. Teaching them to observe all things that I have commanded you; and lo, I am with you always, even to the end of the age."
Matthew 28:19,20

Without the order of Melchizedek being restored, this mandate cannot be fully fulfilled in the earth as it calls for a priestly duty and the kingly authority. Jesus holds the Keyes of the Kingdom and He gave the keys to His sons and daughters to bring His rule and worship to the earth.

"And I will give you the Keys of the kingdom of heaven, and whatever you bind on earth will be bound in heaven, and whatever you lose on earth will be loosed in heaven."
Matthew 16:19

These were the words of Jesus Christ to Peter, one of the disciples. Authority can only return to the church if we first fulfill our priestly duties. Therefore, there is a need to look at the priestly functions carefully. Our responsibility is to bring His rule. Worship and glory will fill the whole earth in the last days, for Him to have a habitation in the Spirit amongst His people. Let Christ rule in you as King. Listen to his Voice and obey Him only. Rule and reign from heavenly realms where we are seated with Him. This is a call to no longer sin but live a lifestyle of holiness as priests before Him. Sin will disqualify you from ruling and carrying authority. There are conditions to be met. The purpose of the order of Melchizedek is for atonement. In the last days God will make clear this New Testament order of Melchizedek as this order needs to rise in the final move of God in the earth.

FUNCTIONS OF A PRIEST

Why do we need to understand this subject? Because Jesus Christ made us priests and kings to His God and Father. We, therefore, have a responsibility to walk in His ways and understand the function that we are called to.

"To Him Who loved us and washed from our sins in His own blood, and has made us kings and priests to His God and Father, to Him be glory and dominion for ever and ever."
Revelation 1:5,6

To be a priest appointed by Jesus Christ is a sacred ministry. We cannot function in our ministry calling until we function as priests. Faithfulness in the priestly will move you into the kingly anointing. Faithfulness and stewarding the priestly functions will usher you into rulership.

"Who then is a faithful and wise servant, whom his master has made ruler over his household, to give them food in due season? Blessed is that servant whom his master, when he comes, will find so doing. Assuredly I say to you that he will make him ruler over all his goods." Matthew 24:45 - 47

These are the words of Jesus Christ. This is His order. What you produce in this phase will determine the next.

Priests sacrifice in the same way Christ sacrificed His life for the eternal atonement of sins. *"I beseech you therefore, brethren, by the mercies of God that you present your bodies as a living sacrifice, holy, acceptable to God, which is your reasonable service. And do not be conformed to this world, but be transformed by the renewal of your mind, that you may prove what is the good, and acceptable and perfect will of God."*
Romans 12:1,2

Our bodies need to be presented on the altar as a living sacrifice for the sake of service. That means you passing out of your own control and ownership to the ownership and control of God. When your body is sacrificed on the altar God has the final say-so over your destiny in Christ.

FUNCTIONS OF A KING

Faithfulness in hardship will promote you to authority. Obedience leads to righteousness; righteousness leads to holiness and holiness leads to eternal life according to *Romans 6*. It is expected of a king to rule and judge righteously as the scepter of the throne of God is righteousness. Righteousness means to be in" right standing" with God. No hindrances or unreported sin. A clear conscience before God. Pure heart. Holy before Him walking in obedience and total surrender. This will cause spiritual authority to rise.

- Kings rule and reign. *"And he who overcomes, and keeps My works until the end, him I will give power over the nations. He shall rule them with a rod of iron, they shall be shed to pieces like the potter's vessels."*
Revelation 2:26 - 27

Kings rule and reign from mount Zion. They rule over a designated area.

- Kings judge. *"Now therefore, o kings, show discernment, take warning, o judges of the earth."* Psalm 2:11

- Kings judge from thrones. *"It is an abomination for kings to commit wicked acts, for a throne is established on righteousness."* Proverbs 16:12

- Kings give stability to the land. *"The king gives stability to the land by justice, but a man who takes bribes overthrows it."* Proverbs 29:4

- Kings search out spiritual matters and the mysteries of God and then reveal it to God's people. *"It is the glory of God to conceal a thing, but the honor of kings to search out a matter."*
Proverbs 25:2

We are preparing for eternity. God's order in the earth is being restored for the church to walk in authority, to legislate and decree.

EFFECTS OF THE ORDER OF MELCHIZEDEK BEING RESTORED

Rest in God. Unbelief and disobedience disqualify us from the rest of God and to enter in. Hearing His Voice, obeying His Word, mixed with faith will cause us to enter into His rest. *"And to whom did He swear that they would not enter His rest, but to those who did not obey? So, we see that they could not enter in because of unbelief."*
Hebrews 3:18,19

When the order of Melchizedek is being followed and we fully fulfill both our priestly and kingly functions, without striving and trying to do things on our own, abiding in the Vine, we will enter His rest. There is a place in Him, when your body is sacrificed as a living sacrifice on the altar and your mind is renewed to a point where the habitation of the soul becomes the Mind of Christ, the sevenfold Holy Spirit, you will obey His Voice and walk in His perfect will. That is when you rest in Him. For this positioning walking in His commandments, being His order and ordinances, He will align you to His perfect will. This is when *Romans 8:28* becomes our portion.

"And we know that all things work together for the good to those who love God, to those who are called according to His purpose." Romans 8:28

At this place God Himself works all things according to the counsel of His will, so that we who trust in Christ will be the praise of His glory. At this place there is no striving. He works it all out for His glory in the earth through your life. However, hearing His Voice, being His commandments, mixed with faith in His Name are the conditions to be met for entering into His rest.

Melchizedek exposed Abram to the life in the Spirit by serving him bread and wine. This was a demonstration of what Jesus did in the New Testament when He instituted communion. Enter His rest, take communion often, examine your heart before taking communion and He will bless you with a complete life, He will keep you from sickness and you will have no weakness in your body. That is how you rest in Him.

CHAPTER 10

THE RISING OF THE SPIRIT OF ELIJAH PREPARING THE WAY OF THE LORD

THE RISING OF THE SPIRIT OF ELIJAH PREPARING THE WAY OF THE LORD:

God is raising up prophets in the last days that will carry the spirit and anointing of the Old Testament prophet, Elijah. For this very reason we need to look into the history of Israel to fully comprehend how this correlates with the last days and how God will again rise up prophets to deliver His people from bondage and to restore the consequences of captivity, corruption and evil that was reigning then and is even reigning now. Even the church is in captivity as it has deviated from the covenant of God and His ways, commandments and governmental order.

When God's covenant, His order, ordinances, commandments and ways are perpetually violated there will be inevitable consequences for the nations and the body of Christ. There is a call right now to "repent" and turn to the Lord to be restored. This call is unto all nations and the church that has deviated from God's original intent. God works in and through the lives of His people for redemption purposes. There is a call to the necessity of obedience to God's covenant and the painful consequences of disobedience are seen all over the world in these last days as the end is approaching. Jesus Christ is calling, a call unto repentance. There will be a remnant that will return to Him with their whole hearts, mind and soul and with all that is within them. There is a call unto obedience which will usher in restoration.

The kingdom under the rulership of king Solomon was a "unified kingdom" and the temple was built to glory, until such time as Solomon became disobedient in marrying foreign wives, which led him into idolatry. The stage was now set for the division of the kingdom and reign of Solomon. A king with a divided heart will leave behind a divided kingdom.

When king Solomon died, those in the northern part of the empire rebelled and started their own nation, known as Israel. In the south, those who remained faithful to the house of David and the former united kingdom of Solomon, formed the nation called Judah. Here is the division now. North is Israel and south is Judah. Judah served as a model of uprightness and Israel went astray under foreign gods and they eventually collapsed.

God is still controlling human affairs and world events. The nation, leader or person who responds to, and obeys the Lord will enjoy the benefits of a relationship with Him. Those who refuse and rebel will experience God's discipline and shaking. God is the Author of redemption and will greatly pardon and restore those who repent and turn to Him. For this very reason the whole world is in turmoil right now, many lives are tormented by anxiety, depression, fear and captivity. Restoration is urgently needed and starts with repentance and a call by the true prophets of God to prepare the way for the Lord's return to rapture His remnant church.

However, there is a failure of the call for the sons and daughters to stand as priests and kings, as well as the failure of the true prophets to arise. These are the days of Elijah where God is calling forth the prophets from their caves to rise and declare.

Christ will reign on the throne of David forever. The tabernacle of David will be restored. His presence in His house will lead the true remnant who are willing to sacrifice their lives.

WHO WAS ELIJAH AND WHAT WAS THE CALL OF ELIJAH

- Elijah is an Old Testament prophet sent by God to deliver Israel out of the suffering and the evil of corrupted kings who ruled over them by the spirit of Jezebel.
- Elijah confronted the evil king Ahab, who was Jezebel's husband. Baal was the god of Jezebel and Ahab. The Baal prophets represented false prophets. Elijah challenged these gods to a showdown at Mount Carmel, to establish who is the true living God as opposed to who is the evil god of Ahab, Jezebel and Baal. Elijah also challenged the false prophets of Baal.

God sent fire onto the altar of Elijah to show his supreme divinity. The fire was followed by rain to end the drought, again showing God's grace.

"Elijah was a man with a nature like ours, and he prayed earnestly that it would not rain, and it did not rain on the land for three years and six months. And he prayed again, and the heavens gave rain and the earth produced its fruit."
James 5:17 - 18

The Israelites lost faith in king Ahab and followed Elijah in trusting the only true God.

This is exactly where we are in history right now. During these last days God will again raise prophets carrying the same power and spirit of Elijah. These will be unknown prophets coming out of their caves and out of the wilderness where they have been prepared through a process of hardship and testing, to stand and establish the reign of the true living God in these last days. It is part of God's end time strategy on the earth to restore and prepare the way for the second coming of the Lord.

- Elijah is a prophet that suffered and endured many hardships, but he was sent as a "restorer". *"Jesus answered and said to them; indeed, Elijah is coming first and will restore things, but I say to you that Elijah has come already, and they did not know him but did to him whatever they wished. Likewise, the Son of man is also about to suffer at their hands."*

Matthew 17:11 - 12

Elijah did not have it easy as he was many a times ill-treated, and the ravens were feeding him. These end time prophets carrying the mantle and power of Elijah will also know suffering, but they will stay true to God. We are in a window period where the true remnant is sanctified, set aside and being restored. All that entails God's original intents for His church will be restored. Therefore, there is a need for this anointing to be released in the last move of God.

- Elijah brought the restoration of unity and reconciliation. Christ is returning for a victorious, pure and spotless bride. Right now, we see the church being defeated. Restoration to victory is coming through the power and spirit of Elijah.

"But you who fear My name, the Son of Righteousness shall arise with healing in its wings; And you shall go out and grow like stall-fed calves. For you shall crackle the wicked, for they shall be ashes under the souls of your feet on the day that I do this, says the Lord of hosts. Behold, I will send you Elijah the prophet before the coming of the great and dreadful day of the Lord. And He will turn the hearts of the fathers to their children, and the hearts of the children to the fathers, lest I come and strike the earth with a curse."
Malachi 4:2 - 6

The opposing spirit to the spirit of Elijah is the spirit of Jezebel and the false prophets of Baal. Jezebel always brings division and strife, manipulation and control and as a result final division between parents and children, husbands and wives, or wherever the spirit gain legal rights, the end result will be division.

Therefore, the opposing spirit of Elijah is to bring reconciliation and unity. The picture in Malachi 4 is a picture of the restoration of the end time church and the healing that God will bring, the restoration of all things unto Himself and especially the restoration between parents and children in the natural as well as a total restoration of the sons and daughters of God to their spiritual authority. This is God's order. He will do it in these last days by the power and the spirit of Elijah.

The church will once again gain strength and authority. As Jezebel usurps and undermines authority. She hates the prophets of God and when this spirit enters the church it gains legal rights within the church, it will betray and undermine all spiritual authority and finally divide and break up the church. The end time remnant church will not be in bed with this spirit. This wicked spirit will be trampled and become ashes under the feet of the remnant church, this will be done by God through the rising and the power of the spirit of Elijah in these last days.

-       Elijah prepared the way for the Lord's coming and make ready a people prepared for the Lord. When the angel Gabriel made known unto John the baptist's father, Zacharias, that his prayers have been heard and his wife, Elizabeth, will bear a son and that they should call him "John", the heavenly persona or true identity of John the baptist was also made known by the angel.

"For he will be great in the sight of the Lord, and shall drink neither wine   nor strong drink. He will also be filled with the Holy Spirit, even from his mother's womb. And he will turn many of the children of Israel to the Lord, their God. He will also go before him in the spirit and power of Elijah, to turn the hearts of the fathers to the children and the disobedient to the wisdom of the just, to make ready a people prepared for the Lord."
Luke 1:15 - 17

John the baptist was born and anointed to usher in the first coming of the Lord Jesus Christ by the spirit of Elijah. By the same spirit of Elijah, the second coming of our Lord Jesus Christ will be ushered in. Therefore, we will see the power and spirit of Elijah rising now.

The power and ministry of John the baptist which was the same anointing that was upon Elijah for the exact same purpose of *"making ready a people for the Lord" will* be an end time anointing that God will release to His end time prophets. The very reason for the sons and daughters to rise as priests and kings, to be set apart and walk in their true identities and authority will also be restored as part of the end time move of God. They will turn many of the children of Israel back to their God to be restored. The spirit of Elijah upon the end time prophets will cause reconciliation as Jezebel will be dealt with in this season. By the spirit and power of Elijah the disobedient will be turned to the wisdom of the just. Unity will be established and restored. The Ecclesia, a people, a remnant who will be willing to fulfill their priestly and kingly functions and obey God's commandments and align themselves to the governing and ruling of the church of Jesus Christ as set out in *Ephesians 4.* They will all be made ready for the coming of our Lord and King.

ELIJAH OVERCOMING JEZEBEL AND THE FALSE PROPHETS

In this end time move of God there will be a definite confrontation between the spirit of Jezebel and the spirit of Elijah. As the spirit of Elijah is preparing the way for the Lord's second return by making ready a people for the Lord and thereby ushering in the second coming of the Lord. The spirit of Jezebel is preparing the way for the anti-Christ and preparing a people for the beast. A people that will follow the mark of the beast which is the number of man 666.

"All who dwell on the earth will worship him, whose names have not been written in the Book of Life of the Lamb slain from the foundation of the earth. If anyone has an ear, let him hear." *Revelations 13:8 – 9*

"He causes all, both small and great, rich and poor, free and slave, to receive a mark on their right hand or on their foreheads, and that no one may buy or sell except one who has the mark or the name of the beast, or the number of his name. Here is wisdom. Let him who has understanding calculate the number of the beast, for it is the number of man: his number is 666."

Revelation 13:16 - 18

There is currently a war going on in the realm of the spirit. We are in an end time war. The preparation of the bride of Christ for His second return to rapture the remnant church, and the preparation of a people to follow the anti-Christ, the beast.

The spirit of Elijah will prepare God's people, and the spirit of Jezebel will prepare a people to succumb to the beast and to take the mark of the beast. Everyone who will not worship the image of the beast will be killed.

"He was granted power to give breath to the image of the beast, that the image of the beast should both speak and cause as many as would not worship the image of the beast to be killed." *Revelation 13:15*

Anyone who worships the beast or who takes the mark of the beast or implant on their right hand or forehead will not enter the kingdom of God. The spirit of Jezebel is preparing the way for the rising of the anti-Christ and the beast in the earth. We can already see this by the micro-chip being prepared to be inserted in the right hands and foreheads of people in order to become a cashless society.

So, we see the two opposing spirits in this final battle on the earth taking place right now. It is time for the Elijah prophets to arise against the control and manipulation of Jezebel. Jezebel massacres the prophets of God.

We are living in perilous times. It is war and there will once again be a final showdown between the true living God and the anti-Christ's rule that is creeping in. Jezebel's strategy is to infiltrate the church and attach herself to leaders in authority to usurp and undermine the authority of God and bring division in the body of Christ. This is the reason why the order must be restored, the governing of the church must be restored, sons and daughters need to be equipped to walk in authority and the priesthood needs to be restored. The apostle and prophet are mantled to confront Jezebel.

There was a final showdown on Mount Carmel during the time when Jezebel killed the prophets of God. Elijah went out and met with king Ahab. Elijah was fierce in his pursuit. *"So Ahab sent for all the children of Israel, and gathered the prophets together on Mount Carmel. And Elijah came to all the people and said: "How long will you falter between two opinions? If the Lord is God, follow Him; but if Baal, follow him. But the people answered him not a word. Then Elijah said to the people, I alone am left a prophet of the Lord, but Baal's prophets are four hundred and fifty men."* *1 Kings 18:20 - 22*

So they prepared the altars with bulls and wood. *"Then Elijah again said: "Then you call on the name of your gods and I will call on the Name of the Lord, and the God who answers before, He is God." "So, all the people answered and said it is well spoken."* *1 Kings 18:24*

"So, the Baal prophets called upon their god and cried aloud, and then cut themselves, as was their custom, with knives and lancets, until the blood gushed out on them. Then they prophesied until the time of the offering of the evening sacrifice. But there was no voice, no one answered. Then Elijah said to all the people, "Come near to me." "So all the people came near to him. And he repaired the altar of the Lord that was broken down."
1 Kings 18:28 - 30

Let us look at the strategy of Elijah. He gathered the people and prepared the altar of the Lord that was broken down. The altar of the Lord is broken down at the moment by the sin and ungodliness that is going on in the church. The altars of the church need to be restored in the Name of the Lord. We cannot defile the altar of the Lord and want victory over the enemy. In these last days the altar of the Lord will be restored to carry His fire. Elijah dug a trench around the altar, and it was filled with water. He poured water on the sacrifice on the altar. Elijah made sure that the altar and the wood, as well as the sacrifice on the altar was altogether wet, and the excess water ran into the trench that was dug.

It is time that the living water of the Spirit of God once again flow from the altar. Elijah, the prophet, came near and said: *"Lord God of Abraham, Isaac and Israel, let it be known this day that You are God in Israel and I am Your servant, and that I have done all these things at Your Word." "Hear me, o Lord, hear me that this people may know that You are the Lord God, and that You have turned their hearts back to You again."*
1 Kings 18:36 - 37

By the miracles and by the power of God displayed through the life of Elijah, the hearts of the people were turned back to God. We are living in the days of Elijah. May the Elijah prophets arise.

"Then the fire of the Lord fell and consumed the burnt sacrifice, and the wood and the stones and the dust, and it licked up the water that was in the trench. Now when all the people saw it, they fell on their faces; and they said "The Lord He is God! The Lord He is God!" "And Elijah said to them, "seize the prophets of Baal! Do not let one of them escape!" So they seized them; and Elijah brought them down to the brook of Kishon and executed them there."
1 Kings 18:44 - 40

This is the power of the spirit of Elijah returning to the end time prophets. The anointing of the spirit of Elijah will once again defeat the Jezebel spirit and the false prophets. The Elijah prophets will carry the Truth and Power of God to expose and deal with all that is false, especially false prophets and heresy swaying God's people away from Him. God's fire will be called down again on all that is false. Every false authority, false foundations, false teachings. It will be exposed and will fall by the fire of God returning to the remnant church.

POWER AND MIRACLES BY THE ANOINTING UPON ELIJAH

- Governmental authority and dominion:

"Elijah said to Ahab: As the Lord God of Israel lives, before Whom I stand, there shall not be dew nor rain these years, except at my word."

1 Kings 17:1

"Elijah was a man just like us and prayed that it would not rain on the earth, and it did not rain for three years and six months. And he prayed again and the heavens gave rain and the earth produced its fruit."

James 5:17 - 18

The end time Elijah prophets will walk in the same governmental authority and power. "They will declare a thing on the earth and it will be established, and light will be on their pathways." Job 22:28

- Supernatural provision:

The Lord commanded Elijah to turn eastward and hide himself by the brook Cherith at the Jordan. "And it will be that you shall drink from the brook, and I have commanded the ravens to feed you there. The ravens brought him bread and meat in the morning; and bread and meat in the evening; and he drank from the brook."
1 Kings 17:3 and 6

In these last days when famine strikes the nations, and we enter into a cashless society, the true remnant will be provided for supernaturally by the same power and anointing that rested upon Elijah. Elijah continually followed the instruction of the Lord. Those who obey Him will walk in power and authority and will be led by the Spirit of God as supernatural abundance will be provided.

- God's revelation to Elijah:

When Elijah hid himself from Jezebel in a cave the Lord spoke to him and said: *"Then He said, "go out and stand on the mountain before the Lord." And behold, the Lord passed by, and a great and strong wind tore into the mountains and broke the rocks in pieces before the Lord, but the Lord was not in the wind; and after the wind an earthquake, but the Lord was not in the earthquake; and after the earthquake a fire, but the Lord was not in the fire; and after the fire, a still small voice. So it was when Elijah heard it, that he wrapped his face in his mantle and went out and stood in the entrance of the cave. Suddenly a voice came to him and said: "What are you doing here, Elijah?"* 1 Kings 19:11 - 13

"Then the Lord gave Elijah an instruction. This was the instruction He gave Elijah: "Also you shall anoint Jehu, the son of Nimsi, as king over Israel. And Elisha, the son of Shaphat, of Abel Meholah you shall anoint as prophet in your place."
1 Kings 19:16

From that day onwards Elisha followed Elijah and he became his servant.

God revealed to Elijah that he had to anoint Elisha as his follower in his place. Elijah threw his mantle upon Elisha and he became an armor bearer and servant to Elijah.

God's revelation to the end time prophets will also come in the still small voice. They will anoint the next generation of Elijah prophets who will carry a double portion of the same power and anointing that was upon Elijah. The youth that are coming unto salvation in this end time harvest will be mantled and anointed to stand and take up their places in the end time army that is rising. God will anoint and mantle the next generation through the end time Elijah prophets. These prophets will honor God and obey His instructions. They will honor the function of anointing, mantling and walking their spiritual sons and daughters to destiny.

- Fire from heaven:

" So Elijah answered and said to them, "If I am a man of God, let fire come down from heaven and consume you and your fifty men." "And the fire of God came down from heaven and consumed him and his fifty."

2 Kings 1:12

Elijah, by the power of God, called fire to come down from heaven and God established his decree on the earth. This is the power and anointing that the end time Elijah prophets will carry during the great move of God on the earth in these last days. God is raising up a company of governmental prophets.

- Dominion and authority - Forthtelling:

Elijah was sent to the widow of Zarephath who had to provide for him. She only had enough for herself and her son for one meal. Elijah then asked for water to drink and that she would give him to eat as well. She gave her last. Elijah then prophesied over her the following words. When you accept a prophet in the name of a prophet or give a prophet a cup of water or something to eat, or a place to sleep, you will receive a prophet's reward. A prophet's reward means that you fulfill the need of the prophet and the prophet brings your need before God and prophecies the mind of God over your circumstances and God will establish it for you. Always receive a true prophet in the name of a prophet, for this is God's will. True prophets many a times carry the key to your destiny.

"For thus says the Lord God of Israel: "The bin of flour shall not be used up, nor shall the jar of oil run dry, until the day the Lord send rain on the earth." "So she went away and did according to the word of Elijah, and she and he and her household ate for many days. The bin of flour was not used up, nor did the jar of oil run dry, according to the Word of the Lord which He spoke by Elijah."   1 Kings 17:14 - 16

These are the days of Elijah that we are entering into. The Ecclesia will have dominion and power over natural circumstances by the hand of the true living God. As priests and kings and as prophets we will decree and declare the mind and voice of the Lord and He shall establish it on the earth. Even in times of difficulty and famine, which are ahead of us, the church will supernaturally overcome by the power and spirit of Elijah released upon the body of Christ and His end time prophets. And the redeemed of the Lord will say so. The church will live naturally by the supernatural. Many supernatural occurrences will take place by the Hand of God overriding the natural. That is the reason why we need to obey His voice and not be influenced by what we see with the natural eye, as we will live supernaturally by faith alone. Faith and the fear of the Lord, together with great discernment, will take us through the end times. He will instruct us continually through His still small voice. When the Joel 2 outpouring of the Spirit takes place, the Voice of the Lord will be everywhere. The prophetic will become very eminent in the last days.

- Elijah transported:

"And it shall come to pass, as soon as I am gone from you that the Spirit of the Lord will carry you to a place I do not know; So when I go and tell Ahab and he cannot find you, he will kill me. But I, your servant, have feared the Lord from my youth."
       1 Kings 18:12

The Spirit of the Lord represents the aspect of the power of the Holy Spirit. By the power of the Holy Spirit Elijah was often transported from one place to another as he was hunted down by Jezebel and the Baal prophets who wanted to kill him. In these last days we can also expect to be transported from one place to another by the Spirit of the Lord when persecution and martyrdom comes against the end time remnant. the church will be a supernatural church and therefore needs to be properly equipped to move in the Holy Spirit.

- Elijah taken up:

Elijah and Elisha were walking together they were discussing what Elijah may do for Elisha before he was taken up into heaven. Elisha asked for the mantle that is upon Elijah to be transferred to him. He also asked for a double portion of the anointing that was upon Elijah. *"Then it happened, as they continued on and talked, that suddenly a chariot of fire appeared with horses of fire, and separated the two of them; and Elijah went up by a whirlwind into heaven."*   *2 Kings 2:11*

Elisha caught the mantle of Elijah when it fell down and received a double portion of the anointing that was upon Elijah to carry on the prophetic ministry of Elijah. In the same way the power and anointing of Elijah will also be transferred to a new generation of believers coming into the kingdom during the final harvest, who will carry the prophetic anointing and do great exploits for God.

- God's provision by the instruction of Elisha and the Spirit of the Lord:

"A certain woman of the wives of the sons of the prophets cried out to Elisha, saying, "Your servant, my husband, is dead, and you know that your servant feared the Lord and the creditor is coming to take my two sons to be his slaves. So Elisha said to her: "What shall I do for you? Tell me, what do you have in the house? And she said, "Your maid servant has nothing in the house but a jar of oil." Then he said, "Go, borrow vessels from everywhere, from all your neighbors - empty vessels, do not gather just a few. And when you have come in, you shall shut the door behind you and your sons, then pour it into all those vessels, and set aside the full ones."

"So she went from him and shut the door behind her and her sons, who brought the vessels to her; and she poured it out. Now it came to pass, when the vessels were full, that she said to her son, "Bring me another vessel." And he said to her, "There is not another vessel." So the oil seized. Then she came and told the man of God. And he said, "Go, sell the oil and pay your debt; and you and your sons live on the rest.   2 Kings 4:1 - 7

God's provision will be supernatural to an obedient remnant. Obedience and a return to following His instructions is of paramount importance in these last days. Empty yourself before Him, let Him fill you. Allow the Spirit of Counsel to give you strategy in these days. Follow His commandments and instructions. Do not leave a back door open. Do as God commands, be led by His Spirit alone and His provision will flow. Believe God as without faith we will not make it through these end times.

The end time church will have faith in Him alone. Follow the Master. Be obedient. Will empty themselves to be pure and holy before Him. His supernatural instruction and provision will be at hand.

However, repentance is needed and a re-alignment to God's original plan and intent. A re-alignment to his commandments, ways and governmental order. It is the times of Elijah to return and be restored. We will see a total rebuilding of the church of Jesus Christ.

CHAPTER 11

THE SHAKING OF ALL THINGS AND THE JUDGEMENT OF GOD

Whenever God's laws are transgressed, His ordinances changed and His everlasting covenant broken, we will see devastating consequences to individuals, families and nations.

This will cause corruption and foundations to be unstable. To correct this state of affairs, it is necessary for God to shake all things in an attempt not to judge His people. However, we will see a final judgment of God upon the earth against all that opposes His plans and purposes.

However here is an "acceptable year of the Lord" However He will help and sustain His remnant. His glory will return to individuals and the church as a result of radical obedience and walking in holiness. At that same time, it will be a day of the vengeance of God to those who oppose Him and reject the blood of Jesus.

We can therefore view the shaking that will take place in these last days as the beginning of God's judgment.

What does the Word of God say about this shaking?

- God's people will be safe.

"The Lord also will roar from Zion; and utter His voice from Jerusalem; the heavens and earth will shake; but the Lord will be a shelter for His people and the strength of the children of Israel"   Joel 3:16

- The heavens and the earth will be shaken. There will be a removal of those things that are being shaken in order for that which cannot be shaken will remain. God's kingdom cannot be shaken and all that is built upon His foundation

"Whose voice then shook the earth; but now He has promised, saying "Yet one more I shake not only the earth, but also the heaven

Now this , *"yet once more"* indicates the removal of those things that are being shaken, as of things that are made; that the things that cannot be shaken may remain. Therefore, since we are receiving a kingdom which cannot be shaken …….   Hebrews 12:26-28

- The sea and the dry land will be shaken

- Nations will be shaken

- Glory will come to the remnant church

"For thus says the Lord of hosts; heaven and earth, the sea and dry land, and I will shake all nations, and they shall come to the desire of all nations and I will fill this temple with glory," says the Lord of hosts" Haggai 2:6,7

- Fear will take a hold of people

"Men's hearts failing them from fear and the expectation of those things which are coming on the earth; for the powers of the heavens will be shaken"
Luke 21:26

- Mountains and islands will be shaken

"I looked when He opened the sixth seal, and behold, there was a great earthquake; and the sun became black as sackcloth of hair and the moon became like blood. Then the sky receded as a scroll when it is rolled up, and every mountain and island was moved out of its place"

Revelation 6:12 &14

No one will be exempted from this shaking. No financial security will secure you against this. The only safety will be in the end time ecclesia of God.

REASONS WHY THIS END TIME SHAKING WILL TAKE PLACE

- These shakings, according to the Word of God in *Isaiah 24:5 & 6,* will happen as a result of His laws being transgressed, the changing of His ordinances which is a pattern set out for us in His Word by which we should live by that has been broken.

His covenant has been broken. Departing from God and the requirements of covenant relationship provokes God's judgment. Also, covenant relationship within families as the institution of "family" has fallen by the wayside.

- Pride is another reason for invoking shaking and God's judgment.

> *"For the day of the Lord of hosts shall come upon everything proud and lofty, upon everything lifted up - and it shall be brought low."*
>
> *Isaiah 2:12*

- God wants to demonstrate a kingdom that cannot be shaken in these last days according to *Hebrews 12*.

- Individual lives will be allowed to be shaken as a result of not being built on a solid foundation of the truth of the Word (Jesus).

- Households and churches will be shaken as they are divided, and the result is unparented children.

> *"But Jesus knew their thoughts and said to them: "Every kingdom divided against itself is brought to desolation, and every city or house divided against itself shall not stand."*

- Any institution not founded on the foundation of Christ - even banks and governments - will fall. We cannot look at these institutions for stability. Stability will only be found within the true remnant built on the Rock Jesus Christ. Religious institutions not being built on the teaching of Jesus will fall in this coming shaking.

- A root cause is degeneration of human character and again pride provokes God's judgment.

> *"But know this, that in the last days perilous times will come: for men will be lovers of themselves, lovers of money, boasters, proud, blasphemous, disobedient to parents, unthankful, unholy, unloving, unforgiving, slanderers, without self-control, brutal, despisers of good, traitors, head-strong, haughty, lovers of pleasure rather than lovers of God, having a form of godliness, but denying its power. And from such people turn away!"*
>
> *2 Timothy 3:1 - 5*

HOW DO WE THEN DEAL WITH PRIDE?

Pride is connected to carnality; it needs to be repented of. Your eternal destiny is at stake. God hates pride and rejects the prideful. Loosing vision of eternity is carnality.

"Confess your trespasses to one another, and pray for one another, that you may be healed. The effective, fervent prayer of a righteous man avails much."
James 5:16

- In *2 Timothy 3:1 - 5* there are eighteen moral blemishes listed which leads to a process of corruption. The only solution is a total new beginning. The love of self, money and pleasure leads to a breakdown of society. Selfishness and the power of mammon dominates society. Justice is not found where riches and wealth is present, unless this is surrendered to Christ. Society uses riches and wealth as protection. Pleasure says if it feels good "do it". This has become a motto.

Having a form of godliness but denying its power. This is a form of denying the power to change people and set them free by the truth of the Word of God. From such people turn away. Don't waste your time with them.

THE JUDGMENT OF GOD

We know that the shaking of all things is related to the end times, and the glory of God in these last days as well as God's judgment.

When the judgment of God comes upon the earth, kings, rich men, men in authority, slaves and every free man will hide themselves in the caves and in the rocks of the mountains. They will cry out for these rocks to fall on them in an effort to hide from Him and from the wrath of the Lamb. No one will be able to stand that day.

"And the kings of the earth, the great men, the rich men, the commanders, the mighty men, every slave and every free man, hid themselves in the caves and in the rocks of the mountains, and said to the mountains and the rocks, "fall on us and hide us from the face of Him Who sits on the throne and from the wrath of the Lamb! For the great day of His wrath has come, and who is able to stand?"

Revelation 6:15 - 17

"It shall come to pass in that day that the Lord will punish on high the host of exalted ones, and on the earth the kings of the earth. They will be gathered together as prisoners are gathered in the pit, and will be shut up in the prison, after many days they will be punished. Then the moon will be disgraced ad the sun ashamed, for the Lord of hosts will reign on

mount Zion and in Jerusalem and before His elders, gloriously".
Isaiah 6:21 - 23

Through the judgment of God His glory will be revealed. let us not loose heart, as there is still time to repent. Let us view all of this as a warning of what is to come and as a cry to align fully to Him and surrender to Christ Jesus. Within the ecclesia there will be safety.

The fear of the Lord will return to the church and the latter days of the church will be greater than the former. Love and unity will be restored. Each son and daughter will take up their place in the *Joel 2* army. His glory will return to the church and the church will finish strong as a spotless bride.

IN CONCLUSION

In the face of perilous times, let our hope arise! Let us call upon the Name of the Lord and repent from all wickedness. Let us serve Him in one accord as He is faithful to restore His church. Let us be meek and trust in the Name of the Lord. Seek righteousness and humility and it may be that you will be hidden in the day of the Lord's anger.

We serve a faithful God Who is merciful. He will be restoring your soul if you come to Jesus for salvation and harken unto His Word. He will restore His end time church, and His glory will be revealed.

There will be safety within the true remnant. Those who follow the Master wholeheartedly. Not a hair from your head will be removed as He protects and provides for His own under His blood covenant. Now unto Him that is able to keep you from falling, and to present you faultless before the presence of His glory with exceeding joy, to the only wise God our Saviour, be glory and majesty, dominion and power, both now and forever. Amen!

Bibliography

1. Jack W. Hayford, Litt.D: (2008): The Holy Bible New King James Version: Printed by SW Press, Korea

2. Prince Derek, (2010):Called to Conquer: Baker publishing group USA

3. Prince Derek, (2010): Prophetic Guide to the End Times: Baker Publishing Group USA

4. Jeff van Wyk, (2012): Anointed for Ministry:Team Impact Publishing Group

5. Dr Jeffrey van Wyk, (2008): The Five Fold Anointing:Published by Joy Ministries SA

6. Dr Ana Mendez Ferrell, (2010): Seated in Heavenly Places: Book Master, OH , USA

7. Jeff van Wyk, (2013): The Power of the Local Church: Team Impact Publishing Group USA

8. Jeff can Wyk, (2012): The Apostolic Anointing: Team Impact Publishing Group USA

9. Benny Hinn, (1995): Welcome Holy Spirit: Published in Nashville Thomas Nelson

10. John Piper, (2001): Seeing and Savouring Jesus Christ: Inter Varsity Press, Lancaster, England

11. Guillermo Maldonado: (2011): How to walk in the Supernatural Power of God: Whitaker House USA

12. Suret Morkel: (2014): The Voice of the Seven Fold Spirit: Formeset Pty Ltd

13. Beale G.K: (1999): The Book of Revelation: Grand Rapids Eerdmans

14. Hitchcock J: (2012): The End: A complete Overview of Bible Prophecy: Nashville Thomas Nelson

15. Eberle H.R. and Trench M. (2006): Victorious Eschatology: Destiny Image Publishers New York